The Good Buy Book

The Good Buy Book

6-State Edition

Illinois	Minnesota
Indiana	Ohio
Michigan	Wisconsin

by Annie Moldafsky

 **Rand McNally & Company**
Chicago • New York • San Francisco

Copyright © 1980 by Annie Moldafsky
All rights reserved
Printed in the United States of America
by Rand McNally & Company

Library of Congress Catalog Card Number: 80-50757

First printing, 1980

THE GOOD BUY BOOK is dedicated to:

my family, who continues to consume, test, and wear GOOD BUY BOOK products with great tolerance and good humor;
the friends who have helped me in the search for GOOD BUY sources;
and the consumers everywhere who want to get the most for their money—and more.

CONTENTS

Introduction • 9
Definitions of GOOD BUY BOOK Terms • 14
Illinois • 17
Indiana • 87
Michigan • 117
Minnesota • 149
Ohio • 187
Wisconsin • 257
Category Index • 303

INTRODUCTION

WE ALL KNOW you can save money by not spending it. But it's the wise consumer who realizes you can save money on most of the things you buy—if you know where to buy.

You can find many of the better things in life and pay a lot less for them in factory outlet stores. Factory outlets, thrift stores, manufacturers' courtesy stores, and seconds stores are those retail facilities where manufacturers sell what they make directly to the consumer. The savings are 20% to 80% every day because you're buying the product as close as possible to the source where it is made.

Manufacturers or retail outlet stores can tag their products with prices that are sometimes even below wholesale cost because they have eliminated the bigger expenses of doing business today. There is no shipping, no packaging, very little advertising, and less promotion. There are no amenities like soft lighting or carpeting. And frequently the dressing room is a small area behind a shower curtain or drape!

Shopping during seasonal sales at regular retail stores can also save you money. But shopping at an outlet has an added element of excitement. There's always the possibility (and the hope) that you'll happen upon the greatest buy of all time at a price so low you can't afford to pass it up.

Our family has tracked down factory outlets in big cities like Detroit and Chicago. We have shopped good buy outlets in suburban shopping malls, on a two-block Main Street in an Indiana town and, once, even in a cornfield. We have found outlets in basements, barns, and garages, and have even found some in conventional stores in urban malls. The Monterey Mills fabric outlet is located in an old Wisconsin sugar beet factory, and one of the Clasgen yarn outlets is in a century-old knitting mill, sitting high on a hill overlooking the Ohio River.

The factory outlet finder, like all bargain hunters, must be equipped with a sense of adventure, insatiable curiosity, and sharp eyes. A good map helps too.

Some outlets are open every day, seven days a week. Others may be open only on weekends or perhaps twice a year for special sales. The most difficult outlets to shop are those that close for lunch at a different hour every day. It's also hard, even for a veteran outlet shopper, to keep track of moving outlets. In ten years, I have followed Glen of Michigan back and forth across Lake Michigan three times!

For those who have never been in a factory outlet store, a brief explanation is in order. Outlets are not like department stores. They do not deliver, ever, and they offer no extra services. Some manufacturers simply set off a space in the factory or in an adjoining small room and furnish it minimally with tables, racks, bins, or boxes.

The larger the outlet, the more amenities the manufacturer provides. West Bend Company, a Wisconsin appliance manufacturer, and Haeger Potteries in Dundee, Illinois, have checkout counters, cash registers, shopping baskets, and even take-home bags. But don't get spoiled. In one bakery outlet, you are expected to provide your own bags for your purchases.

There are other differences too, like the levels of quality in outlet store merchandise. First quality can be samples, overruns, overstock, discontinued styles, or last season's goods.

In the case of food packagers such as the Kitchens of Sara Lee and Stouffer's, the product sold in the outlets may also be "test product." These are new items that are test-marketed before they become part of the regular product line.

Labels of *irregular, second, as is, imperfect,* or *o.k.* mean that the product did not meet the manufacturer's standards of quality and therefore cannot be shipped to a regular retail account. A quality reject might be a plaid skirt with the match off one-eighth of an inch or a luxuriously quilted spread with topstitching of varying lengths.

Second products are often the best buys in factory outlets. The West Bend or Sunbeam appliance with a *second* or *irregular* stamp may be a first quality product, but the design printed on the outside enamel could be off center, off color, or smudged. Or the inside surface of a cooking utensil might be marred by a small scratch from the spinning or polishing process. In both cases, the flaw does not affect the use or the durability of the product. The second carries the same manufacturer's guarantee as the first quality product, but the price is now 40% to 50% less.

Major manufacturers sell through factory outlets for different reasons. Some companies use their outlets to create good will in the small communities where they operate their factories. They sell direct to the consumer at close to wholesale prices because there are no other retail sources for their products in that area. Other manufacturers, such as food processors and bakeries, see their outlets as an opportunity to recoup the raw material cost of their test products or day-old baked goods.

Clothing and furniture manufacturers welcome an opportunity to sell, at clear-out prices, all the materials left over after the production runs: fabrics, buttons, zippers, linings, and trims. Factory outlets offer incredible savings on quality materials for home sewers or craftpersons. Fabrics, for instance, can be bought in a wide variety of money-saving ways: by the bolt, the yard, the piece, the bag, and even by the square!

How Do You Know a Good Buy?
Shopping in GOOD BUY BOOK sources is not like shopping in your favorite department or discount store. Price tags usually indicate only one price—not an original price crossed out and the marked-down sale price written in. However, you probably know the normal price range for the item you're interested in and, if you're shopping in the outlet store of a particular manufacturer, you know what to look for in the manufacturer's product line.

There are many reasons the product in the outlet store is being sold at a lower price, so visually check each item you want to buy. If you have any questions about the product or its price, ask a salesperson. Most salespeople in outlet stores are friendly and full of information about what they sell. If the item fits your needs and the lower price has enabled you to save money, you have made a *good buy!*

There are a few factory outlet shopping suggestions I'd like to share with you:

1. *Save yourself time and money* by checking the address for each source and the hours it is open *before* you go. Call ahead if there is any question. Outlets have been known to quietly move upstairs, downstairs, across the street, or even close permanently, on a few days' notice.

2. *Don't be intimidated* by the sometimes overwhelming quantities of merchandise in factory outlets. Start with the aisle on your left and just walk up and down the aisles slowly, stopping only to check those items in which you have a real interest.

3. *Know your correct size.* The ready-to-wear in outlets is sold right off the pipe rack, and fitting rooms are not always available. Some shoppers do their field work in regular retail stores to determine whether a size 7 or 8 dress in a certain style will fit. I have a card, which I carry in my wallet, on which I have written the sizes of each member

12 • Introduction

of my family, along with their height, weight, and color preferences. Then, when I see a good buy, I always know what size to bring home.

4. *Check each item carefully before you buy it.* Few outlets have a merchandise return policy. What you buy may be yours to keep—forever. If the product is marked *second* or *irregular* and you can't find the flaw, ask the salesperson. In ready-to-wear, the flaw may be in the stitching or in the setting in of a pocket, zipper, or cuff. It often pays to turn the garment inside out and check the seams and pockets.

5. *Nothing is a bargain if you can't use it.* One of the biggest problems in shopping factory outlets is the temptation to buy everything simply because it all seems so cheap. Resist the urge and, if necessary, jam your hands in your pockets until the moment of weakness passes.

6. *If you find something you want* or can use, buy it. Factory outlet stock changes constantly and you may not get that second chance to make a good buy.

7. *Many factory outlets sell on a cash-only basis.* However, some outlets take American Express, Diner's Club, Master Charge, Visa, traveler's checks, and even personal checks with proper identification. Be sure, before you leave home, that you have enough money with you or the proper credit cards.

Where Do You Find the Good Buys?

We've traveled thousands of miles and shopped hundreds of sources in each state to find the good buys listed in this edition of THE GOOD BUY BOOK. In each case, we have tried to track down the place where you can buy a manufactured product at the lowest possible price. Only those sources that are open to the public at specified times, provide real savings, and are prime outlets for a named manufacturer are included.

Bakery outlets and day-old product thrift stores are good sources for saving. Today, most large commercial bakeries like Buttermaid, Butternut, and Wonder Bread maintain outlets for the sale of day-old products. Because there are so many more bakery outlets, we have limited those listed in THE GOOD BUY BOOK to the specialty bakeries. We suggest you check your local telephone directory for the additional names and addresses of those commercial outlets near your home.

How Do You Use THE GOOD BUY BOOK?

Check the category index of products at the back of the book for the items you want to buy. The index will give you the page numbers for the sources selling those items.

Introduction • 13

All GOOD BUY BOOK sources are listed geographically by the name of the city in which they're located. Some companies have outlets in several cities or in other states. Products sold in these outlets are described under the first source listing or under the listing of the main factory.

The days and hours that each source is open for business are indicated under the name and address of that source. A few factories are open to the public for selling only during certain periods of the year. Some are open on one day of the week or month only. Please check each listing carefully to save yourself time or a needless trip.

Hours and addresses have been checked and verified up to the time this book was printed. But hours and locations can change. And company stores do go out of business. If you find any of these changes, please let us know.

THE GOOD BUY BOOK describes what each source sells, what the savings are, how you can pay for your purchases, and where you can park. Many sources now accept credit cards; these sources and the charge cards they accept are identified in the listings.

We have continued to enjoy the sharing and swapping of favorite sources with those of you who've written in since the first publication of THE GOOD BUY BOOK in 1974. And we've learned a lot about GOOD BUY BOOK extras from you. Many readers tell us they keep a copy of the book in their car glove compartment "just in case we happen to be passing near a source while we're on the road."

Friends get together and share the fun—and expenses—of day-long good buy shopping trips to nearby cities. And both social and philanthropic groups have written to say they've helped their group treasuries by purchasing items they need from GOOD BUY BOOK sources.

If we've overlooked some source you think should be included, please share it with us. Just write to me in care of Rand McNally & Company, P.O. Box 7600, Chicago, Illinois 60680.

Factory outlet shopping may not be the answer to everyone's tight money problems. But for those of us who are addicted to bargain hunting, the ultimate happiness comes in being able to say, "Look at this great buy. Would you believe? I got it for 50 percent off."

Here's hoping that every buy you make is a good buy!

ANNIE MOLDAFSKY

Definitions of GOOD BUY BOOK Terms

Cancellations or discontinueds: Goods that are no longer being produced. Usually first quality.

Dents: First quality product in dented cans.

Irregulars: Goods with imperfections or flaws such as crooked stitching, gradation of color, etc., which probably will not affect the item's use.

Manufacturer's closeouts: Discontinued production. May be of first or second quality.

Mill-ends, bolt-ends, remnants, cuttings, piece goods, findings: Material not used up in production. Usually first quality.

Overrun, overstock, over-cut, surplus: Amounts manufactured beyond the amount of orders sold. Usually first quality.

Samples: One-of-a-kind items made but never mass-produced, such as manufacturer's samples and salesman's samples; also, samples used for display or advertising.

Seconds: Goods that do not conform to the manufacturer's standards. If **imperfect,** the flaws may or may not affect the use or wearability of the product.

The Good Buy Book

ILLINOIS

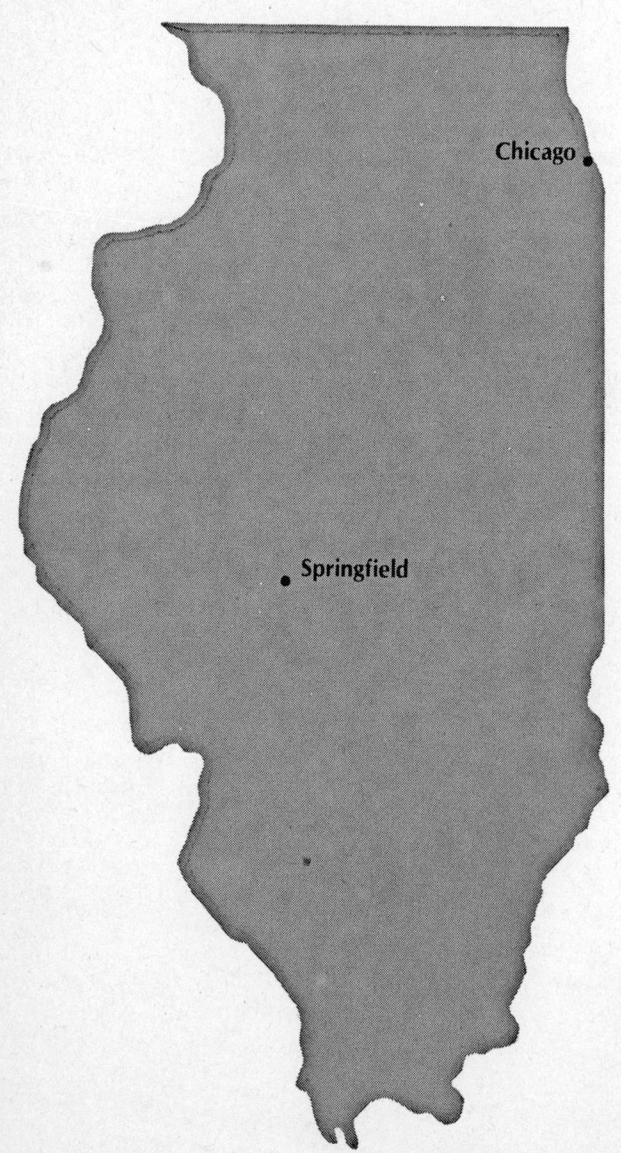

Algonquin

STORY, INC.
790 West Chicago Street
Algonquin, Illinois 60102   phone: 312-658-5626

Hours: Monday–Friday, 9 am–4 pm
       Saturday, 9 am–1 pm

Manufacturer of quality quilted spreads in full, twin, queen, and king sizes. Sells "reject" spreads (minor flaws such as spots in lining, crooked seams, fabric flaws) in such quilted fabrics as acetates, cottons, velvets, antique satins, linen, and chintz. Wide selection of colors and patterns.
Savings: 50% and more.

First quality fabric sold by the yard. Also: quilted strips and remnants for pillows and patchwork, polyester fiber batts for quilting, foam in several thicknesses, and, on occasion, ready-made drapes.

Payment: Cash, check with identification, Master Charge, Visa.
Parking: Lot next to building.

Antioch

PICKARD CHINA
782 Corona Street
Antioch, Illinois 60002   phone: 312-395-3800

Hours: Monday–Friday, 8:30 am–4 pm

Manufacturers of quality dinnerware in 24 patterns and white. Dinnerware and decorative accessories with slight imperfections are available in the showroom sales area. Dinnerware, platters, bowls, candy dishes, bonbon dishes, and candlesticks available at different times.
Savings: Average 40%.

Payment: Cash only.
Parking: Lot.

Aurora

ARBETMAN BROTHERS AND BLAIR
1620 East Mountain Street
Aurora, Illinois 60507   phone: 312-898-2500

Illinois residents only: Write to be placed on mailing list for notice of seasonal sales. Out-of-state residents can send stamped, self-addressed number ten sized envelopes for notice of spring and fall sales.

Arbetman manufactures good quality women's coats, primarily in larger sizes (10½ to 24½, 46 to 52), which are available for sale to the public only during their regularly scheduled weekend sales in the spring and fall. (Note: They have a very limited selection in sizes 8 to 20.)
Savings: 50% and up.

Also: Excellent savings on fabric remnants and sample piece goods during the scheduled sales.

Payment: Cash, check for exact amount with identification.
Parking: Lot.

PREVUE FASHIONS
11 South Broadway
Aurora, Illinois 60507   phone: 312-892-6963

Hours: Monday-Saturday, 9:30 am-5 pm
       Open Friday evenings until 8 pm

Larger of the two Prevue Fashions stores in Aurora, this is an outlet for R. M. Kaufmann, a division of Russ Toggs, Inc.

First-quality closeouts, samples, and seconds in Lady Laura, Toni Todd, and Vicky Vaughan. Dresses, suits, and pantsuits in sizes 1 to 15, 2 to 20, 12½ to 24½.
Savings: 50% and more, with closeouts priced at wholesale.

Also: End-of-bolt remnants and fabric pieces from 3 to 7 yards in polyesters, cotton, and acrylic knits selling for less than $1.00 a yard and up.

Payment: Cash, check, Master Charge, Visa.
Parking: Difficult. Park in municipal lot or in bank lots on Wednesday.

PREVUE FASHIONS
Northgate Shopping Plaza
Lake Street
Aurora, Illinois 60507   phone: 312-892-7200

Hours: Monday-Friday, 9:30 am-9 pm
        Saturday, 9:30 am-5:30 pm
        Sunday, 12 noon-5 pm

Stock basically like the Prevue Fashions on South Broadway. More samples in size 9 and 10 here and, sometimes, samples in size 12, usually priced under $20.
Savings: About 50%.

Payment: Cash, check, Master Charge, Visa.
Parking: In front of store.

Batavia

H. W. GOSSARD COMPANY FACTORY OUTLET STORE
8 West Wilson Street
Batavia, Illinois 60519   phone: 312-879-2992

Hours: Monday-Saturday, 8:30 am-5 pm

Outlet store for the H. W. Gossard Company, manufacturers of quality sleepwear, loungewear, and lingerie in small to extra-large sizes, and foundations and bras. Primarily overstocks, discontinueds, and a few irregulars. No seconds.

Wide selection of colors, prints, and fabrics in long and short nightgowns, sleep coats, pajamas, long and short robes in quilted and unquilted fabrics, slips, brief and bikini underpants, body suits, girdles, bras, and support panties. Also sell at-home loungewear and mix-and-match peignoir sets with matching slippers. Two fitting rooms.

Also: Women's support and panty hose, men's socks in all colors and stretch sizes, children's anklets and knee socks, and some fabrics and lace trims.
Savings: 30% to 70%.

Men's knit shirts from small to extra large and boy's knit shirts from sizes 4 to 6 and up to 20. Also, men's and boy's sweaters.

Payment: Cash, check with an Illinois driver's license, Master Charge, Visa.
Parking: Street parking in front of store.

Belleville ───────────────

THE FACTORY LETOUT
R. Fox Ltd.
301 South First Street
Belleville, Illinois 62220   phone: 618-233-1631

Hours: Monday-Friday, 8 am-4 pm
       Saturday, 9 am-2 pm

Retail outlet for R. Fox, Ltd., manufacturers of men's dress trousers in sizes 27 to 72.
Savings: Up to 50% on overruns and first quality.

Also: Cutting ends under 3 yards at great savings.

Payment: Cash, check for exact amount with identification.
Parking: Use factory lot on Saturdays. Park on street at other times.

Belvidere ───────────────

FACTORY FASHION CENTER
405 South State Street
Belvidere, Illinois 61008   phone: 815-547-8552

Hours: Monday-Saturday, 9 am-5:30 pm
       Open Friday evenings until 8 pm

See: Chicago, Illinois, Factory Fashion Center.

Savings: Average 50% on samples, overruns, and discontinueds—usually current styles.

Fitting rooms.

Payment: Cash only.
Parking: Street.

Bensenville ───────────────

BEELINE FASHIONS
375 Meyer Road
O'Hare Industrial Park
Bensenville, Illinois 60106   phone: 312-860-3200
(Off York Road.)

Warehouse is open twice a year, fall and spring, for a two-weekend warehouse sale. Write or call to have name put on mailing list for advance notice of sales.

BeeLine Fashions are sold through the BeeLine party plan and include a complete line of juniors (sizes 7 to 15) and misses (sizes 6 to 18) clothing including dresses and sportswear coordinates in polyesters, wool, and cotton blends. Some men's wear and children's jeans, T-shirts, and sweatshirts are also available during the warehouse sales.
Savings: From 20% to 50%, sometimes more, on first quality overruns.

Payment: Cash, check for exact amount with identification.
Parking: Lot.

Berwyn

MISS AMERICA STORE
Carmen Foundations, Inc.
6300 West 22nd Street
Berwyn, Illinois 60402   phone: 312-788-1800

Hours: Monday-Friday, 9 am-6 pm
　　　　Saturday, 9 am-5 pm

See: Chicago, Illinois, Carmen Foundation Factory Store.

This outlet sells bras, girdles, lingerie, and panty hose for the fuller figured woman.

Also: Double knit blouses (sizes 8 to 20, 38 to 46), and slacks (sizes 8 to 20, 16½ to 24½, 42 to 54).
Savings: 30% to 50% on irregulars, seconds, discontinueds, and overruns in misses' and half sizes. (No junior sizes.)

Payment: Cash, check for exact amount with identification.
Parking: Street.

Bloomington

BEICH'S CANDY
Interstate 55 and Interstate 74
Bloomington, Illinois 61701   phone: 309-828-1311

Hours: Monday-Friday, 8 am-4:30 pm
Manufacturers of candy for fund-raising programs and retail sales.

Quality products include Katydids, Truffles, Golden Crumbles, Taffy Caramels, and party nuts.
Savings: Up to 50% on seconds and overproduction.

Tours of the plant are scheduled at 45-minute intervals between 9:15 am and 2:15 pm, except on weekends and holidays.

Payment: Cash, check with identification.
Parking: Lot.

Carol Stream

SEARS CATALOG SURPLUS STORE
455 South Schmale Road
Carol Stream, Illinois 60187   phone: 312-690-7200

Hours: Monday-Friday, 9:30 am-9 pm
        Saturday, 9:30 am-5 pm
        Sunday, 11 am-5 pm

See: Chicago, Illinois, Sears Catalog Surplus Store.

Larger selection of merchandise at this location.
Savings: 20% to 80%.

Payment: Cash, check with identification, Sears charge card.
Parking: Lot.

Carpentersville

GRIST "MILL ENDS" AND THINGS
39 East Main Street
Carpentersville, Illinois 60110   phone: 312-426-6455

Hours: Monday-Friday, 9 am-5 pm
        Saturday, 9:30 am-3:30 pm

Located in the Old Grist Mill, which dates back to 1846, Grist "Mill Ends" and Things does machine quilting for decorators and individuals and custom makes bedspreads and draperies.
Savings: 40% and up on discontinued and sample bedspreads and pillows.

Also: Good savings on pieces of quilted fabric, quilting materials, and antique satin, cotton, and velvet fabrics in a range of colors and prints.

Payment: Cash, check with identification, Master Charge, Visa.
Parking: Lot.

Cary

HARVEY MANUFACTURING COMPANY
1122 North Silver Lake Road
Cary, Illinois 60013   phone: 312-639-2166

Hours: Monday-Friday, 8 am-4:30 pm

Manufacturers of quality wicker accessories including hampers, wastebaskets, wall shelves, and tissue dispensers in six colors and varying weaves.
Savings: 50% and more on seconds and overruns.

Payment: Cash only.
Parking: In front of building.

Champaign

BASS SHOE FACTORY OUTLET
Burgess Shoe Store
503 South Mattis Street
Champaign, Illinois 61820   phone: 217-359-7351

Hours: Monday-Saturday, 9 am-9 pm
         Sunday, 10 am-6 pm

Shoes and boots for men and women. Seconds, overruns, and some discontinueds with all merchandise guaranteed. Returns and exchanges permitted, with receipt, on merchandise that has not been worn.
Savings: Up to 50% on Bass overruns and discontinueds.

Payment: Cash, check, Master Charge, Visa.
Parking: Lot.

CHAMPAIGN MATTRESS FACTORY
104 South Second Street
Champaign, Illinois 61820   phone: 217-356-9071

Hours: Monday-Friday, 8 am-6 pm
         Saturday, 8 am-3 pm

Manufacturer of foam and innerspring mattresses and box springs in Medium Firm, Regular Firm, Firm Best, and Extra Firm categories, and twin, full, queen, and king sizes.
Savings: Up to 50% when compared to normal retail prices for comparable quality product.

Free delivery in the city of Champaign; delivery charges beyond the city area.

Payment: Cash, check for exact amount with identification, Master Charge, Visa.
Parking: Back of the store.

Chicago

ADVANCE UNIFORM COMPANY
1132 South Wabash Avenue
Chicago, Illinois 60603   phone: 312-922-1797

Hours: Monday-Friday, 8 am-5:30 pm
       Saturday, 8 am-3 pm

Men's and women's uniforms and career apparel for police, postal workers, chauffeurs, bellhops, hospital workers, factory and store security personnel, bank tellers, receptionists, and salespersons. Five fitting rooms.

For men: jackets in sizes 36 to 52, pants in sizes 29 to 54, and shirts in sizes 14½ to 19.

For women: jackets in sizes 6 to 20, skirts and pants in sizes 6 to 20, and blouses in sizes 30 to 38.

Note: Advance also manufactures made-to-measure uniforms for other than standard sizes.
Savings: Average 25%.

Payment: Cash, check with identification, Master Charge, Visa.
Parking: On street or S.E. corner of Roosevelt and Wabash.

AFFY TAPPLE, INC.
7110 North Clark Street
Chicago, Illinois 60626   phone: 312-338-1100

Hours: Monday-Saturday, 7 am-5 pm
Savings: 50% on taffy apple seconds.

Also: Savings on slightly bruised or discolored fresh apples when available

Payment: Cash only.
Parking: In front.

Illinois • Chicago

AMERICAN FAMILY SCALE COMPANY, INC.
3718 South Ashland Avenue
Chicago, Illinois 60609   phone: 312-376-6811

Hours: Monday-Friday, 8:30 am-4 pm

Manufacturers of molded plastic baby seats; kitchen, nursery, diet, and peddler scales; and kitchen timers. Hanging peddler household scales, perfect for hanging plants, artificial flower or fruit arrangements, are bright red, green, or black. Kitchen scales are antiqued in red, green, or black.
Savings: 30% off retail on all products.

Payment: Cash only.
Parking: Lot or street.

ANDREWS CARAMEL APPLES
3258-60 West Fullerton Avenue
Chicago, Illinois 60622   phone: 312-772-7484

Hours: Monday-Friday, 7 am-4 pm
       Saturday, 7 am-1 pm

Savings: 50% on caramel apple seconds, when available.

Payment: Cash only.
Parking: In rear.

ARMOUR DIAL MEN'S CLUB STORE
1344 West 31st Place
Chicago, Illinois 60608   phone: 312-247-0016
(Located 2 blocks east of Ashland, ½ block south of 31st.)

Hours: Monday-Friday, 9 am-4 pm
       Saturdays, 9 am-12 noon

Armour Dial outlet store selling soaps, detergents, dry bleach, water softener, prewash products, sizing, floor wax, and wax remover. Also some Armour meat products.
Savings: Up to 60% on unwrapped Dial soap in bath and hand sizes, white and colors, sold in bags of one dozen each.

Also: Small savings on Armour meat products, when available, with greater savings during store case-lot specials.

Payment: Cash only.
Parking: Street and lot.

ARROW SOAP
7116 South Troy Street
Chicago, Illinois 60629   phone: 312-776-6917

Hours: Monday-Friday, 3:30 pm-5:30 pm

Special formula, powdered, low sudsing, biodegradable laundry detergent, dishwashing liquid, and Blue Fluff fabric softener.

Sold by telephone order only and delivered to the home at a small extra charge in the Chicago metropolitan area and suburbs: south to Joliet, west to Schaumburg, and north to the Wisconsin state line.
Savings: Average at least 25% for a quality detergent product.

Payment: Cash, check.

ARVEY PAPER AND SUPPLIES CENTER
A Division of Arvey Corporation
3555 North Kimball Avenue
Chicago, Illinois 60618   phone: 312-463-0822

Hours: Monday-Friday, 8 am-5:30 pm
       Saturday, 9 am-1 pm

This self-service warehouse store sells paper and paper products to churches, schools, organizations, and small businesses. The store stocks mimeo and bond papers (watermarked and unwatermarked) in several textures and weights and in white or colors. It also stocks envelopes, business cards and file cards, social announcements, white and manila envelopes in all sizes from 2¼" to 10"×15", printing supplies and equipment, office supplies, hot and cold paper cups, and some janitorial supplies. Paper is sold by the ream (500 sheets to a package) and envelopes in boxes of 500. Manila envelopes may be purchased in quantities of 100.
Savings: At least 33⅓% on paper supplies and more on the half-price table, which features weekly specials.

Payment: Cash, check for exact amount with identification.
Parking: Lot.

BALTIC BAKERY
4627 South Hermitage Avenue
Chicago, Illinois 60609   phone: 312-523-1510

Hours: Monday-Friday, 7 am-8 pm
        Saturday, Sunday, 7 am-7 pm

Baker of all varieties of breads, cakes, and rolls for supermarket chains.
Savings: 30% to 50% on day-old product.

Payment: Cash, check for exact amount.
Parking: Across the street.

BESLEY TIE SHOPS, INC.
17 North Wabash Avenue
Chicago, Illinois 60602   phone: 312-236-8182

Hours: Monday-Friday, 9 am-5:15 pm
        Saturday, 9 am-3:30 pm

Manufacturers of first quality men's neckties in cotton, silk, polyester, and wool fabrics and in knits, reps, foulards, solids, and patterns. Besley also has women's original design, hand-painted scarves in silk and polyester. (Priced from around $6.00 to $25.00.)
Savings: 33⅓% to 50%.

Payment: Cash, check for exact amount with identification.
Parking: City underground on South Michigan Avenue.

BESLEY TIE SHOPS, INC.
123 South Franklin Street
Chicago, Illinois 60606   phone: 312-726-4238

Hours: Monday-Friday, 8 am-5:30 pm
        Saturday, 8 am-12 noon
Savings: 33⅓% to 50%.

Payment: Cash, check for exact amount with identification.
Parking: City lot next door.

BUTCHER BLOCK & MORE FACTORY STORE
The Schoenheit Company
1600 South Clinton Avenue
Chicago, Illinois 60616   phone: 312-421-1138
(Factory Store is on second floor.)

Hours: Monday-Saturday, 9 am-4 pm

Manufacturers of chopping blocks and boards and butcher block tables, benches, shelves, and chopping bowls.
Savings: 20% to 40% on seconds in cutting blocks, boards, and table tops.

Payment: Cash, check for exact amount with identification.
Parking: Lot.

B & W GOLF BALL COMPANY
6244 West Belmont Avenue
Chicago, Illinois 60634   phone: 312-283-7111

Hours: Monday-Friday, 9 am-8 pm
       Saturday, 9 am-6 pm

Driving range golf balls, x-max flite, and B & W solid balls. First quality.
Savings: 25% to 50%.

Payment: Cash, check.
Parking: In back.

CARMEN FOUNDATIONS FACTORY STORE
411 South Sangamon Street
Chicago, Illinois 60607   phone: 312-829-1801
(Right off Van Buren.)

Hours: Monday-Friday, 9 am-3:30 pm

Carmen Foundations manufactures foundation garments for the fuller figured woman. These include bras (sizes 34B to 54D) and girdles (sizes 32 and up), which are sold through leading national retailers.
Savings: 30% to 50% on irregulars, seconds, discontinueds, and overruns in bras, girdles, lingerie, panty hose, and tank-style bathing suits in misses' and half sizes. (No junior sizes.)

Payment: Cash, check for exact amount with identification.
Parking: Street.

Illinois • Chicago

CHARLES HOLLENBACH, INC.
2653 Ogden Avenue
Chicago, Illinois 60608   phone: 312-521-2500

Hours: Monday-Friday, 7:30 am-3:30 pm

Unsliced dry salami, pepperoni, pizza sausage, Genoa, soft summer sausage, thuringer, and Old Smoky Beef, in whole sausages and smaller pieces.
Savings: Up to 25%.

Payment: Cash, check for exact amount with identification.
Parking: Street, and difficult.

CHERNIN'S SHOES
606 West Roosevelt Road
Chicago, Illinois 60607   phone: Men's shoes,
(At Jefferson.)   312-922-4545
                             Women's/Children's shoes,
                             312-939-4080

Hours: Monday-Saturday, 9 am-6 pm
       Sunday, 9:30 am-5 pm

To request catalog for mail order, call:
   Illinois Residents: 312-922-4545
   Toll Free Number: 800-621-5454

Chernin's, an outlet for the Florsheim Shoe Company, sells first quality, discontinueds, and factory damaged shoes and boots from many of America's best name manufacturers and some imports. Included in the labels found in Chernin Shoes are Bally, Allen Edwards, Nettleton, and Stacey Adams for men; Air Step, Caresse, S.R.O., Bass, Custom Craft, Herbert Levine, Louis Jourdan, Pappagallo, and Selby's for women.

Each Chernin's store (there are four in the Chicago area) carries a large inventory of men's, women's, and children's casual, dress, sport, and work shoes; athletic shoes; and fashion, hiking, and bad weather boots. Sizes for women: 5 to 11, AAA to D. For men: 5½ to 15, AA to EEE and some EEEEE.
Savings: 30% to 60% and even greater during frequent store sales.

Payment: Cash, check with identification, Master Charge, Visa.
Parking: Lot.

CHICAGO KNITTING MILLS
3344 West Montrose Avenue
Chicago, Illinois 60618   phone: 312-463-1464

Hours: Monday-Friday, 8 am-4:30 pm
        Saturday, 9 am-4:30 pm

Chicago Knitting Mills manufactures varsity, cheerleader, and school sweaters and jackets including a 100% wool, excellent weight button-down or v-necked classic slipover in 18 colors (in a combination of white and one color), which can be made to order within four weeks.
Savings: At least 30% on the 100% wool, custom made sweaters.

Sweaters also available through mail order.

Payment: Cash, check.
Parking: Street.

CHICAGO SHOE OUTLET
4422 West Belmont Avenue
Chicago, Illinois 60641   phone: 312-736-1144

Hours: Monday-Friday, 10 am-8 pm
        Saturday, 10 am-6 pm
        Sunday, 11 am-5 pm

Outlet for Florsheim Shoe Company. Dress, sport, and work shoes and boots for men and women including (for men) such labels as Design Collection and Royal Imperial. Chicago Shoe Outlet price range: $25 to $75.
Savings: About 30% and up on first quality footwear.

Payment: Cash, check, American Express, Master Charge, Visa.
Parking: Lot.

CRACKER JACK
4800 West 66th Street
Chicago, Illinois 60638   phone: 312-767-6800

Hours: Monday-Friday, 9 am-3:30 pm

Cracker Jacks and Campfire Marshmallows sold in case quantity only. Twelve 1-lb. bags of marshmallows in a case; 50 or 100 boxes of Cracker Jacks in a case.
Savings: 33⅓% average on case quantity.

Payment: Cash only.
Parking: Lot.

CRATE & BARREL
850 North Michigan Avenue
Chicago, Illinois 60611 phone: 312-787-5900
(Seconds Room is located in lower level.)

Hours: Monday, Thursday, 10 am-7 pm
Tuesday, Wednesday, Friday, Saturday, 10 am-6 pm
Sunday, 12 noon-5 pm

Crate & Barrel, the Tiffany of the kitchen world, sells well-designed contemporary living accessories that include cookware, glassware, dinnerware, flatware, and stemware. Many of the items are imports from England, Ireland, France, Germany, Italy, Denmark, Sweden, and China.

An important department in each Crate & Barrel store is the Seconds Room for Arabia seconds, Copco seconds, and inexpensive machine-made glass.
Savings: 30% to 70% on seconds, discontinueds, and closeouts.

Payment: Cash, check with identification, Crate & Barrel charge, Master Charge, Visa.
Parking: Private or city garages within two block area.

CRATE & BARREL WAREHOUSE STORE
1510 North Wells Street
Chicago, Illinois 60610 phone: 312-787-4775

Hours: Monday-Saturday, 10 am-6 pm
Sunday, 12 noon-5 pm

Seconds, discontinueds, and closeouts from all the regular Crate & Barrel stores, plus factory closeouts from Pilgrim Glass, seconds from Leyse, and seconds from other manufacturers of cookware, dinnerware, glassware, and flatwear. Also: Marimekko linen seconds and closeout patterns.
Savings: 30% to 70% on well-designed home accessories.

Payment: Cash, check with identification, Crate & Barrel charge, Master Charge, Visa.
Parking: Metered parking on street. Private garage one block north.

CRAWFORD SAUSAGE COMPANY
2314 South Pulaski Road
Chicago, Illinois 60623   phone: 312-277-3905

Hours: Monday-Friday, 1 pm-3 pm
        Saturday, 9 am-12 noon

Crawford makes 45 different kinds of sausage, which are sold by the whole sausage only. Frankfurters are available in 5-lb. boxes.
Savings: 20% and up.

Payment: Cash only.
Parking: Lot.

DANIELSON FOOD PRODUCTS
215 West Root Street
Chicago, Illinois 60609   phone: 312-285-2111

Hours: Monday-Friday, 7 am-3 pm

Five-pound packs of frozen pork sausage and Italian sausage in long links, short links, and patties; fresh hamburger patties; beanless chili mix with meat; and barbecued beef, Italian beef, and roast beef with gravy.

An excellent value is the chili mix, sold in 2½-lb. "bricks," each of which makes a half gallon of beanless chili with the addition of a quart of water.
Savings: 25% and more.

Payment: Cash, check for exact amount with identification.
Parking: Lot on Wells.

DAVIDSON'S BAKERIES SURPLUS STORE
5921 North Broadway
Chicago, Illinois 60660   phone: 312-561-8055

Hours: Monday-Saturday, 7 am-6 pm

Rye and white, sliced and unsliced breads; and rolls, layer cakes, coffee cakes, and sweet rolls.
Savings: About 50% on day-old when available.

Payment: Cash only.
Parking: Metered—dimes, quarters.

DRESSEL'S BAKERY
6630 South Ashland Avenue
Chicago, Illinois 60636			phone: 312-434-5300
(Main plant store.)

Hours: Monday-Friday, 9 am-5:30 pm
        Saturday, 9 am-5 pm

Complete restaurant line of whipped-cream cakes, dessert cakes (9"), coffee cakes, sweet rolls, and Danish; special-order decorated cakes; cookies; and seasonal specialty items.
Savings: 33⅓% to 50% on seconds.

Payment: Cash, check with identification, food stamps.
Parking: Metered—nickels, dimes.

DRESSEL'S BAKERY
5859 West Irving Park Road
Chicago, Illinois 60634			phone: 312-685-4124

Hours: Monday-Friday, 9:30 am-6 pm
        Saturday, 9 am-5:30 pm
        Sunday, 9:30 am-3 pm
Savings: 33⅓% to 50% on seconds.

Payment: Cash, check with identification, food stamps.
Parking: Lot.

E. J. BRACH AND SON
Division of American Home Products Corporation
4656 West Kinzie Avenue
Chicago, Illinois 60624			phone: 312-626-1200

Hours: Monday-Friday, 9 am-4:30 pm

Chocolates, hard candies, and holiday specialties sold by the pound and in bulk.
Savings: 35% and more on such specialties as the 25-lb. "grocery mix" of multi-flavored candies (no chocolates included).

Payment: Cash only.
Parking: Street, and very difficult.

FACTORY FASHION CENTER
2926 North Pulaski Avenue
Chicago, Illinois 60641   phone: 312-283-8000

Hours: Monday-Saturday, 9 am-5 pm

Factory outlet for a Chicago-based manufacturer of popular priced women's ready-to-wear in junior sizes (5 to 15), misses' sizes (8 to 20), and half sizes (12½ to 20½). Line includes dresses, pantsuits, slacks, blouses, jackets, coats, and long dresses. Three fitting rooms.
Savings: Average 50% on samples, overruns, and discontinueds— usually current styles.

Payment: Cash only.
Parking: Street.

FANNIE MAY CANDIES
1137 West Jackson Boulevard
Chicago, Illinois 60607   phone: 312-243-2700

Hours: Monday-Friday, 8:30 am-5 pm
       Saturday, 9 am-2 pm

Fannie May chocolates, caramels, creams, nut clusters, mints, and assorted confections are made at this location.
Savings: Up to 50% on seconds, but shop early for best selection.

Payment: Cash only.
Parking: Street.

FANNIE MAY CANDIES
1813 West Montrose Avenue
Chicago, Illinois 60613   phone: unlisted

Hours: Monday-Friday, 8 am-6 pm
       Saturday, 9 am-6 pm
       Sunday, 10 am-4 pm

Savings: Up to 50% on seconds.

Shop Tuesday, Thursday, Friday, and Sunday for best selection.

Payment: Cash, check for exact amount with identification.
Parking: Street

FASANO PIE THRIFT STORE
6201 West 65th Street
Bedford Park
Chicago, Illinois 60638 phone: 312-767-8760

Hours: Monday-Friday, 9 am-6 pm

Fasano bakes fresh and frozen berry and fruit pies primarily for restaurants and institutions in a 9" size. Varieties include apple, blueberry, cherry, peach, pineapple, pumpkin, and custard pies. Frozen pies by the case only: 6 pies of one flavor only to each case.
Savings: Average 33⅓% on fresh, broken pies, sold individually. Selection varies daily.

Payment: Cash, check for exact amount with identification.
Parking: In front.

FLAVOR KIST
Schulze and Burch Biscuit Company
Main Plant
1133 West 35th Street
Chicago, Illinois 60609 phone: 312-927-6622

Hours: Monday-Saturday, 8 am-11 pm

Bakers of saltines and unsalted crackers; sandwich, bar, oatmeal, chocolate, marshmallow, raisin, plain, and frosted cookies; packaged cookies; and parfait dessert cakes.
Savings: Up to 50% on fresh misformed or broken cookies and crackers in 3-lb. bags and boxes.

Also: New product test runs, when available.

Payment: Cash only.
Parking: Side lot.

FLAVOR KIST
Schulze and Burch Biscuit Company
6001 South Kedzie Avenue
Chicago, Illinois 60629 phone: 312-476-9477

Hours: Monday-Saturday, 8:30 am-6 pm
       Open Fridays until 7 pm
Savings: Up to 50%.

Payment: Cash only.
Parking: Street.

GEORGIA NUT COMPANY
3325 North California Avenue
Chicago, Illinois 60618   phone: 312-539-0240

Hours: Monday-Friday, 7:30 am-4:30 pm

Complete line of nut meats, salted and unsalted, including cashews, filberts, pecans, peanuts, pistachios, walnuts, and mixed nuts. Also: Candies and dried fruits including apricots, dates, papaya, pineapple, prunes, and raisins.
Savings: From 30% to 50% on quality sized nut meats; greater savings on broken pecans and walnuts for baking.

Payment: Cash, check for exact amount with identification.
Parking: Street.

GINGISS FORMALWEAR WAREHOUSE
555 West 14th Place
Chicago, Illinois 60607   phone: 312-829-1188

Hours: Monday-Saturday, 9:30 am-5 pm

Gingiss is the world's largest seller and renter of formalwear and accessories including tuxedos, trousers, dinner jackets, fancy shirts, vests, cummerbunds, ties, and accessories in sizes 3 to 60.
Savings: 40% and better on irregular formal shirts, tuxedos, etc.

Greater savings on sales of used formalwear during the once-a-year advertised warehouse clearance sale usually held in February or March.

Payment: Cash, check with identification, Master Charge, Visa.
Parking: Lot.

GRAPHIC TWO
247 East Ontario Street
Chicago, Illinois 60611   phone: 312-944-7572

Hours: Monday-Friday, 8 am-4 pm

Graphic Two stocks and sells papers, envelopes, and supplies for printers and small business concerns. Inventory includes reams of

paper (500 sheets in a ream) and envelopes from 2½" up to 10" in boxes of 500 in white and colors and service weights.
Savings: Average at least 30% and more when compared to prices in regular retail stationery sources.

Payment: Cash, check for exact amount with identification.
Parking: Difficult. Temporary parking in driveway or in front of loading dock.

GUARANTY CLOCK COMPANY
6422 West Belmont Avenue
Chicago, Illinois 60634   phone: 312-282-6730

Hours: Monday, Thursday, 9 am-9 pm
        Tuesday, Wednesday, Friday, Saturday, 9 am-5:30 pm

Grandfather, chime, cuckoo, and decorator wall clocks.
Savings: 25% to 35% off list price on floor clocks and 20% off list price on all other clocks.

Note: Guaranty services all clocks it sells.

Payment: Cash, check for exact amount, Master Charge, Visa.
Parking: Street and rear of building.

KITCHENS OF SARA LEE THRIFT STORE
7654 West Touhy Avenue
Chicago, Illinois 60648   phone: unlisted

Hours: Monday-Thursday, 9 am-6 pm
        Friday, 9 am-9 pm
        Saturday, 9 am-5 pm

See: Deerfield, Illinois, Kitchens of Sara Lee Thrift Store.
Savings: 20% to 50%, with greater savings on specials.

Deliveries every day but Saturday.

Payment: Cash only.
Parking: Lot.

KOSHER ZION SAUSAGE COMPANY
5511 North Kedzie Avenue
Chicago, Illinois 60625　　　　　　phone: 312-463-3351

Hours:　Monday-Thursday, 8 am-5:30 pm
　　　　　Friday, 8 am-3 pm
　　　　　Sunday, 8 am-5 pm
　　　　　Closed Saturdays.

Complete delicatessen line of pure beef kosher products including corned beef, tongue, pepper beef, roast beef, cold cuts, sausage, bologna, pastrami, and hot dogs. Meats sliced at no extra cost.
Savings: 25% and more on rejects—product that doesn't meet size or perfect appearance standards.

Also: As an extra service, Kosher Zion packages whole salamis in a special tube for mailing anywhere in the country.

Payment: Cash, check for exact amount with identification.
Parking: Lot.

KROCH'S AND BRENTANO'S BARGAIN BOOK CENTER
62 East Randolph Street
Chicago, Illinois 60601　　　　　　phone: 312-263-2681

Hours:　Monday, Thursday, 9 am-7 pm
　　　　　Tuesday, Wednesday, Friday, Saturday, 9 am-6 pm

First stop for several publisher's remainders or overstocks. Large selection of popular titles, subject headings, reference, and art books, remainders, reprints, and imports.
Savings: 50% to 80% and more with a wide selection of varying specials available all the time.

Payment: Cash, check, Kroch's charge card, Master Charge, Visa.
Parking: Private lots within one block. Underground parking in Grant Park lot.

LASSER BEVERAGE COMPANY
2452 North Sheffield Avenue
Chicago, Illinois 60614　　　　　　phone: 312-549-0400

Hours:　Monday-Friday, 7:30 am-5:30 pm
　　　　　Saturday, 7:30 am-4:30 pm

Lasser makes soft drinks according to old family recipes in 10-ounce and quart bottles and in 12-ounce cans. The product, which is sold by

the case only (one flavor to a case), includes such all-time favorites as black cherry, cream, grape, orange, sarsaparilla, strawberry, ginger ale, sparkling water, and tonic. There are also more unusual flavors (in 10-ounce bottles) like apple/champagne, cranberry, peppermint, root beer, and maple.
Savings: At least 25% and more on favorite "old-time" flavors.

Also: Savings on beers from smaller area breweries and wines from Austria and Germany, which are sold by the case only at wholesale prices.

Payment: Cash, check for exact amount with identification.
Parking: Street. Difficult on Saturdays.

LAVA SIMPLEX INTERNATIONALE, INC.
1650 Irving Park Road
Chicago, Illinois 60613   phone: 312-528-6000

Hours: Monday-Friday, 8:30 am-5 pm
Manufacturers of Lava-Lites, Gemlites, The Wave, Roto Lite, and Infinity Lite. The Lava Simplex process permanently seals oils and chemicals into glass, and a motorized base permits the sealed material to flow and create changing patterns within the enclosed shape. Firsts and some seconds are sold here.
Savings: About 40%.

Payment: Cash, check for exact amount.
Parking: Side streets.

LEO'S ADVANCE THEATRICAL COMPANY
125 North Wabash Avenue
Chicago, Illinois 60602   phone: 312-772-7150

Hours: Monday-Friday, 9:30 am-5:30 pm
       Saturday, 9:30 am-2:30 pm
       Closed Saturdays in June and July
Theatrical supply house. Carries Danskin discontinueds in leotards and tights. Assorted sizes but limited colors.
Savings: Almost 50% on Danskin discontinueds.

Also: Discontinued and irregular leotards and ballet slippers under Leo's own label in a wider range of colors and sizes.
Savings: 25% to 35%.

Payment: Cash, check with identification.
Parking: City underground on South Michigan Avenue.

LOOMCRAFT TEXTILES
4892 North Clark Street
Chicago, Illinois 60640   phone: 312-275-1414

Hours: Monday-Friday, 9 am-5 pm
        Saturday, 10 am-4 pm
        Closed Saturdays in June, July, and August

Loomcraft, a wholesale distributor of drapery and upholstery fabrics and an importer of fabrics from mills all over the world, sells to furniture manufacturers, retailers, and the public. They offer a large selection of bolt fabrics (priced from $2 to $15 per yard) in a wide variety of colors, weaves, finishes, and patterns. Bolts range from 15 to 180 yards and fabrics may be purchased by the yard or by the bolt.
Savings: 50% to 75% on first quality fabrics.

Payment: Cash, check for exact amount with identification.
Parking: Metered.

MAMA COOKIE BAKERIES, INC.
7200 South Kostner Avenue
Chicago, Illinois 60629   phone: 312-767-8200

Hours: Monday-Saturday, 9 am-5 pm

Assorted cookies, in bulk or boxed, in 2- and 5-lb. quantities.
Savings: 33⅓% to 50% on broken cookies and seconds.

Payment: Cash only.
Parking: Large lot.

MATERNITY FACTORY OUTLET
Dan Howard Maternity Clothes
7th Floor
710 West Jackson Boulevard
Chicago, Illinois, 60606   phone: 312-263-6700

Hours: Monday-Friday, 12 noon-5 pm
        Saturday, 9 am-3 pm

Outlet for manufacturer of quality maternity clothes in sizes 4 to 26, including sportswear, career clothing, bathing suits, and lingerie. Fitting rooms.
Savings: 20% to 50% on first quality production overruns and samples. Greater savings on irregulars and seconds.

Payment: Cash, check with identification, Master Charge, Visa.
Parking: Lot at corner of Adams and Desplaines.

MONASTERY HILL BINDERY
1751 West Belmont Avenue
Chicago, Illinois 60657   phone: 312-525-4126

Send self-addressed postcard for notification of sales.

Manufacturers of leather goods and novelties including picture frames, wastebaskets, photo albums, binders, some books, and limited edition sets of cloth bound books.
Savings: 50% and more on discontinued quality merchandise at special scheduled sales.

Payment: Cash, check for exact amount with identification.
Parking: Street.

MONTGOMERY WARD CATALOG LIQUIDATION CENTER
618 West Chicago Avenue
Chicago, Illinois 60610   phone: 312-467-8902
(First floor and basement budget store in Montgomery Ward Headquarters building.)

Hours: Monday, Friday, 9:30 am-7:30 pm
        Tuesday, Wednesday, Thursday, Saturday, 9:30 am-5 pm
        Open Friday evenings until 8:30 pm

Main outlet for Montgomery Ward catalog surplus and merchandise return including clothing for all members of the family and a large selection of furniture. Furniture is sold on the first and eighth floors and in the basement budget store.
Savings: Average 50%.

Payment: Cash, check for exact amount with identification, Montgomery Ward Charge-All.
Parking: Free in garage across the street.

PHIL MAID, INC.
1033 West Van Buren Street
Chicago, Illinois 60607   phone: 312-829-2772

Four-times-a-year warehouse sale.

Write or call to be placed on mailing list for regularly scheduled warehouse sales held in the main plant.

Phil Maid manufactures lingerie; sleepwear; loungewear; dusters; full, half, and evening slips; panties, briefs, and bikinis; robes and shifts; and sleep shirts. Sizes range from petite to extra large.
Savings: 20% to 80% on samples, overstocks, discontinueds, and some irregulars.

Also: Large selection of fabrics by the yard, scrap bags, quilt squares, laces, buttons, zippers, and threads at excellent savings.

Payment: Cash, check for exact amount with identification.
Parking: Street.

PICK FISHERIES, INC.
702 West Fulton Market
Chicago, Illinois 60606   phone: 312-226-4700

Hours: Monday-Friday, 7 am-5 pm
        Saturday, 7 am-2 pm

Over 500 different species of fresh and frozen seafood including white fish, trout, pike, pickerel, herring, crab, eel, grouper, cod, carp, catfish, shrimp, lobster, clams, and frog legs. Fish will be cut and filleted at an additional charge of 15¢ per pound.
Savings: Up to 25%.

Also: Frozen vegetables, fruits, turkey products, onion rings, mushrooms, and orange juice concentrates at some savings.

Payment: Cash, check.
Parking: Street, and difficult.

RANDOLPH PACKING COMPANY
158 North Sangamon Street
Chicago, Illinois 60607   phone: 312-421-3320

Hours: Monday-Friday, 7 am-2 pm
        Saturday, 7 am-11 pm

Pork products only. Wide selection of sausages sold in 5-lb. boxes.
Savings: Up to 20%.

Also: Swiss, muenster, brick, cheddar, provolone, and American cheeses, in blocks and sliced, at some savings.

Payment: Cash, check for exact amount with identification.
Parking: Street.

Illinois • Chicago

RICCI NUTS
162 West Superior Street
Chicago, Illinois 60610   phone: 312-787-7660

Hours: Monday-Friday, 7 am-4:30 pm
       Saturday, 7 am-11:30 am

Ricci roasts and sells nuts to retail stores and well-known food service companies. Premium-sized nuts, salted and unsalted, are available here in every variety, except macadamia nuts.
Savings: Up to 40% less than normal retail prices for quality nuts. Greater savings on broken pecan and walnut pieces for baking.

Call ahead to place order.

Payment: Cash, check for exact amount with identification.
Parking: Front loading zone.

ROYAL KNITTING MILLS
Factory Outlet Store
20th and South California Avenue
Chicago, Illinois 60608   phone: 312-247-6300

Hours: Monday-Friday, 10 am-3:30 pm
       Saturday, 9 am-12 noon

Classically styled wool, acrylic, and cotton sweaters for men, women, and children (sizes 8 to 20).
Also: Men's and women's chenille warm-up jackets and sweaters, gloves, hats, dickeys, and vests.
Savings: 20% to 60% on first quality and sample sweaters; greater savings on irregulars.

Payment: Cash, check for exact amount with identification.
Parking: Lot.

ROYAL KNITTING MILLS
2nd Floor
Off Center Shopping Center
300 West Grand Avenue
Chicago, Illinois 60610   phone: 312-329-1433

Hours: Monday-Saturday, 10 am-5 pm
       Sunday, 11 am-5 pm

Savings: 20% to 60% on first quality men's and women's sweaters and some samples.

Chicago • Illinois

Payment: Cash, check for exact amount with identification, Ma
Charge, Visa.
Parking: Street or private lots.

RUBENS BABY FACTORY
2340 North Racine Avenue
Chicago, Illinois 60614   phone: 312-348-6200

Hours: Monday-Friday, 9 am-4 pm
Factory outlet store for infants' undergarments, diapers, underwear, waterproof pants, and kimonos. Made for hospitals and institutional use.
Savings: Up to 50% on irregulars or seconds.

Mail orders accepted.

Payment: Cash, check for exact amount with identification.
Parking: Street.

SEARS CATALOG SURPLUS STORE
5555 South Archer Avenue
Chicago, Illinois 60638   phone: 312-284-3200

Hours: Monday-Friday, 9 am-9 pm
       Saturday, 9 am-5 pm
       Sunday, 11 am-5 pm
Outlet store for Sears catalog surplus and returns including clothing for all members of the family, footwear, fashion accessories, housewares, and home accessories.
Savings: 20% to 80%.

Payment: Cash, check with identification, Sears charge card.
Parking: Lot.

SILVESTRI CORPORATION
2720 North Paulina Street
Chicago, Illinios 60614   phone: 312-871-5200

Hours: October—Monday-Saturday, 10 am-3:30 pm
       November, December—Monday-Saturday, 10 am-4 pm
       Open Thursday evenings until 6 pm
       Not open from January through September
Manufacturers of Christmas novelties including ornaments, lights,

and trees. Also importers of jewelry and giftware from around the world.

Factory is open to the public for the three months preceding the Christmas holiday for the sale of contemporary and traditional holiday decorations.
Savings: 40% to 80% on new merchandise.

Payment: Cash only.
Parking: Lot.

SLOTKOWSKI SAUSAGE COMPANY
2021 West 18th Street
Chicago, Illinois 60608   phone: 312-226-1667

Hours: Saturdays only, 7 am-11:30 am

More than 65 varieties of sausages sold by the whole piece or slab (no slicing). Also hams and hot dogs.
Savings: 20% to 25%.

Self service: 3/4- to 3-lb. packs of chubs and liver sausage.

Payment: Cash only.
Parking: Lot.

SMOLER BROTHERS, INC.
2300 West Wabansia Street
Chicago, Illinois 60647   phone: 312-384-1200
(Located in basement.)

Hours: Monday-Friday, 9 am-4 pm
       Saturday, 9 am-3 pm

Overruns, discontinueds, and some seconds in polyesters and bonded fabrics. Garments include dresses, pants, pantsuits, robes, sweaters, skirts, and blouses. Sizes: 8 to 20 and 14½ to 24½.
Savings: 35% to 60%.

Also: Polyesters, wools, cottons sold by the yard.

Payment: Cash, check for exact amount with identification.
Parking: Street, best on Saturday.

SPARRER SAUSAGE COMPANY
4325 West Ogden Avenue
Chicago, Illinois 60623 phone: 312-762-3334
(On the corner.)

Hours: Monday-Friday, 7:30 am-3 pm

Dry sausages sold by the piece: hard salami, smoked beef, summer sausage, thuringer, and variations. Pieces weigh from 3 to 10 lbs. with a 6-lb. average.
Savings: 20% and up to 50% on seconds, products with split or broken casings.

Payment: Cash only.
Parking: By side entrance.

SPECIALTY TRUNK AND SUITCASE COMPANY
443 North Clark Street
Chicago, Illinois 60610 phone: 312-642-1446

Hours: Monday-Friday, 8:30 am-4:30 pm
       Saturday, 8:30 am-2 pm

Manufacturer of salesmen's sample cases and decorative plywood trunks covered in sheet metal and finished in silver or brass with brass corners, locks, and hardware.

Trunks come in two sizes: a 17" x 17" x 17" cube (perfect for a coffee table) and 24" x 18" x 24" (for use as a lamp, TV, or side table). Specialty also manufactures trunks and foot lockers in all sizes.
Savings: 25% to 50%.

Also: A complete line of luggage, attaché cases, and garment bags.
Savings: Average 20%.

Payment: Cash, check for exact amount with identification.
Parking: Metered on side streets. Temporary parking in alley behind store.

SUNBEAM APPLIANCE SERVICE COMPANY
Sunbeam Oster Company
Main Plant
5340 West Roosevelt Road
Chicago, Illinois 60650 phone: 312-854-4605

Hours: Monday-Friday, 8 am-5 pm

Courtesy and service store for Sunbeam Oster, manufacturers of clocks, irons, mixers, coffee makers, frying pans, toasters, blenders,

can openers, ice crushers, kettles, griddles, waffle irons, electric knives, air filters, hot combs and brushes, hair curlers, electric toothbrushes, hair dryers, and make-up mirrors.
Savings: Up to 40% on scratched appliances or appliances in damaged cartons. Full guarantee on all appliances.

Largest selection of "as is" Sunbeam appliances available at the plant.

Payment: Cash, check for exact amount with identification.
Parking: Lot

TOM TOM TAMALE AND BAKERY COMPANY
4750 South Washtenaw Avenue
Chicago, Illinois 60632   phone: 312-523-5675

Hours: Monday-Friday, 9 am-4 pm
Saturday, 9 am-2 pm

Wholesale to the public: all-beef tamales, red hots, hamburger patties, Polish sausage, chili, buns, mustard, relish, hot peppers, sliced pickles, and catsup.

Relishes are sold in gallon containers; red hots, in 6-lb. boxes with 10 to 12 red hots per pound, depending on size; Polish sausage (5 to a pound) is sold in 2-lb. and 10-lb. packages. Minimum tamale order is 25.
Savings: 33⅓% to 50%.

Red hots are good quality—85% meat.

Prices are posted as you enter. You order from the posted list and someone quickly fills your order.

Payment: Cash only.
Parking: In front.

VIENNA SAUSAGE MANUFACTURING COMPANY
The Sausage Shop
2501 North Damen Avenue
Chicago, Illinois 60647   phone: 312-235-6652

Hours: Monday-Friday, 9 am-5 pm
Saturday, 9 am-4 pm

Pure beef, Kosher style products including corned beef, bologna,

pastrami, salami, hot dogs, and a variety of cold cuts. Vienna also makes a Kosher line under the Wilno label.
Savings: Average 33⅓% on factory irregulars, when available, in salami ends, corned beef and roast beef ends, beef bacon and sausage ends. Daily specials also available.

Note: The Sausage Shop also serves a complete menu of hot and cold deli sandwiches for snacking on the spot.

Payment: Cash only.
Parking: Lot.

VIENNA SAUSAGE MANUFACTURING COMPANY
1215 South Halsted Street
Chicago, Illinois 60607 phone: 312-226-4288

Hours: Monday-Saturday, 8 am-5:30 pm
Sunday, 9 am-3 pm
Savings: Average 33⅓%.

Payment: Cash only.
Parking: Street, metered.

VOLNA LIMITED
Mark-It Eng Corporation
2901 North Pulaski Avenue
Chicago, Illinois 50541 phone: 312-282-7200

Hours: Monday-Friday, 10 am-4:30 pm
Saturday, 10 am-2:30 pm

Manufacturer of home accessories in glass and ½" thick acrylic in three finishes: clear, smoked, and white. Items include coffee tables, parsons tables, cubes, pedestals, shelves, wine and magazine racks, etageres, and table, vertical (up to 7' tall), and bubble aquariums. Also: Chime, battery, electrical, and digital grandfather clocks.
Savings: 50% to 75% on samples and seconds.

(Note: Small scratches on the acrylic pieces marked *seconds* can usually be successfully removed by diligent rubbing with toothpaste.)

Payment: Cash, check for exact amount with identification.
Parking: On street.

Chicago Heights

STEAD TEXTILE COMPANY, INC.
Warehouse Annex
18 East Sauk Trail
Chicago Heights, Illinois 60411

phone: Illinois residents,
800-942-6739
Outside Illinois,
800-323-9176

Call toll free numbers for advance notice of the periodic "oops we goofed" factory closeout sales.

Stead, manufacturer of custom draperies, periodically opens the Warehouse Annex for the sale of closeouts, seconds, discontinueds, and "goofs" (factory made up wrong size or used wrong color or fabric in filling order) in draperies and bedspreads.
Savings: Up to 50% less than the wholesale price.

Also: Fabric remnants priced for closeout at 25¢ per yard and up. Stead will custom make drapes to your measurement from your sale fabric selection and ship them to your home via United Parcel Service. (The charge for labor is also reasonable.)

Payment: Cash, check with identification, Master Charge, Visa.
Parking: Lot.

Cicero

LINGERIE AND FABRIC SHOP
Phil Maid, Inc., Outlet Store
6104-06 Cermak Road
Cicero, Illinois 60650

phone: 312-863-0255

See: Chicago, Illinois, Phil Maid, Inc.
Savings: 20% to 80% on women's lingerie and sleepwear samples, overstocks, discontinueds, and some irregulars.

Also: Overstocks and discontinueds in men's coats (up to size 46).
Savings: 50% and up.

Note: There is a larger selection of fabrics, craft materials, and home sewing project ideas in this outlet store.

Sign mailing list in store for notice of the Phil Maid four-times-a-year warehouse sales.

Payment: Cash, check for exact amount with identification.
Parking: Street.

Clinton

PAUL REVERE SHOPPE
Revere Copper and Brass, Inc.
Clinton Division
Junction of Illinois Routes 54 and 10 and US 51
Clinton, Illinois 61727   phone: 217-935-3822

Hours: Monday-Saturday, 9 am-5 pm
        Sunday, 12 noon-5 pm

Manufacturer of quality cookware including copperclad and stainless steel bottom skillets, pots and pans of all sizes, and tea kettles; a solid copper and brass gourmet line; and kitchen tool sets.
Savings: 50% off regular retail prices on factory irregulars, discontinueds, and first quality closeouts.

Also: Pewter, Oneida stainless, sterling, and silverplate accessories.
Savings: At least 33⅓% off list.

Payment: Cash, check with identification, Master Charge, Visa.
Parking: At door.

Collinsville

MARTHA MANNING COMPANY
1700 St. Louis Road
Collinsville, Illinois 62234   phone: 618-344-7131

Hours: Monday-Saturday, 9:30 am-5 pm

Manufacturers of casual wear, skirts, slacks, vests, and jackets in polyesters and blends in sizes 5 to 15, 8 to 20, 12½ to 26½. Labels

include Martha Manning, Paula Brooks, Carole King, Mr. Simon, and Glen Echo. Five dressing rooms.
Savings: 40% and more.

Also: Savings on bolt fabrics and remnants.

Payment: Cash, check for exact amount with identification, Master Charge.
Parking: Factory lot.

Countryside

FLAVOR KIST
Schulze and Burch Biscuit Company
22 East Plainfield Road
Countryside, Illinois 60525   phone: 312-354-9704

Hours: Monday-Saturday, 9 am-6 pm
        Open Friday until 7 pm
See: Chicago, Illinois, Flavor Kist.

Savings: Up to 50% on fresh, misformed, or broken cookies and crackers in 3-lb. bags and boxes. Also, new product test-runs, when available.

Payment: Cash only.
Parking: Lot.

Crystal Lake

JEWEL CATALOG OUTLET MERCHANDISE CLEARANCE CENTER
301 Virginia Street
Crystal Lake, Illinois 60014   phone: 815-455-0333

Hours: Monday, Tuesday, 9 am-5 pm
        Wednesday, Thursday, Friday, 9 am-8 pm
        Saturday, 9 am-5 pm
        Sunday, 10 am-3 pm

Jewel's Home Shopping Service merchandise is sold by home salespersons and through catalogs. Discontinued, overstocks, returned merchandise, and private label items packaged under the Jewel name are sold here. Goods include clothing for all members of the family,

appliances, floor coverings, linens, shop tools, sports equipment, seasonal items, and toiletries.
Savings: 33⅓% to 50% on most items, including many name-brand products. Extra savings on specials.

Payment: Cash, check, Master Charge, Visa.
Parking: Lot.

Cullom

HAHN INDUSTRIES
South Walnut Street
Illinois 116 off Interstate 57
Cullom, Illinois 60929   phone: 815-689-2133

Hours: Monday-Saturday, 8:30 am-4 pm
       Sundays, 1 pm-5 pm

Manufacturers of ornamental concrete objects: figurines, lanterns, garden statuary, bird baths, and flower pots in various sizes.
Savings: Up to 50%.

Payment: Cash, check.
Parking: Available.

Decatur

DECATUR GARMENT COMPANY OUTLET STORE
620 East Eldorado Street
Decatur, Illinois 62521   phone: 217-429-5221

Hours: Monday-Saturday, 9 am-4:45 pm

Manufacturers' outlet for women's wash dresses in cotton and polyester blends. Sizes 10 to 20, 40 to 52, 12½ to 32½. Large selection of first quality, but some seconds selling for less than $4 and up. Fitting rooms.
Savings: 33⅓% and up.

Also: Exquisite Form bras and girdles, fabrics, zippers, notions, laces, and trims at good savings.

Payment: Cash, check, Master Charge, Visa.
Parking: Lot at corner of Eldorado and Broadway.

Deerfield

KITCHENS OF SARA LEE THRIFT STORE
500 Waukegan Road
Deerfield, Illinois 60015   phone: unlisted

Hours: Monday-Thursday, 9 am-6 pm
        Friday, 9 am-9 pm
        Saturday, 9 am-5 pm

Outlet for Sara Lee, manufacturers of quality, all-butter frozen baked goods. Products include coffee cakes; cheesecakes; whipped-cream, layer, and sheet cakes; dessert cakes; brownies; fruit and Bavarian cream pies; sweet rolls; and dinner rolls. Baked products are available in standard and institutional sized packages.
Savings: 20% to 50% with greater savings on specials.

Product sold in store varies, but all products are seconds, samples, or tests.

Call the Kitchens of Sara Lee Tour Office (312-945-2525) to inquire about reservations for guided tours through the Deerfield Plant. (Children under 12 are not permitted on tours.)

Payment: Cash only.
Parking: Large lot.

Des Plaines

J. B. SANFILIPPO AND SON, INC.
300 East Touhy Avenue
Des Plaines, Illinois 60018   phone: 312-298-1510
(1½ miles west of Mannheim.)

Hours: Monday-Friday, 8:30 am-4:30 pm
        Saturday, 9:30 am-2 pm

Top-quality nuts—shelled and unshelled, raw and salted—sold in bags, cello packages, and vacuum packed cans. Giant cashews; pistachios; blanched, redskin, and Spanish peanuts; pecans (halves, pieces, and in the shell); blanched, unblanched, sliced, and slivered almonds; walnut halves and pieces; blanched and unblanched filberts; Brazil nuts; and mixed nuts for baking.
Savings: 20% and up for top size and quality nutmeats.

Sanfilippo carries a variety of Evon label candy specialty items.
Savings: 20% to 25% on seconds—items returned from regular retail sources.

Also: Chocolate pecan turtles, dried fruits, and health food mixes (similar to trail and California mixes) at some savings.

Payment: Cash only.
Parking: Lot.

Downers Grove

CHERNIN'S SHOES
Finley Square
Butterfield Road and Finley Road
Downers Grove, Illinois 60515   phone: 312-620-1400
Hours: Monday-Friday, 10 am-9:30 pm
        Saturday, Sunday, 10 am-6 pm
See: Chicago, Illinois, Chernin's Shoes.
Savings: 30% to 60% and even greater during frequent store sales.

Mail orders accepted. See Chicago listing.

Payment: Cash, check with identification, Master Charge, Visa.
Parking: Lot.

FLAVOR KIST
Schulze and Burch Biscuit Company
1705 Ogden Avenue
Downers Grove, Illinois 60515   phone: 312-969-9694
Hours: Monday-Friday, 9 am-6 pm
        Saturday, 9 am-5 pm
See: Chicago, Illinois, Flavor Kist.
Savings: Up to 50% on fresh, misformed or broken cookies and crackers in boxes and 3-lb. bags.

Payment: Cash only.
Parking: Lot.

KITCHENS OF SARA LEE THRIFT STORE
Ogden and Belmont Avenues
Downers Grove, Illinois 60515   phone: unlisted

Hours: Monday-Thursday, 9 am-6 pm
        Friday, 9 am-8 pm
        Saturday, 9 am-5 pm

See: Deerfield, Illinois, Kitchens of Sara Lee Thrift Store.

Savings: 25% to 50%.

Payment: Cash only.
Parking: Lot.

MATERNITY FACTORY OUTLET
Dan Howard Maternity Clothes
2019 Ogden Avenue
Downers Grove, Illinois 60515   phone: 312-969-4666
(1 mile west of Main Street.)

Hours: Tuesday, Wednesday, Friday, Saturday, 10 am-5 pm
        Monday, Thursday, 10 am-9 pm
        Sunday, 12 noon-4 pm

See: Chicago, Illinois, Maternity Factory Outlet.

Savings: 20% to 50% on first quality production overruns and samples. Greater savings on irregulars and seconds.

Payment: Cash, check with identification, Master Charge, Visa.
Parking: Lot.

PEPPERIDGE FARM THRIFT STORE
748 Ogden Avenue
Downers Grove, Illinois 60515   phone: 312-964-6380

Hours: Monday-Friday, 9 am-6 pm
        Saturday, 9 am-5 pm
        Sunday, 10 am-4 pm

Bakery outlet store for day-old and imperfect baked goods including breads, rolls, cakes, cookies, stuffing, and snacks. Also frozen products such as cakes, pastry shells, and fruit turnovers.
Savings: 25% to 50%.

Also: Bulk pack croutons are always good buys, and the stores now carry first quality items from the Pepperidge Farm Gourmet Line—usually available only through their mail order division—at small savings. Included are pancake flour and bread mixes; jellies and jams; and blueberry, strawberry, cherry, and peach soups, as well as the more conventional black mushroom and black bean, chicken curry, and lobster soups and clam chowder.

Payment: Cash, check for exact amount with identification.
Parking: Lot

SUNBEAM APPLIANCE SERVICE COMPANY
Sunbeam Oster Corporation
1644 West Ogden Avenue
Downers Grove, Illinois 60515   phone: 312-852-1550

Hours: Monday, 8:30 am-8 pm
        Tuesday-Friday, 8:30 am-5 pm
See: Chicago, Illinois, Sunbeam Appliance Service Company.
Savings: 40% on "as is" appliances that are slightly scratched or appliances in damaged cartons. All appliances are covered by full guarantees.

Payment: Cash, check for exact amount with identification.
Parking: Lot.

WINONA KNITTING MILLS, INC., OUTLET STORE
1524 Butterfield Road
Finley Square Mall
Downers Grove, Illinois 60515   phone 312-495-9560

Hours: Monday, Tuesday, Thursday, Friday, 10 am-5:30 pm
        Wednesday, 10 am-9 pm
        Saturday, 10 am-5 pm
        Sunday, 11 am-5 pm
Winona is a manufacturer of wool and acrylic knitwear. The outlet store sells berber, rag, and tundra wool sweaters for men and women, velour and knit shirts, mittens, scarves, gloves, hats, and socks for men, women, and children.
Savings: Up to 50% on firsts and overruns; more on seconds and irregulars.

Payment: Cash, check with identification, Master Charge, Visa.
Parking: Lot.

East Dundee

HAEGER POTTERIES
7 Maiden Lane
East Dundee, Illinois 60118 phone: 312-426-3441

Hours: Monday-Saturday, 8 am-4:30 pm
Sunday, 10 am-5:30 pm

Very large, very commercial outlet store for Haeger Potteries. Manufacturers of lamps, vases, planters, pottery sculpture, figurines, table pottery, serving pieces, cookie jars, ceramic lighters, bean pots, and large ornamental urns. Supermarket carts are provided for shopping selection.

Savings: 20% to 50% on firsts, seconds, and discontinueds. Greater savings on specials.

Tours of plant on regular schedule Monday through Friday.

Payment: Cash, check, Master Charge, Visa.
Parking: Large lot.

Effingham

H. W. GOSSARD COMPANY FACTORY OUTLET STORE
106 West Washington Street
Effingham, Illinois 62401 phone: 217-342-2902
(Northwest corner of square.)

Hours: Monday-Saturday, 8:30 am-5 pm

See: Batavia, Illinois, H. W. Gossard Company Factory Outlet Store.

Savings: 30% to 70% on women's quality sleepwear, lingerie, and loungewear.

Payment: Cash, check with an Illinois driver's license.
Parking: Street.

Elgin

BRODY, INC.
630 Congdon Avenue and Illinois 25
Elgin, Illinois 60120   phone: 312-741-7940

Hours: Monday-Saturday, 9 am-5 pm
Open Sundays from the middle of September through January, 11 am-4 pm

Outlet store for Brody, manufacturer of women's quality coats under the Sycamore label, and a large selection of nationally advertised men's and women's coats, first quality and irregulars, which are discounted here.

Women's coats (sizes 6 to 20) in long and short lengths: all-wool tweeds, plaids, solids, twills, worsteds, knits; man-made furs; fur trimmed; leather; and shearling.

Men's long and short coats in leathers, shearlings, and all-weather fabrics.

All coats are marked as samples, overruns, and/or seconds and all flaws are described on the price tag.

Savings: Average 30% on name brand merchandise. Savings of up to 75% in the Special Sale Area.

Payment: Cash, personal check with identification, traveler's checks.
Parking: Street or lot.

PREVUE FASHIONS
4 Douglas Avenue
Elgin, Illinois 60120   phone: 312-742-8883
(Just north of the downtown mall.)

Hours: Monday-Friday, 9:30 am-5:30 pm
Open Monday and Thursday evenings until 9 pm

See: Aurora, Illinois, Prevue Fashions.

First quality closeouts, samples, and seconds in Lady Laura, Toni Todd, and Vicky Vaughan dresses, suits, and pantsuits in sizes 5 to 15, 10 to 20, 14½ to 24½.

Savings: 50% and more, with closeouts priced at near wholesale cost.

Payment: Cash, check, Master Charge, Visa.
Parking: Metered—pennies, nickels. Also, Civic Center parking lot. Bring in ticket for free-parking stamp.

Elk Grove Village

ACE PECAN COMPANY
1180 Pratt
Elk Grove Village, Illinois 60007   phone: 312-364-3275

Hours: Monday-Friday, 8 am-4:30 pm
       Saturday, 8 am-12 noon

Ace shells and roasts 28 varieties of nuts under the brand name County Fair.
Savings: 33⅓% on seconds—broken nuts in 12-oz. or 1-lb. bags; 50% on dented cans of roasted nuts.

Payment: Cash, check for exact amount.
Parking: In front of plant.

G. & G. D. HASSELMAN SUPREME MEADOW MUSHROOMS
1225 East Oakton Avenue
Elk Grove Village, Illinois 60007   phone: 312-439-8186

Hours: Monday-Saturday, 8:30 am-6 pm

Mushroom growers now selling directly to the consumer. Top quality mushrooms, picked fresh daily, in graded sizes of small (average 50 per lb.), medium (average 25 to 30 per lb.), and large (about 5 or 6 per lb.). Available all year.
Savings: At least 33⅓% for true gourmet quality.

Note: You can test the freshness of a mushroom by breaking open the cap. A fresh mushroom is crisp and pink under the gills.

Payment: Cash only.
Parking: Front of building.

GENERAL BATHROOM PRODUCTS CORPORATION
Factory Warehouse Outlet
1443 Jarvis Avenue
Elk Grove Village, Illinois 60007   phone: 312-439-1800

Irregularly scheduled weekend warehouse clearance sales of discontinued styles. Call or write for the date of the next sale.
General Bathroom Products manufactures bathroom cabinetry, vanity bases, and marbleized tops; decorative lighting fixtures; medicine

chests; faucets and hot and cold handles; towel and soap holders in brass, pewter, gold plate, and antique gold finishes.
Savings: 50% and up on cash and carry discontinued merchandise during the warehouse clearance sale.

Payment: Cash, check for exact amount with identification.
Parking: Lot.

Evergreen Park

SUNBEAM APPLIANCE SERVICE COMPANY
Sunbeam Oster Corporation
3523 West 95th Street
Evergreen Park, Illinois 60642   phone: 312-425-7134

Hours: Monday-Friday, 8:30 am-5 pm
       Saturday, 9 am-1 pm
See: Chicago, Illinois, Sunbeam Appliance Service Company.
Savings: Up to 40% on "as is" appliances.

Payment: Cash, check.
Parking: Nearby lot.

Franklin Park

MONTGOMERY WARD HOME IMPROVEMENT SALES CENTER
3101 Inland Drive
Franklin Park, Illinois 60131   phone: 312-562-8450
(Back of Inland Container.)

Hours: Monday-Saturday, 9 am-5 pm

Warehouse outlet for home improvement materials such as sinks; wood burning stoves; furnaces; fireplaces; plumbing, heating, and building materials; built-ins; cabinets; tile; and patio materials.
Savings: Average about 50% for "as is" merchandise.

Payment: Cash, check with identification, Montgomery Ward Charge-All.
Parking: Lot.

MONTGOMERY WARD FRANKLIN PARK WAREHOUSE LIQUIDATION CENTER
10601 West Seymour Street
Franklin Park, Illinois 60131 phone: 312-678-4991

Hours: Monday, Tuesday, Saturday, 8:45 am–5 pm
Wednesday, Thursday, Friday, 8:45 am–9 pm
Sunday, 11 am–5 pm

Warehouse outlet for Montgomery Ward overstock including large appliances such as refrigerators, dryers, stoves, TVs, furniture, and carpeting.
Savings: Up to 50%.

Payment: Cash, check with identification, Montgomery Ward Charge-All.
Parking: Lot.

Hanover Park

ENTENMANN'S, INC., THRIFT STORE
2005 West Irving Park Road
Hanover Park, Illinois 60103 phone 312-289-1006

Hours: Monday–Saturday, 9 am–6 pm
Sunday, 9 am–2 pm

Bakers of fresh coffee cakes; carrot, devil's food, and layer cakes; pound, ranch, and iced cakes. Also Danish pastries, doughnuts, and cookies.

Thrift store sells fresh product overruns and slightly irregular product ("red-line") and day-old items returned from regular store routes ("black-line").
Savings: 25% to 40%.

Wednesday Special Prices: 50% off box prices on all "black-line" items (day-old product) and 25% off box prices on "red-line" items (fresh irregulars or overruns).

Payment: Cash only.
Parking: Lot.

Herrin

HERRIN APPAREL RETAIL STORE
Division of Smoler Brothers
712 East Monroe Street
Herrin, Illinois 62948   phone: 618-942-2191

Hours: Monday-Saturday, 9:30 am-4:30 pm

Manufacturer of women's dresses, pantsuits, blouses, skirts, slacks, shorts, and coats in sizes 8 to 24½. Four fitting rooms.
Savings: 50% and up on samples, overruns, discontinueds, and seconds.

Also: Fabrics by the yard and by the pound, zippers, buttons, and trims.

Payment: Cash, check for exact amount with identification.
Parking: Lot.

Hillside

ARVEY PAPER AND SUPPLIES CENTER
A Division of Arvey Corporation
500 Mannheim Road
Hillside, Illinois 60162   phone: 312-544-0705

Hours: Monday-Friday, 8 am-5:30 pm
       Saturday, 9 am-1 pm

See: Chicago, Illinois, Arvey Paper and Supplies Center.

Savings: At least 33⅓% on paper supplies such as mimeo and bond papers purchased in reams (500 sheets) and envelopes in boxes of 500. Greater savings on the half-price table, which features weekly specials.

Payment: Cash, check for exact amount with identification.
Parking: Lot.

Homewood

MATERNITY FACTORY OUTLET
Dan Howard Maternity Clothes
17932 South Halsted Avenue
Washington Park Plaza
Homewood, Illinois 60430　　　　　　phone: 312-798-4347

Hours:　Tuesday, Wednesday, Friday, 10 am-5 pm
　　　　Monday, Thursday, 10 am-9 pm
　　　　Saturday, 9 am-5 pm
　　　　Sunday, 12 noon-4 pm

See: Chicago, Illinois, Maternity Factory Outlet.
Savings: 20% to 50%.

Payment: Cash, check with identification, Master Charge, Visa.
Parking: Lot.

LaGrange Park

BROWNBERRY OVENS THRIFT STORE
1103 East 31st Street
LaGrange Park, Illinois 60525　　　　phone: 312-482-8384

Hours:　Monday-Friday, 8:30 am-5:30 pm
　　　　Saturday, 8:30 am-5 pm
　　　　Open Thursday evenings until 7 pm

Outlet for Catherine Clark's Brownberry Ovens products made with no preservatives including white bread in sandwich and extra thin slices; bran, great grain, health nut, oatmeal, raisin cinnamon, and raisin nut; rye, hearth grain rye, and hearth grain wheat; rolls; bread cubes; herb and sage and onion stuffings; croutons in onion, garlic, seasoned, and cheddar cheese flavors; bread sticks in sesame, onion, garlic, cheese, and salted flavors.

Also: Snack items; cookies; Brownberry preserves and jams in strawberry, red raspberry, cherry, apricot, and orange marmalade; and natural peanut butter in plain and chunky styles.
Savings: 33⅓% and up on day-old bread and seconds. Small savings on other items.

Payment: Cash only.
Parking: In front.

Lake Forest

THE BARTLEY COLLECTION, LTD.
747 Oakwood Avenue
Lake Forest, Illinois 60045   phone: 312-295-2535

Hours: Monday-Saturday, 10 am-5 pm

Manufacturer of finely crafted 18th century antique reproduction kits for home assembly and finishing. Included are kits for making chests; tray, candle, and dining tables; chairs; mirrors; and benches.

Some kits bear the Henry Ford Museum and Greenfield Village seal of quality and authenticity of reproduction.

Savings: 50% and more on kit seconds (wood may be knotted or slightly flawed). The variety of seconds depends upon items being made.

Payment: Cash, check, Master Charge, Visa.
Parking: Street.

Lake Zurich

R. A. BRIGGS AND COMPANY
650 Church Street
Lake Zurich, Illinois 60047   phone: 312-438-2345
(Midlothian Road.)

Hours: Monday-Friday, 9 am-4 pm

This is a seconds store for Briggs, manufacturers of printed terry, beach, bath, and kitchen towels; bath mat sets; dish cloths; aprons; and pot holders.

Savings: Better than 50%.

Also: Bags of terry-cloth pieces for household wiping or polishing cloths.

Fill out postcard for notification of special sales, when items are sold at even greater savings.

Payment: Cash only.
Parking: Factory lot.

Libertyville

BERGGREN TRAYNER CORPORATION
624 East Park Avenue
Libertyville, Illinois 60048   phone: 312-367-0064

Hours: Monday-Saturday, 9 am-4 pm

Manufacturer of decorated English ironstone in four patterns including the well known Swedish Christmas: complete place settings, coffee mugs, and some serving pieces.

Also: Decorated ceramic tiles, tile planters and trays, cutting boards, and cannister sets.

Savings: Average 50% on seconds and some "o.k.'s."

Payment: Cash, check with identification.
Parking: Lot at side of building.

GRAPHIC 14
Bradley Road
Libertyville, Illinois 60048   phone: 312-362-9650
(In Industrial Park off Illinois 176—near the Tri-State Tollway.)

Hours: Monday-Friday, 8 am-5 pm

See: Chicago, Illinois, Graphic Two.

Savings: Average at least 30% on reams of paper (500 sheets in a ream) and boxes of envelopes (500 in box).

Payment: Cash, check for exact amount with identification.
Parking: Lot.

Lindenhurst

FACTORY FASHION CENTER
Linden Plaza
Lindenhurst, Illinois 60046   phone: 312-356-2532

Hours: Monday-Friday, 9:30 am-8 pm
       Saturday, 9:30 am-5:30 pm
       Sunday, 10 am-3 pm

See: Chicago, Illinois, Factory Fashion Center.

Savings: Average 50% on samples, overruns, and discontinueds—usually current styles.

Fitting rooms.

Payment: Cash only.
Parking: Lot.

Macomb

MACOMB POTTERY COMPANY
Division of Haeger Potteries, Inc.
411 West Calhoun Street
Macomb, Illinois 61455   phone: 309-833-2171

Hours: Monday-Saturday, 8 am-5 pm
       Sunday, 10 am-5 pm

Savings: 50% on seconds in pottery items, lamps, and planters.

Also: Frequent specials on the Dundee line of ashtrays; figurines and artware; and first quality artificial flowers, baskets, woodenware, and glassware.

Payment: Cash, check, Master Charge, Visa.
Parking: Lot.

Mascoutah

MARTHA MANNING COMPANY
175 East Harnett Street
Mascoutah, Illinois 62258   phone: 618-566-2199

Hours: Monday-Friday, 9:30 am-5:30 pm
       Saturday, 9:30 am-5 pm

See: Collinsville, Illinois, Martha Manning Company.

Savings: 40% and up.

Fitting rooms.

Payment: Cash, check for exact amount with identification, Master Charge, Visa.
Parking: Lot.

Matteson

CHERNIN'S SHOES
Lincoln Highway at Crawford Avenue
Matteson, Illinois 60433   phone: 312-481-7070

Hours: Monday-Friday, 10 am-9:30 pm
       Saturday, Sunday, 10 am-6 pm
See: Chicago, Illinois, Chernin's Shoes.
Savings: 30% to 60% and even greater during frequent store sales.

Mail orders accepted. See Chicago listing.

Payment: Cash, check with identification, Master Charge, Visa.
Parking: Lot.

Melrose Park

BOWL OF BEAUTY THRIFT STORE
Division of Amling Florist
1957 North George Street
Melrose Park, Illinois 60100   phone: 312-344-2140
(Across from the Winston Park Shopping Center main entrance.)

Hours: Monday-Friday, 8:30 am-4 pm

Amling's factory surplus store for artificial centerpieces, stem flowers, green leaves, green plant accessories, and ming trees; dried flowers; and a variety of floral containers.
Savings: Average 50% and more on specials.

Payment: Cash only.
Parking: In front.

SEARS RETAIL STORE OUTLET
2065 George Street
Melrose Park, Illinois 60100   phone: 312-865-4411
(Street poorly marked. It's north of North Avenue and behind Amling's.)

Hours: Monday-Saturday, 9 am-5:30 pm

Outlet for merchandise from Sears' normal retail store operations

including appliances, TVs, furniture and carpeting, home improvement materials, and plumbing and heating equipment.
Savings: 33⅓% to 80%.

Payment: Cash, Sears charge card.
Parking: Lot.

Mendota

CARON YARN COMPANY
Mendota Mill Outlet
US 51
Mendota, Illinois 61342 phone: 815-538-3171
(About 5 blocks north of US 34.)

Hours: Monday-Saturday, 9 am-5 pm

Synthetic and wool yarns in bulk and pull skeins in all weights—4 ply, 3 ply, 2 ply, bulky, and homespun; machine yarns on cones; crewel yarns by the skein or by the pound; and macrame yarns in all weights. Also a complete line of latch hooks, canvas, and closeouts of needlework kits.
Savings: Average 50% on overruns, seconds, and tangled skeins.

Write to be placed on mailing list for notice of special sales.

Payment: Cash, personal check with identification, traveler's checks.
Parking: Lot.

Moline

CARON YARN OUTLET STORE
1711 Fifth Avenue
Moline, Illinois 61265 phone: 309-762-9068

Hours: Monday-Friday, 9:30 am-5:30 pm
Saturday, 9:30 am-5 pm
See: Mendota, Illinois, Caron Yarn Company.
Savings: Average 50% on overruns, seconds, and tangled skeins in synthetic and wool yarns in all weights.

Payment: Cash, personal check for exact amount with identification, traveler's checks.
Parking: Behind store on Fourth Avenue.

Monmouth

THE POTTERY BARN
Western Stoneware Company
South D Street and Sixth Avenue
Monmouth, Illinois 61462   phone: 309-734-6980

Hours: Monday-Saturday, 12 noon-4:30 pm
       Sunday, 12 noon-5 pm

Outlet for firsts and seconds in stoneware and kitchenware including bean pots, bowls, oval bakers, casseroles, cheese crocks, cookie jars, cups and mugs, jars, pitchers, and vases. Available in white, brown, yellow, blue, green, and assorted finishes.

Western has begun to make items from old molds including "milk pails" which are really 8", 10", and 12" bowls that are perfect for making bread.

Savings: About 25% on first quality and much more on seconds.

Payment: Cash, check, Master Charge, Visa.
Parking: Lot.

Morton Grove

CHERNIN'S SHOES
Dempster Street and Waukegan Road
Morton Grove, Illinois 60053   phone: Men's shoes,
                                        312-966-4655
                                        Women's/Children's shoes,
                                        312-966-7276

Hours: Monday-Friday, 10 am-9:30 pm
       Saturday, Sunday, 10 am-6 pm

See: Chicago, Illinois, Chernin's Shoes.

Savings: 30% to 60% and even greater during frequent store sales.

Mail orders accepted. See Chicago listing.

Payment: Cash, check with identification, Master Charge, Visa.
Parking: Lot.

ENTENMANN'S, INC., THRIFT STORE
6947 West Dempster Street
Morton Grove, Illinois 60053   phone: 312-967-9420

Hours: Monday-Saturday, 9 am-6 pm
Sunday, 9 am-2 pm
See: Hanover Park, Illinois, Entenmann's, Inc.
Savings: 25% to 40% on fresh and day-old baked goods.

Wednesday Special Prices: 50% off box prices on all "black-line" items (day-old product) and 25% off box prices on "red-line" items (fresh irregulars or overruns).

Payment: Cash only.
Parking: Lot.

Mount Prospect

KITCHENS OF SARA LEE THRIFT STORE
106 West Northwest Highway
Mount Prospect, Illinois 60056   phone: unlisted

Hours: Monday-Thursday, 9 am-6 pm
Friday, 9 am-9 pm
Saturday, 9 am-5 pm
See: Deerfield, Illinois, Kitchens of Sara Lee Thrift Store.
Savings: 25% to 50%.

Payment: Cash only.
Parking: Lot.

Mount Vernon

FACTORY OUTLET STORE
102 North Ninth Street
Mount Vernon, Illinois 62864   phone: 618-242-2990

Hours: Monday-Saturday, 10 am-5 pm
See: Collinsville, Illinois, Martha Manning Company Outlet.
Dresses and sportswear in sizes 5 to 15, 8 to 20, 12½ to 26½. Six dressing rooms.
Savings: 40% and up on first quality overruns, with all labels removed. 40% to 60% on bolt and remnant fabrics.

Payment: Cash, check with identification, Master Charge, Visa.
Parking: Metered—pennies, nickels.

Mundelein

CONDECOR, INC.
444 East Cortland Street
Mundelein, Illinois 60060   phone: 312-566-4444

Send a business-sized, stamped, self-addressed envelope for notice of the five-times-a-year factory sales. Address your request to Factory Sale—Personnel Department.

Condecor manufactures wooden and metal decorator and picture frames, family album frames, and framed prints, which are normally sold through major retailing chains. Frame sizes range from 2" x 3" to 3' x 4'.

Savings: 50% and more on discontinueds, overstocks, and seconds during the three-hour sales, which are normally scheduled to coincide with Christmas, Valentine's Day, graduation, back-to-school, and Mother's Day.

Payment: Cash only.
Parking: Lot.

Naperville

ENTENMANN'S, INC., THRIFT STORE
1175 East Ogden Avenue
Naperville, Illinois 60540   phone: 312-357-7670

Hours: Monday-Saturday, 9 am-6 pm
        Sunday, 9 am-2 pm

See: Hanover Park, Illinois, Entenmann's, Inc., Thrift Store.

Savings: 25% to 40% on fresh and day-old baked goods.

Wednesday Special Prices: 50% off box prices on all "black-line" items (day-old product) and 25% off box prices on "red-line" items (fresh irregulars or overruns).

Payment: Cash only.
Parking: Lot.

Niles

MATERNITY FACTORY OUTLET
Dan Howard Maternity Clothes
9026 Milwaukee Avenue
Niles, Illinois 60648   phone: 312-824-9018

Hours: Monday, Thursday, 11 am-9 pm
       Tuesday, Wednesday, Friday, 11 am-5 pm
       Saturday, 9 am-5 pm

See: Chicago, Illinois, Maternity Factory Outlet.

Savings: 20% to 50%.

Fitting rooms.

Payment: Cash, check, Master Charge, Visa.
Parking: Large lot.

PEPPERIDGE FARM THRIFT STORE
Lawrencewood Shopping Center
Waukegan and Oakton Streets
Niles, Illinois 60648   phone: 312-965-5333

Hours: Monday-Friday, 10 am-6 pm
       Saturday, 9 am-5 pm
       Sunday, 11 am-4 pm

See: Downers Grove, Illinois, Pepperidge Farm Thrift Store.

Savings: 25% to 50%.

Payment: Cash, check for exact amount with identification.
Parking: Lot.

SKOKIE PAPER POINT
5677 Howard Street
Howard Industrial Center
Niles, Illinois 60648   phone: 312-677-3817

Hours: Monday-Friday, 8 am-5 pm

Skokie Paper Point stocks and sells papers for the printer and small business person. Paper, in many weights and qualities, sold by the ream (500 sheets) and envelopes (in all sizes) are sold in boxes of 500.
Savings: About 30% and up on first quality papers and envelopes.

Payment: Cash, check for exact amount with identification.
Parking: Lot.

74 Illinois • Niles

SUNBEAM APPLIANCE SERVICE COMPANY
7427 North Harlem Avenue
Niles, Illinois 60648   phone: 312-647-8250

Hours: Monday–Friday, 8:30 am–5 pm
         Saturday, 9 am–1 pm
See: Chicago, Illinois, Sunbeam Appliance Service Company.
Savings: Up to 50% on "as is" appliances.

Also: Appliance exchange program. Small allowance given on new product price with trade-in of old Sunbeam appliances.

Payment: Cash, check, Master Charge, Visa.
Parking: Very small lot.

Norridge

RESALE COOKIE COMPANY
Maurice Lennell Cookies
4474 North Harlem Avenue
Norridge, Illinois 60656   phone: 312-456-6500

Hours: Monday–Friday, 8 am–9 pm
         Saturday, 8 am–6 pm
         Sunday, 9 am–6 pm
Cookies, plain and fancy, in all flavors including chocolate chip, butterscotch, etc. Sold loose, bagged, in boxes, and in tins.
Savings: 33⅓% to 50% on experimentals and broken cookies.

Payment: Cash only.
Parking: Lot.

Northbrook

ALPHA-BATICS
3324 Commercial Avenue
Northbrook, Illinois 60062   phone: 312-498-4620

Send self-addressed postcard for notification of sale—usually held second weekend in June.
Manufacturer of the Children's Alphabet on clothes racks, bulletin boards, and books. Some clothes racks are personalized with children's names; others spell out slogans.

Note: Factory is open to the public only during the once-a-year sale.
Savings: Up to 60% on overstocks, discontinueds, and some seconds.

Payment: Cash, check with identification.
Parking: Lot.

BOOK VALUE INTERNATIONAL, INC.
Subsidiary of Quality Books, Inc.
400 Anthony Trail
Northbrook, Illinois 60062   phone: 312-498-4000
(Sky Harbor Industrial Park.)

Annual warehouse outlet book sale begins about Thanksgiving and continues through the day before Christmas.

Hours: Open weekends only during this sale period.
        Saturday, Sunday, 1 pm–5 pm

On sale are current fiction and non-fiction best sellers; do-it-yourself guides; general reference works; artbooks, cookbooks, and gardening texts; sports and travel books; and gothics, mysteries, romances, and science fiction books.
Savings: Average 20% on current best sellers; up to 90% off list on selected titles.

Payment: Cash, check, Master Charge, Visa.
Parking: Lot.

Oak Brook

CRATE & BARREL
54 Oak Brook Mall
Oak Brook, Illinois 60521   phone: 312-986-1300
(Oak Brook Shopping Center.)

Hours: Monday–Friday, 9 am–9:30 pm
        Saturday, 9 am–5:30 pm
        Sunday, 12 noon–5 pm

See: Chicago, Illinois, Crate & Barrel.

Savings: 30% to 60% on seconds, closeouts, and discontinueds.

Payment: Cash, check with identification, Crate & Barrel charge, Master Charge, Visa.
Parking: Large lot.

Oak Lawn

DRESSEL'S BAKERY
9028 South Cicero Avenue
Oak Lawn, Illinois 60454   phone: 312-423-8373

Hours: Monday-Friday, 9:30 am-6 pm
　　　　Saturday, 9 am-5:30 pm
　　　　Sunday, 9:30 am-3 pm
See: Chicago, Illinois, Dressel's Bakery.
Savings: 33⅓% to 50% on seconds.

Payment: Cash, check with identification, food stamps.
Parking: Lot.

ENTENMANN'S, INC., THRIFT STORE
10800 South Cicero Avenue
Oak Lawn, Illinois 60454   phone: 312-857-7151

Hours: Monday-Saturday, 9 am-6 pm
　　　　Sunday, 9 am-2 pm
See: Hanover Park, Illinois, Entenmann's, Inc., Thrift Store.
Savings: 25% to 40% on fresh and day-old baked goods.

Wednesday Special Prices: 50% off box prices on all "black-line" items (day-old product) and 25% off box prices on "red-line" items (fresh irregulars or overruns).

Payment: Cash only.
Parking: Lot.

PEPPERIDGE FARM THRIFT STORE
9900 Southwest Highway
Oak Lawn, Illinois 60453   phone: 312-424-5655

Hours: Monday-Friday, 10 am-6 pm
　　　　Saturday, 9 am-5 pm
　　　　Sunday, 10 am-4 pm
See: Downers Grove, Illinois, Pepperidge Farm Thrift Store.
Savings: 25% to 50%.

Payment: Cash, check for exact amount with identification.
Parking: Lot.

Oregon

CARON YARN OUTLET STORE
White Pines Road
White Pines Plaza
Oregon, Illinois 61061　　　　　　　　phone: 815-732-2007
(Right side of factory.)

Hours: Monday-Saturday, 9 am-5 pm
See: Mendota, Illinois, Caron Yarn Company.
Savings: Average 50% on overruns, seconds, and tangled skeins in all weights of synthetic and wool yarns.

Payment: Cash, personal check for exact amount with identification, traveler's checks.
Parking: Front and back of building.

Peru

THE WESTCLOX COMPANY
315 Fifth Street
Peru, Illinois 61354　　　　　　　　　phone: 815-224-5000
(East end of plant.)

Hours: Saturdays only, 8:30 am-12 noon
Manufacturer of watches, clocks, clock radios, digital and alarm clocks, and home weather instruments.
Savings: Average 50% on overruns, reconditioneds, and closeouts. Selection varies from week to week.

Ask about the "mad warehouse sales," when everything is closed out at incredible savings.

Payment: Cash, check with identification.
Parking: Lot.

Pinckneyville

PINCKNEYVILLE GARMENT COMPANY
404 South First Street
Pinckneyville, Illinois 62274　　　　　phone: 618-357-2141

Hours: Monday-Saturday, 9:30 am-5:30 pm
Factory outlet for first quality overstocks. Dresses, separates, blouses,

slacks, skirts in sizes 5 to 15, 12 to 20, and 12½ to 24½ in polyesters, blends, and double knits.
Savings: Average 50% and up.

Also: Piece goods, trims, threads, and notions. Excellent savings for sewers.

Payment: Cash, check for exact amount with identification, Master Charge, Visa.
Parking: Lot.

Prospect Heights

BROWNBERRY OVENS THRIFT STORE
4 East Camp McDonald Road
Prospect Heights, Illinois 60070   phone: 312-392-8874
(Right off Illinois 83.)

Hours: Monday-Friday, 9:30 am-5:30 pm
       Saturday, 9 am-5 pm
See: LaGrange Park, Illinois, Brownberry Ovens Thrift Store.

Savings: 33⅓% and up on day-old bread and seconds. Extra 10% savings on Tuesdays and Fridays.

Payment: Cash only.
Parking: In front.

Riverside

ELENHANK DESIGNERS
347 Burlington Street
Riverside, Illinois 60546   phone: 312-447-7933
(East Burlington is ½ block west of Harlem and runs parallel to the Burlington Railroad.)

Hours: Open to the public one day of the month only.
       First Wednesday of each month, 10 am-5 pm, 7 pm-9 pm

Elenhank Designers design and print custom fabrics for the contract/design trade. They silk screen on linen, cotton, and cotton and polyester blend fabrics.
Savings: Up to 75% on printed fabric overruns, nonstandard colors,

seconds, and samples and on unprinted fabrics of linen, cotton, and polyester blends. Available from remnant sizes to bolt lengths.

Payment: Cash, check for exact amount with identification.
Parking: In front.

MATERNITY FACTORY OUTLET
Dan Howard Maternity Clothes
North Riverside Park Plaza
7305 West 25th Street at Harlem
Riverside, Illinois 60546   phone: 312-447-2772

Hours: Tuesday, Wednesday, Friday, Saturday, 10 am–5 pm
       Monday, Thursday, 10 am–9 pm
       Sunday, 12 noon–4 pm

See: Chicago, Illinois, Maternity Factory Outlet.

Savings: 20% to 50% on first quality production overruns and samples. Greater savings on irregulars and seconds.

Payment: Cash, check with identification, Master Charge, Visa.
Parking: Lot.

Rochelle

V.I.P. YARN OUTLET
US 51 and Illinois 38
Rochelle, Illinois 61068   phone: 815-562-5900
(Near the Vagabond.)

Hours: Monday–Saturday, 9:30 am–5:30 pm
       Sunday, 12 noon–5 pm

Outlet for Caron, International, synthetic and wool yarns. Sold on cones, in packages, and in skeins. Rug kits, crewel, needlework, sportsweight, fingering, and afghan yarns. Also rug backing and kits.
Savings: 25% to 50% on overruns, seconds, and tangled skeins. Greater savings on closeout counter.

Write to be placed on mailing list for notice of special sales.

Also: Free mini-demonstrations are given each week, and there are classes in crewel, crocheting, knitting, macrame, and needlepoint.

Payment: Cash, personal check with identification, traveler's checks, Master Charge, Visa.
Parking: Lot.

Rolling Meadows

MONTGOMERY WARD CATALOG OUTLET
3225 Kirchoff Road
Rolling Meadows, Illinois 60008   phone: 312-259-6900

Hours: Monday-Friday, 9:30 am-9 pm
        Saturday, 9:30 am-5:30 pm
        Sunday, 12 noon-5 pm

See: Chicago, Illinois, Montgomery Ward Catalog Liquidation Center.

Savings: Average 50%.

Payment: Cash, check with identification, and Montgomery Ward Charge-All.
Parking: Lot.

Schaumburg

ENTENMANN'S, INC., THRIFT STORE
275 West Golf Road
Schaumburg, Illinois 60172   phone: 312-884-9049

Hours: Monday-Saturday, 9 am-6 pm
        Sunday, 9 am-2 pm

See: Hanover Park, Illinois, Entenmann's, Inc., Thrift Store.

Savings: 25% to 40% on fresh and day-old baked goods.

Wednesday Special Prices: 50% off box prices on all "black-line" items (day-old product) and 25% off box prices on "red-line" items (fresh irregulars or overruns).

Payment: Cash only.
Parking: Lot.

MATERNITY FACTORY OUTLET
Dan Howard Maternity Clothes
32 East Golf Road
Schaumburg, Illinois 60172   phone: 312-884-9626
(K-Mart/Dominick's Shopping Center, northeast corner, Illinois 58 and Roselle Road.)

Hours: Monday-Wednesday, 11 am-5 pm
        Thursday, Friday, 11 am-9 pm
        Saturday, 9 am-5 pm
See: Chicago, Illinois, Maternity Factory Outlet.
Savings: 20% to 50%.

Fitting rooms.

Payment: Cash, check, Master Charge, Visa.
Parking: Large lot.

PEPPERIDGE FARM THRIFT STORE
700 East Higgins Road
Hippodrome Plaza
Schaumburg, Illinois 60172   phone: 312-882-0242

Hours: Monday-Friday, 9 am-6 pm
        Saturday, 9 am-5 pm
        Sunday, 11 am-4 pm
See: Downers Grove, Illinois, Pepperidge Farm Thrift Store.
Savings: 25% to 50%.

Payment: Cash, check for exact amount with identification.
Parking: Lot.

SCHAUMBURG MATTRESS FACTORY
520 Lunt Avenue
Schaumburg, Illinois 60193   phone: 312-529-0118
(Located in Centex Industrial Park.)

Hours: Monday, Thursday, 8:30 am-8 pm
        Tuesday, Wednesday, Friday, Saturday, 8:30 am-5:30 pm
Manufacturers of quality mattresses and box springs in five grades: Gold (top luxury line); Silver (softer luxury line); Hotel (durable

hotel/motel quality); Rainbow (firm line); and Standard (medium firm line). Twin, full, queen, and king sizes in firm, extra firm, and super firm; also Delux Foam mattresses.
Savings: 30% and up as compared to comparable quality available in leading department stores.

Payment: Cash, check for exact amount with identification, Master Charge, Visa. Company will deliver COD.
Parking: Lot.

Thomasboro

SAND-MAN COUCH COMPANY
R. R. 1
Thomasboro, Illinois 61878   phone: 217-643-7860

Hours: Monday-Saturday, 8 am-5 pm

Manufacturers of sofa beds, chairs, and couches. Large selection of factory closeout first quality upholstery fabrics in velvet, tweed, herculon, nylon, rayon, and vinyl.
Savings: Up to 50%.

Also: Good savings on upholstery supplies including polyfoam.

Payment: Cash, check with identification.
Parking: Lot.

Vernon Hills

CRATE & BARREL
Hawthorne Center
Off Illinois Routes 60 and 21
Vernon Hills, Illinois 60061   phone: 312-367-1333

Hours: Monday-Friday, 10 am-9 pm
       Saturday, 10 am-5:30 pm
       Sunday, 12 noon-5 pm
See: Chicago, Illinois, Crate & Barrel.
Savings: 30% to 60% on seconds, closeouts, and discontinueds.

Payment: Cash, check with identification, Crate & Barrel charge, Master Charge, Visa.
Parking: Large lot.

Villa Park

J C PENNEY CATALOG OUTLET STORE
North Park Mall
Villa Park, Illinois 60181　　　　　　phone: 312-279-2300
(1 mile west of Illinois 83 on North Avenue.)

Hours:　Monday-Friday, 9 am-9 pm
　　　　Saturday, 9 am-6 pm
　　　　Sunday, 11 am-5 pm

Outlet store for J C Penney catalog surplus and returned merchandise including clothing for all members of the family, housewares, furniture, and bedding.
Savings: 30% and up, with big savings on seasonal specials.

Payment: Cash, check with identification, J C Penney charge card, Visa.
Parking: Lot.

Wauconda

JEWEL CATALOG OUTLET MERCHANDISE CLEARANCE CENTER
476 Liberty Street
Wauconda, Illinois 60084　　　　　　phone: 312-526-2247

Hours:　Monday, Tuesday, 9 am-5 pm
　　　　Wednesday, Thursday, Friday, 9 am-8 pm
　　　　Saturday, 9 am-5 pm
　　　　Sunday, 9 am-3 pm

See: Crystal Lake, Illinois, Jewel Catalog Outlet.
Savings: 30% to 60% on many recognized, name brand items.

Payment: Cash, check, Master Charge, Visa.
Parking: Lot.

Wheeling

FACTORY OUTLET STORE
General Time Service
599 South Wheeling Road
Wheeling, Illinois 60090　　　　　　phone: 312-541-3700

Hours: Saturday, 10 am-3 pm

Manufacturers of clocks, radios, stereos, and watches. Portable, AM/FM clock and digital, cordless, pocket, and table radios. Also tape

recorders; radio headsets; stereo changers and speakers; Big Ben, Baby Ben, keywound, and electric alarm clocks; tape and solid state digital alarm clocks; pocket watches; 17-jewel LED, LCD wrist watches; and electric and battery powered wall clocks.
Savings: 50% to 75% off list prices.

Payment: Cash, check for exact amount with identification.
Parking: Lot.

SEARS CATALOG SURPLUS STORE
903 Dundee Road
Dunhurst Shopping Center
Wheeling, Illinois 60090   phone: 312-541-2910

Hours: Monday-Friday, 9 am-9 pm
       Saturday, 9:30 am-5:30 pm
       Sunday, 11 am-5 pm
See: Chicago, Illinois, Sears Catalog Surplus Store
Savings: 25% to 80%.

Note: Special accommodations for the handicapped, including parking area in front.

Payment: Cash, check with identification, Sears charge card.
Parking: Lot.

Wilmette

CRATE & BARREL
1515 North Sheridan Road
Plaza Del Lago
Wilmette, Illinois 60091   phone: 312-256-2723

Hours: Monday-Saturday, 10 am-5:30 pm
       Sunday, 12 noon-5 pm
       Open Thursday evenings until 9 pm
See: Chicago, Illinois, Crate & Barrel.
Savings: 30% to 60% on seconds, closeouts, and discontinueds.

Payment: Cash, check with identification, Crate & Barrel charge, Master Charge, Visa.
Parking: Large lot.

Willowbrook

DRESSEL'S BAKERY
6940 Kingery Road
Illinois 83
Willowbrook, Illinois 60514   phone: 312-654-9048

Hours: Monday-Friday, 9:30 am-6 pm
       Saturday, 9 am-5:30 pm
       Sunday, 9:30 am-3 pm

See: Chicago, Illinois, Dressel's Bakery.

Savings: 33⅓% to 50% on seconds. Additional discounts on selected bakery goods on Wednesdays.

Payment: Cash, food stamps.
Parking: Lot.

Zion

SEWING FACTORY OUTLET STORE
Zion Sewing Factory
3441 South Sheridan Road
Zion, Illinois 60099   phone: 312-872-8988

Hours: Monday-Saturday, 9 am-5 pm
       Sunday, 12 noon-5 pm

Outlet store for well-known manufacturer of robes in fur-pile and velour fabrics, caftans, and front-snap housecoats. Also pants, skirts, pantsuits, and blouses in sizes 6 to 20, 38 to 44, and 14½ to 24½. Fitting rooms.

Savings: 50% and more. Even greater savings during the twice-yearly, one-cent sales (held in January/February and July/August). The first item sells for the ticketed price; the second item costs 1¢.

Also: Good savings on remnants and end-of-bolt fabrics including corduroy, denim, fur pile, suede, velour, printed knits and sheers, linings, and trims.

Payment: Cash, check with identification, Master Charge, Visa.
Parking: Lot.

WHITESIDE DRAPERY FABRICATORS, INC.
2701 Deborah Avenue
Zion, Illinois 60099 phone: 312-746-5300

Hours: Monday-Friday, 7 am-3 pm

Drapery fabricating workroom specializing in custom made, ready-to-hang lined and unlined draperies for decorators and individual customers. Whiteside stocks fabric samples and sample books or will make draperies from fabrics provided by the client.

Savings: Average 33⅓% and up, depending on fabric choice for made-to-your-own measurement draperies. Also, excellent savings on linings by the yard, which Whiteside buys "by the truckload."

Payment: Cash, check for exact amount with identification.
Parking: Street.

ZION INDUSTRIES
27th and Ebenezer Avenues
Zion, Illinois 60099 phone: 312-872-4581

Hours: Monday-Friday, 8:45 am-4 pm

Cookies made for different labels, in bulk and packaged. Chocolate chip, pecan, coconut, peanut butter, lemon, and molasses. Also blueberry, fig, oatmeal, date, dutch apple, raspberry, strawberry, and cherry bars.

Savings: About 33⅓%.

Payment: Cash, check with identification.
Parking: Lot.

INDIANA

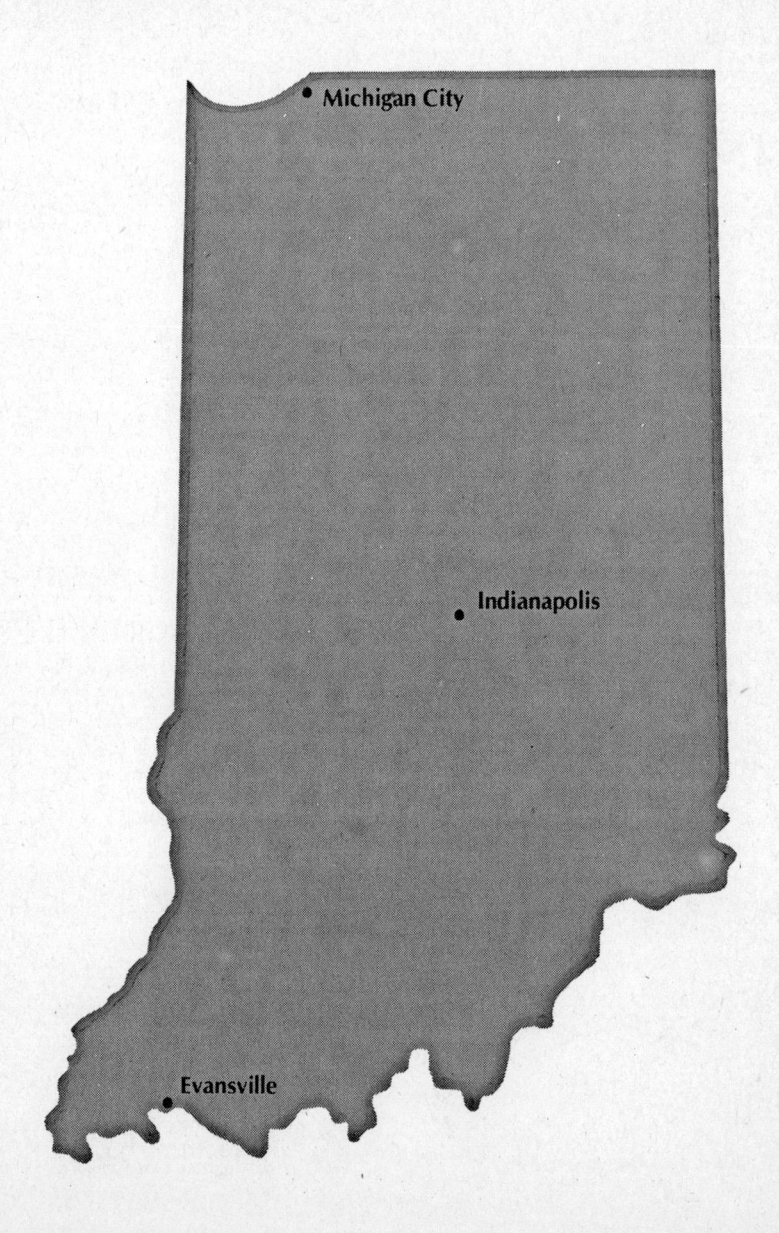

Berne

BERCO, INC.
104 East Main Street
Berne, Indiana 46711   phone: 219-589-3136

Hours: Monday-Friday, 8 am-5 pm

Manufacturer of one-piece overalls for leading retailers. Coveralls have two-way zippers, long or short sleeves, and come in blue cotton denim, blue cotton and polyester blend, grey and blue herringbone polyester blends, and in green or white polyester and cotton. Sizes 36 to 46, short, regular, or tall.

Savings: 50% on seconds, which, when available, are sold at the front desk of the factory. No try ons.

Also: Savings on fabrics when available.

Payment: Cash, check for exact amount with identification.
Parking: Street.

FABRIC GALLERY
164 West Main Street
Berne, Indiana 46711   phone: 219-589-8566

Hours: Monday-Saturday, 10 am-4 pm

The Fabric Gallery handles first quality remnant and bolt fabrics and wood veneer and cut ends from Dunbar Furniture Corporation of Indiana, manufacturers of fine quality furniture for home and office.

Fabrics—including cottons, mohair, nylon and rayon blends, silks, and wools—are sold by the piece, by the yard, or by the bolt. Leather is sold in pieces that range from small scraps to 30 square feet. Walnut wood cuts are available in odd sizes, and small veneer pieces—which range in size from 4" × 4" to 15" × 20" and sometimes 6" × 24"—are sold (depending upon availability) in acacia, ash, cherry, English oak, mahogany, oak, poplar, rosewood, and walnut.

Savings: At least 50% and up on Dunbar remnants and wood ends.

Also: Pillows and Marimekko fabrics (about 30 patterns).
Savings: Up to 50%.

Dacron and feather tickings and a line of knock-down rustic furniture are priced well.

Payment: Cash, check for exact amount with identification, Visa.
Parking: Behind store.

LIECHTY'S FOODS, INC.
Home Style Canned Meats
424 East Main Street
Berne, Indiana 46711 phone: 219-589-2849

Hours: Monday-Friday, 9 am-5 pm
Closed for lunch 11:30 am-12:30 pm

Canned meat products, sold by the case, include canned beef chunks, barbecued beef, beef in gravy, turkey, pork chunks, beef and chicken broth, beef stew, noodles and beef, and hot-dog sauce.

Special Christmas six-pack assortment sold in December.
Savings: 20% and more on full case orders depending on items purchased.

Payment: Cash, check with identification.
Parking: Street.

YAGER FURNITURE COMPANY
117 West Main Street
Berne, Indiana 46711 phone: 219-589-3101

Hours: Monday-Saturday, 9 am-5:30 pm
Open Monday and Friday evenings until 9 pm

Retail furniture store that carries all Berne Furniture Company's fabric remnants and fabric overruns. Also carries a complete line of Berne upholstered furniture, in addition to other nationally advertised furniture lines.
Savings: 50% or more on Berne Company fabric remnants and overruns including velvets and upholstery fabric blends in plains, plaids, and textures from 3-yard pieces to almost full bolts.

Also: Berne upholstered furniture showroom samples, when available.
Savings: 50%.

Payment: Cash, check with identification, Master Charge, Visa.
Parking: Lot.

Carmel

THE DRAPERY MART
The Aero Company Outlet Store
12166 North Meridian Street
Carmel, Indiana 46032   phone: 317-844-7731

Hours: Monday–Saturday, 9 am–6 pm
       Open Thursday evenings until 9 pm

The Aero Company manufactures and wholesales ready-made and made-to-measure decorator draperies. This large outlet (20,000 feet of selling space) sells overruns, closeouts, and specials in made-up decorator draperies; custom-made bedspread samples and seconds; decorator pillows; and a large inventory of fabrics including seamless, imported fabrics and fabric designs that are "tests" for new drapery lines.
Savings: 50% and up on overruns, closeouts, specials, and samples.

Also: Excellent savings in woven wood cut-offs from Roman Shades. These can be used for placemats, wastebaskets, flowerpot covers, and other home accessory projects.

Payment: Cash, check for exact amount with identification, Master Charge, Visa.
Parking: Lot.

Columbia City

THE CORRAL
Blue Bell—Wrangler Outlet
128 West Van Buren Street
Columbia City, Indiana 46725   phone: 219-244-7737
(Across from courthouse.)

Hours: Monday–Saturday, 9 am–5:30 pm
       Open Friday evenings until 8 pm

Blue Bell, Wrangler, and Lady Wrangler casualwear for all members of the family. Jeans, slacks, pants, jackets, skirts, sweaters, T-shirts, blouses, mix-and-match outfits, underwear, and socks. Boys' sizes 1 to 18; girls', to size 14; women's, 5 to 20 and blouses to size 44; and men's sizes to 46. Four fitting rooms.
Savings: Average 40% on discontinueds, irregulars, and closeouts. Up

to 75% on "ridiculous markdowns" during inventory sales after Christmas and after the summer season.

Payment: Cash, check, Master Charge, Visa.
Parking: Street.

Columbus

COSCO COMPANY STORE
2525 State Street
Columbus, Indiana 47201 phone: 812-372-0141
(Outlet store located in Cosco factory. Enter lot from Gladstone Street side.)

Hours: Monday-Friday, 10 am-5 pm
       Open Saturdays before Christmas only.

Cosco manufactures a variety of items. Juvenile products include high chairs, play pens, baby carriers, booster seats, jumpers, walkers, and strollers. Home products include bar and counter stools; step stools; serving, utility, and buffet carts; folding tables and chairs; and plastic pantry ware and household accessories. Cosco produces a line of baby products under the Peterson label.

They also manufacture and sell items from the Cosco Chemical line including concrete, fiberglass, and porcelain cleaners, septic system solution, humidifier descaler, and water treatment products.

This very small store displays available merchandise. When item is selected for purchase, it is filled from stock. Items are often packed in shipping containers.
Savings: 33⅓% to 50% on discontinueds and returns.

Payment: Cash, check for exact amount with identification.
Parking: Lot.

SAP'S BAKERIES, INC.
2741 Central Avenue
Columbus, Indiana 47201 phone: 812-372-4443
(Enter off Central or US Highway 31.)

Hours: 7 days a week, 6 am-11 pm
Bakers of breads, rolls, pastries, doughnuts, and cookies (including oatmeal, peanut butter, chocolate chip, sugar, and molasses).

Available are day-old products (often baked the night before) in boxed specials, such as 3 dozen doughnuts or 8 dozen cookies to the box.
Savings: About 50% on day-old or "reject" (seconds) products.

Also: Small savings on fresh specials.

Payment: Cash only.
Parking: Lot.

Delphi

PETERS-REVINGTON MANUFACTURING COMPANY
1100 North Washington Street
Delphi, Indiana 46923   phone: 317-564-2586

Write for notice of special warehouse sales.

Manufacturers of a better-quality line of living room, coffee, and end tables. Sold to the public only during scheduled warehouse sales.
Savings: Average 50% on discontinueds, overruns, and some factory seconds.

Payment: Cash, check with identification.
Parking: At front gate.

Dunkirk

INDIANA GLASS COMPANY
Subsidiary of Lancaster Colony Corporation
South Main Street
Dunkirk, Indiana 47336   phone: 317-768-6789

Hours: Monday-Thursday, Saturday, 10 am-6 pm
       Friday, 10 am-8 pm
       Sunday, 12 noon-6 pm

Outlet store for Indiana Glass overruns, discontinueds, and seconds. Products include glasses, bowls, snack sets, ice cream and dessert dishes, ginger jars, salad bowl and serving sets, pitchers, planters, flower bowls and vases, and carnival glass. Also, candles and candle rings.
Savings: 33⅓% to 50%. More on special closeouts.

Payment: Cash only.
Parking: Lot.

Elkhart

BLESSING'S SCHOOL
Music, Inc.
721 Riverview Avenue
Elkhart, Indiana 46514 phone: 219-293-6332
(East side of the Industrial Park.)

Hours: Monday-Friday, 9 am-5 pm
Saturday, 9 am-12 noon

Blessing's sells and rents musical instruments, "anything you need to make a band or orchestra go," and offers lessons. Many of the instruments made in Elkhart may be purchased here at a courtesy discount.

Olds, King, Bach, Armstrong, Schilke, Selmer, Magnavox, and De Ford are just a few of the line represented.
Savings: Discounts vary but can be up to 25% on the more popular instruments in stock. There may be a wait for delivery of special order instruments.

Payment: Cash, check for exact amount with identification.
Parking: Lot.

FACTORY FASHION CENTER
Boris Smoler and Sons Factory Outlet Store
916-918 North Michigan Street
Elkhart, Indiana 46514 phone: 219-293-8012

Hours: Monday-Saturday, 9 am-5 pm

Outlet for Smoler easy-care, polyester dresses in sizes 10 to 20, 14½ to 22½. Labels include Joan Curtis, Jean Leslie, and Round the Clock.
Savings: 50% and up.

Also: Fabrics at good savings and quilt scraps for less than 25¢ a pound.

Payment: Cash, check for exact amount with identification, Master Charge, Visa.
Parking: Lot.

Elnora

GRAHAM CHEESE CORPORATION
Indiana 57
Elnora, Indiana 47529   phone: 812-692-5230
(Red brick building with brown roof on east side of highway.)

Hours: Monday–Saturday, 8 am–6 pm

Cheddar, sharp cheddar, colby, and an aged colby with its own special good taste are made at this plant.
Savings: Average 25% and up on fresh product.

Payment: Cash only.
Parking: Lot.

Evansville

BUNNY BREAD COMPANY THRIFT STORE
Main Plant
520 North Fulton
Evansville, Indiana 47710   phone: 812-425-4642
(Corner of North Fulton Street and Michigan Street.)

Hours: Monday–Saturday, 9 am–5 pm

Supermarket style bakery outlet, complete with shopping carts. Breads, rolls, buns, Danish, etc. Bring your own shopping bag, or pay 10¢ for each bag.
Savings: 50% and better. Even greater savings on Tuesday, "bargain day."

Payment: Cash, food stamps.
Parking: Lot.

CARHARTT MIDWEST FACTORY OUTLET
201 North 9th Avenue and Franklin Street
Evansville, Indiana 47712   phone: 812-422-2545

Hours: Monday–Friday, 9 am–5 pm
       Saturday, 8:30 am–4 pm

Factory outlet store for men's and boys' shirts, pants, coats, vests, and bib overalls and women's blouses, pants, sweaters, and jumpsuits.

Men's sizes 28 and up (to 54 in some items); boys', 2 to 18; and women's, 8 to 18.
Savings: 30% to 50% on first quality and some irregulars.

Payment: Cash, check for exact amount with identification.
Parking: Lot.

COLONIAL THRIFT STORE
Evansville Colonial Baking Company
1321 Cobert Avenue
Evansville, Indiana 47714 phone: 812-476-0435

Hours: Monday-Saturday, 8:30 am-6 pm
Outlet for day-old rye, French, New World, old fashioned, and giant Colonial breads, rolls, buns, snack cakes, and cookies.
Savings: 33⅓% to 50% on day-old baked goods.

Payment: Cash, food stamps.
Parking: Lot.

COLONIAL THRIFT STORE
Evansville Colonial Baking Company
1507 North Green River Road
Evansville, Indiana 47714 phone: 812-479-6934

Hours: Monday-Saturday, 8:30 am-6 pm
Savings: 33⅓% to 50% on day-old baked goods. Special savings on Tuesdays.

Payment: Cash, food stamps.
Parking: Lot.

EDWARDS MANUFACTURING COMPANY
324 N. W. Sixth Street
Evansville, Indiana 47708 phone: 812-423-5224

Hours: Monday-Friday, 10 am-4 pm
Saturday, 10 am-5 pm
Sunday, 12 noon-5 pm
Ladies' sportswear, primarily polyester, in sizes 6 to 20: pants, pantsuits, four-piece suits (jackets, pants, vests, and skirts), and coor-

dinating blouses. Also shell blouses in sizes 40 to 44 and slacks in waist sizes 32 to 38.
Savings: 35% and up on first quality, current styles.

Payment: Cash, check for exact amount with identification, Master Charge, Visa.
Parking: Street.

HONEY FLUFF DONUT SHOP
621 North Fulton Avenue
Evansville, Indiana 47710   phone: 812-422-1725
(Corner of Delaware and Fulton.)

Hours: Monday-Friday, 12 midnight-11 pm
        Saturday, close at noon and reopen at 11 pm
        Sunday, 12 midnight-11 pm

Bakers of Honey Fluff Donuts, including round, filled, iced, and sugared doughnuts, long johns, and bismarcks. Also Danish and small novelty cookies.
Savings: About 50% on day-old doughnuts.

Best time to shop for day-olds is Sunday morning because the plant bakes Saturday night.

Payment: Cash only.
Parking: Street.

SHANE UNIFORM FACTORY OUTLET
Division of Superior Surgical Company
2015 West Maryland Street
Evansville, Indiana 47712   phone: 812-425-8171

Hours: Monday-Friday, 9 am-5 pm
        Saturday, 9 am-4 pm

Lab coats, uniforms on order, and polyester and cotton knit fabrics in remnants and by the yard.
Savings: 25% and up on first quality uniforms. Excellent savings on fabrics.

Payment: Cash, check for exact amount with identification.
Parking: Lot.

UNCLE CHARLIE'S MEATS
Plant Outlet Store
2420 Morgan Avenue
Evansville, Indiana 47712
(½ block from K-Mart.)

phone: 812-424-5568

Hours: Monday-Saturday, 9 am-5 pm
      Open Friday evenings until 6 pm

Frozen meat and specialty food items including pizza, sirloin steaks, bacon-wrapped beef patties, breaded mushrooms and onion rings, catfish, etc. Meat products packed in plastic freezer bags.
Savings: 20% and up with weekly specials.

Payment: Cash, check for exact amount with identification.
Parking: Lot.

Fort Branch

FACTORY OUTLET STORE
Elder Manufacturing Company
103 McCreary Street
Fort Branch, Indiana 47648

phone: 812-753-4929

Hours: Monday-Saturday, 9:30 am-4:30 pm

Company-owned factory outlet store for Tom Sawyer, Eldorado, Tough Guys, and other labels. Boys' sizes 3 to 12 and waist sizes 25 to 30 in regular and slim. Men's sizes 25 to 46 and young men's sizes to 20.

Included are suits, pants, vests, sport coats, ski and winter jackets, dress and knit shirts, T-shirts and undershirts, jeans, ties, and some underwear.
Savings: 50% and better on first quality overstocks, samples, and discontinueds. Closeout prices on seconds.

Payment: Cash, check, Master Charge.
Parking: Lot.

Franklin

CARTER'S FACTORY OUTLET STORE
Northwood Plaza Shopping Center
US Highway 31
Franklin, Indiana 46131 phone: 317-736-8667

Hours: Monday-Saturday, 10 am-5 pm
Sunday, 1 pm-5 pm

Outlet store for Carter's, manufacturers of infant's wear and accessories: girls' clothing and underwear, sizes from birth to size 14; boys' underwear, sizes from birth to size 20; and women's bikini and spanky underpants.
Savings: 30% to 60% on Carter samples, closeouts, and irregulars.

Also: Closeouts from other manufacturers, which might include Camp Togs, Purity, Tidykins, etc., at good savings.

Payment: Cash, check for exact amount with identification.
Parking: Lot.

Gary

QUALITY DISCOUNT APPAREL
8040 East Melton Road
Dunes Shopping Plaza
Gary, Indiana 46403 phone: 219-938-0474

Hours: Monday, Tuesday, Wednesday, Friday, 11 am-5 pm
Thursday, 11 am-8 pm
Saturday, 10 am-5 pm
Sunday, 12 noon-5 pm

Outlet for Hart Schaffner and Marx, manufacturers of medium to better priced clothing for men and women.

Outlet store sells first quality overruns and overstocks for Hart Schaffner and Marx Divisions including men's slacks, sport coats, suits, jackets, raincoats, and sweaters. Labels might include: Glen Eagle, Great Western, Escadrille, Society Brand, Austin Reid, Christian Dior, and Jack Nicklaus.
Savings: 50% on first quality clothing.

Note: Not all items are available all the time. Call first if you are looking for a specific item.

Payment: Cash, check for exact amount with identification, American Express, Master Charge, Visa.
Parking: Lot.

Highland

SEARS CATALOG SURPLUS STORE
8401 Indianapolis Boulevard
Highland, Indiana 46322　　　　　　　phone: 219-972-0202

Hours: Monday-Friday, 9 am-9 pm
　　　　Saturday, 9 am-5 pm
　　　　Sunday, 11 am-5 pm

See: Chicago, Illinois, Sears Catalog Surplus Store.
Savings: 20% to 80%.

Payment: Cash, check with identification, Sears charge card.
Parking: Lot.

Hobbs

RAY BROTHERS AND NOBLE CANNING COMPANY
Hobbs, Indiana 46047　　　　　　　　phone: 317-675-7451

Hours: Monday-Friday, 8 am-4:30 pm
　　　　Closed for lunch, 12 noon-1 pm

Canner of whole tomatoes, tomato juice, and ketchup. Product sold in case lots only.

First quality, fancy, and dents (first quality product in dented cans) when available.
Savings: 25% to 50%.

Payment: Cash only.
Parking: Lot.

Howe

BRIGHTON MUSHROOM FARM
R. R. #3
Howe, Indiana 46746　　　　　　　　phone: 219-367-2112
(2 miles east of Brighton on State Road 120.)

Hours: Monday-Friday, 7 am-4 pm
　　　　Saturday, 7 am-11 pm

Mushrooms picked fresh daily.
Savings: Up to 30% less than normal retail store price for superior quality and freshness.

Payment: Cash only.
Parking: Lot.

Huntingburg

H. W. GOSSARD COMPANY FACTORY OUTLET STORE
316 Fourth Street
Huntingburg, Indiana 47542　　　　　phone: 812-683-2426

Hours: Monday-Saturday, 9 am-5 pm
See: Batavia, Illinois, H. W. Gossard Company Factory Outlet Store.
Savings: 30% to 70%.

Two fitting rooms.

Payment: Cash, check for exact amount with identification, Master Charge, Visa.
Parking: Street.

Indianapolis

AERO BLINDS AND DRAPERIES
Cox Manufacturing Company
846 North Senate Avenue
Indianapolis, Indiana 46202　　　　　phone: 317-639-6551

Hours: Monday-Friday, 8 am-5 pm
　　　　 Saturday, 8 am-12 noon

Showroom outlet for Aero draperies, curtains, quilted bedspreads, and decorative pillows.
Savings: 50% on seconds and unclaimed custom orders.

Payment: Cash, check for exact amount with identification.
Parking: Lot.

ARVEY PAPER AND SUPPLIES CENTER
A Division of Arvey Corporation
1021 North Pennsylvania Street
Indianapolis, Indiana 46204   phone: 317-634-3227

Hours: Monday-Friday, 8:30 am-5:30 pm
       Saturday, 9 am-1 pm

See: Chicago, Illinois, Arvey Paper and Supplies Center.

Savings: At least 33⅓% on mimeo and bond paper bought by the ream (500 sheets) and envelopes bought by the box (500 envelopes); greater savings on the monthly specials featured in the "sales-mailers."

Payment: Cash, check for exact amount with identification.
Parking: Lot.

FARM AND HOME SADDLERY
3449 South Harding Street
Indianapolis, Indiana 46217   phone: 317-632-4554

Hours: Monday-Friday, 8:30 am-5 pm
       Saturday, 8:30 am-2 pm

Manufacturer of Fits-Em saddlery, halters, bridles, and leads.
Savings: Average 30% on first quality.

Payment: Cash, check with identification.
Parking: Lot.

LANE BRYANT OUTLET STORE
2300 Southeastern Avenue
Indianapolis, Indiana 46201   phone: 317-266-3318

Hours: Monday-Saturday, 9:45 am-6 pm
       Open Thursday evenings until 8:30 pm

Outlet for Lane Bryant catalog services including Hayes Half-Size Fashions, Lane Bryant Tall Girls, and Lane Bryant Larger Sizes.

Dresses, sportswear, coordinates, lingerie, fashion accessories, uniforms, and formal wear.
Savings: 50% to 80% on styles that are one season behind.

Payment: Cash, check for exact amount with identification, Lane Bryant credit card, Master Charge, Visa.
Parking: Lot.

ROSELYN BAKERY SURPLUS STORE
3702 East 10th Street
Indianapolis, Indiana 46202   phone: 317-635-7778

Hours: Tuesday-Saturday, 8 am-7 pm
       Sunday, 8 am-6 pm

Outlet for "second-day" bread, pies, cakes, doughnuts, Danish pastries, and cookies returned from Roselyn Bakeries, Inc., fresh bake stores.
Savings: 40% to 60%.

Payment: Cash, check for exact amount with identification.
Parking: Lot.

ROSELYN BAKERY SURPLUS STORE
2901 North Keystone Avenue
Indianapolis, Indiana 46206   phone: 317-923-2933

Hours: Tuesday-Saturday, 8 am-7 pm
       Sunday, 8 am-6 pm

Savings: 40% to 60%.

Payment: Cash, check for exact amount with identification.
Parking: Lot.

STAUB AND SMITH MEAT MARKET AND PACKING COMPANY
2210 Kentucky Avenue
State Road 67
Indianapolis, Indiana 46204   phone: 317-241-6341

Hours: Monday-Saturday, 8 am-6 pm

Meat packer and retail meat market. Weekly specials on choice beef or pork bundles. Sells 20-lb. pork, 20-lb. beef, and 13-lb. steak bun-

dles. Also, old fashioned cure whole hams and half hams, eggs, and a full line of produce.
Savings: 20% and more on weekly specials.

Payment: Cash, Master Charge, Visa, food stamps.
Parking: Lot.

Jasper

HOFFMAN OFFICE SUPPLY, INC.
116 East 7th Street
Jasper, Indiana 47541 phone: 812-482-4224

Hours: Monday-Friday, 8 am-5 pm
       Saturday, 8 am-1 pm

Local retail office and business machine company serves as a courtesy outlet for major office furniture manufacturers in the area including Indiana Desk, Indiana Chair, Hoosier Desk, Jasper Chair, Jasper Table, Kimball Office Furniture, DMI, Jasper Seating Company, etc.

Samples, closeouts, and discontinueds are carried in the lower level display area.
Savings: About 40% off list price on items ordered through Hoffman, with approximate delivery within four to six weeks.

Payment: Cash, check for exact amount with identification.
Parking: Lot.

JASPER GLOVE COMPANY, INC.
611 Main Street
Jasper, Indiana 47546 phone: 812-482-4473
(Next to Schneider's Furniture in main square.)

Hours: Monday-Friday, 8 am-4 pm

Up one flight of stairs. Manufacturers of work gloves under the Jasper, Jet 99, Fli-Hi, and JG labels. Cotton and leather-palmed gloves sold by dozen only.

Also: Leather, rubber, and plastic aprons for welding, shop, and home craft work.
Savings: 35% to 50% on discontinueds, closeouts, and some seconds.

Payment: Cash, check for exact amount with identification.
Parking: Street.

LaPorte

FACTORY FASHION CENTER
510 Lincolnway Avenue
LaPorte, Indiana 46350   phone: 219-362-9635

Hours: Monday-Saturday, 9:30-5:30 pm
Open Friday evenings until 7:30 pm

See: Chicago, Illinois, Factory Fashion Center.

Savings: Average 50% on samples, overruns, and discontinueds—usually current styles—in women's sportswear and dresses.

Six fitting rooms.

Payment: Cash, check for exact amount with identification.
Parking: Metered—pennies, nickels.

Logansport

H. W. GOSSARD COMPANY FACTORY OUTLET STORE
316 Sixth Street
Logansport, Indiana 46947   phone: 219-753-2808
(Located in basement.)

Hours: Monday-Saturday, 8:30 am-5 pm

See: Batavia, Illinois, H. W. Gossard Company Factory Outlet Store.

Savings: 30% to 70%.

Fitting rooms.

Payment: Cash, check for exact amount with identification.
Parking: Street.

Merrillville

QUALITY DISCOUNT APPAREL
6136 Broadway Avenue
Merrillville, Indiana 46410   phone: 219-980-3980
(Off Interstate 65 at the 61st Street exit.)

Hours: Monday, Tuesday, Wednesday, Friday, 11 am-5 pm
Thursday, 11 am-8 pm
Saturday, 10 am-5 pm
Sunday, 12 noon-5 pm

See: Gary, Indiana, Quality Discount Apparel.

Savings: 50% on first quality overruns and discontinueds in men's clothing from Hart Schaffner and Marx clothing divisions.

Note: Not all items are available all the time. Call first if you are looking for something specific.

Payment: Cash, check for exact amount with identification, American Express, Master Charge, Visa.
Parking: Lot.

Michigan City

EASTMOOR COMPANY FACTORY OUTLET STORE
800 Chicago Street
Michigan City, Indiana 46360   phone: 219-874-5231

Hours: Monday-Friday, 9 am-3:30 pm
        Saturday, 9 am-12 noon

Store carries women's sportswear in sizes 8 to 20 and junior sportswear in sizes 3 to 15, including pants, pantsuits, blouses, and skirts.

Clothing is usually first quality but one season behind retail stores in styling. Two fitting rooms.
Savings: 50% on first quality, more on seconds.

Also: 2- and 3-yard sample cut fabrics and buttons, bindings, and trims at very good savings.

Payment: Cash, check for exact amount with identification.
Parking: Lot.

FACTORY OUTLET STORE
Jaymar-Ruby, Inc.
209 West Michigan Boulevard
Michigan City, Indiana 46360   phone: 219-879-7341
(Across from the post office.)   (Ask for outlet store.)

Hours: Thursday and Friday, 10 am-8 pm
        Saturday and Sunday, 10 am-4 pm

Outlet for Jaymar-Ruby, manufacturer of better priced men's sportswear and pants under the Jaymar, Sansabelt, and Nino Cerutti Sport labels.

Outlet sells samples, discontinueds, and some seconds in men's slacks (sizes 28 to 60); sweaters, vests, blazers, jackets, and suits (sizes

36 to 54 in regular, long, and extra long); and shirts. Items sold in outlet store are usually about two months behind regular retail source items in styling.
Savings: Average 50% on quality men's sportswear samples, discontinueds, and some seconds.

Payment: Cash, check for exact amount with identification, Master Charge, Visa.
Parking: Lot on west side of store.

FREDERIC H. BURNHAM COMPANY
1602 Tennessee Street
Michigan City, Indiana 46360   phone: 219-874-5205
(Enter through dock area.)

Hours: Monday-Friday, 8 am-12 noon
                     1 pm-4 pm
       Saturday, 8 am-12 noon

Manufacturers and distributors of gloves for men, women, and children including leather dress gloves, work gloves, ski gloves, and mittens. Also, battery heated socks and mittens under the Stronghold and Sportster labels.

Gloves sold by the dozen or by the individual pair.
Savings: 50% on first quality overruns; greater on seconds or irregulars.

Payment: Cash, check for exact amount with identification.
Parking: Side street.

SOCIETY LINGERIE, INC.
Springland and Roeske Avenue
Michigan City, Indiana 46360   phone: 219-872-7206
(Enter outlet through main lobby.)

Hours: Monday-Friday, 9 am-5 pm
       Saturday, 9 am-1 pm

Manufacturer of women's sleepwear in petite to large sizes including long and short gowns, long and short robes, and baby-doll pajamas.
Savings: Average 50% on first quality; slightly more on seconds.

Also: Design room sample pieces of cotton and polyester blends and nylon jersey crepe sets, and laces at excellent savings.

Payment: Cash, check for exact amount with identification.
Parking: Lot.

Middlebury

GOHN BROTHERS MANUFACTURING COMPANY
Main Street
Box 111
Middlebury, Indiana 46540   phone: 219-825-2400

Hours: Monday-Saturday, 7:30 am-5:30 pm

Clothing, dry goods, and notions store carrying good quality clothing for the Amish trade. Men's broadfall work pants in blue or gray denim are made in the factory upstairs. (Broadfall pants, a favorite item of clothing on college campuses, have no zippers. They feature a broad, inside pocket in the front and button much like sailor's pants.)

Store carries well-priced zippered nylon jackets, denim overshirts lined with blanket cloth, and sheepskin vests.
Savings: About 33⅓% on simple, good quality, sturdy clothing.

Also: Take mail orders. Write to request price sheet.

Payment: Cash, check for exact amount with identification.
Parking: Street.

Nashville

KIRBY'S OUTLET
Corner of Van Buren and Washington Streets
Nashville, Indiana 62263   phone: unlisted

Hours: Monday-Saturday, 9 am-5 pm
        Open Sundays during the summer, 9 am-5 pm
See: North Vernon, Indiana, Kirby's.
The Nashville store carries acrylic, cotton, nylon, and polyester yarns

from Regal Rug Company and a very limited selection of smaller decorator rugs from Regal.
Savings: 60% and up on yarns.

Some savings on Nelson McCoy pottery irregulars.

Payment: Cash, check for exact amount with identification, American Express, Master Charge, Visa.
Parking: Street.

THE POTTERY CUPBOARD #13
Main Street at Artist Drive
Nashville, Indiana 47448   phone: 812-988-7633
(Old Route 46.)

Hours: Winter—Tuesday-Sunday, 10 am-5 pm
              Closed Mondays
        Summer—Monday-Saturday, 9 am-6 pm
              Sunday, 10 am-5 pm

The Pottery Cupboards are subsidiaries of the Anchor Hocking Corporation and carry first quality, closeouts, and seconds in glass bakeware and tableware; ceramic, glass, and plastic micro-wave ovenware; gourmet cooking items and giftware; and Taylor, Smith and Taylor dinnerware.
Savings: 50% and more on Taylor, Smith and Taylor seconds in 20 and 45 piece sets. Small savings on first quality dinnerware.

Payment: Cash, check for exact amount with identification, Master Charge, Visa.
Parking: Street.

New Castle

THE COMPANY STORE
Bofel, Ltd.
2200 Troy Avenue
New Castle, Indiana 47362   phone: 317-521-2613
(Trojan Industrial Park just off Grand Avenue. The Company Store is located in the back of the factory.)

Hours: Monday-Saturday, 9 am-5 pm
        Sunday, 12 noon-5 pm

Outlet for women's separates and coordinates in sizes 6 to 20, and 12½ to 26½ in wool blends and polyester and cotton blends. Some

items are made in this factory, but store also discounts name brand sportswear and hosiery. Fitting rooms.
Savings: 50% to 70% on first quality discontinueds and overruns.

Also: Good savings on first quality cotton and polyester fabric sold by the yard.

Payment: Cash, check for exact amount with identification.
Parking: Lot.

North Vernon

KIRBY'S
250 East Hoosier Street
North Vernon, Indiana 47265   phone: 812-346-3500
(Corner of Madison and Hoosier.)

Hours: Monday-Saturday, 9 am-5 pm
Outlet for Regal area rugs from 17" x 24" to 4' x 6'. Also, bathroom carpeting, tank sets, and toilet lid covers.
Savings: 45% and up on first quality closeouts and discontinueds.

Also: Acrylic, cotton, nylon, and polyester yarns for home handicraft projects and pottery irregulars from McCoy.
Savings: 60% and up on yarns and good savings on pottery.

Payment: Cash, check for exact amount with identification, American Express, Master Charge, Visa.
Parking: Front and side of store.

Ossian

HEYERLY BAKERY COMPANY, INC.
Jefferson Street
Ossian, Indiana 46777   phone: 219-622-4196

Hours: Monday-Saturday, 7 am-11 pm
Wholesale, quality baker of rolls, sweet rolls, breads, cakes, and cookies.
Savings: 50% on all baked goods on "leftover" table.

Especially recommended is the freshly baked Texas Doughnut, about

8" or 10" in diameter, a good buy even at its fresh price.

Also: Free help-yourself coffee service available to waiting customers.

Payment: Cash only.
Parking: In front.

OSSIAN CANNING COMPANY, INC.
713 West LaFever Street
Ossian, Indiana 46777   phone: 219-622-4172
(Off Jefferson Street behind the lumber company.)

Hours: Monday-Friday, 8 am-5 pm

Canners of fancy tomatoes and quality tomato juice, sold by the case only.

Savings: 25% on first quality product and more than 50% on dents (first quality product in dented cans), when available.

Bundles of tomato plants, 50 to a bundle, available at very low prices in May of each planting year. Ask about the new variety of tomato plant—less acid in the fruit—now being marketed.

Payment: Cash only.
Parking: Lot.

Paoli

BRITTANY FURNITURE INDUSTRIES
Rural Route 3, Box 14 A44A
Paoli, Indiana 47454   phone: 812-723-4702

Factory is not open to the public. However, Brittany occasionally sells manufacturing overruns to the public at an announced public sale date.

Write and enclose a business sized, stamped, self-addressed envelope and request notification of sale, whenever it is scheduled.

Manufacturer of upholstered sofas, loveseats, chairs, and ottomans.
Savings: Up to 50% on samples, discontinueds, and overruns at infrequently scheduled public sales.

Payment: Cash, check for exact amount with identification.
Parking: Lot.

Richmond

NETTLE CREEK INDUSTRIES
40 Peacock Road
Richmond, Indiana 47374　　　　　　　　phone: 317-962-1555

Hours: Monday-Friday, 8 am-4:30 pm
　　　　Saturday, 9 am-3 pm

Nettle Creek manufactures luxuriously quilted bedspreads in twin, full, queen, and king sizes; decorative pillows in all sizes; padded headboards; and draperies. Also, a home decorative accessory line, Gallery Classics, including framed art reproductions, sculpture, mirrors, and wall accessories.
**Savings: 50% and up on design samples and factory seconds.
Seconds flaws are marked on price tags.**

Incredible savings on fabric bolt ends (some for less than $1 a yard), which are brought into the store every morning.

Payment: Cash, check for exact amount with identification.
Parking: Lot.

Roachdale

WILSON BROTHERS
Off US 231 in town of Raccoon
Roachdale, Indiana 46172　　　　　　　　phone: 317-596-3455

Hours: Seven days a week, 8 am-5 pm

Growers of geraniums, African violets, and a wide variety of house and exotic plants.
Savings: 20% to almost 50% on prices of comparable sized plants sold by local florists and garden supply stores.

Also sell through a mail order catalog at smaller savings.

Payment: Cash, check for exact amount with identification, Master Charge, Visa.
Parking: Lot.

Rochester

EDMONTON MANUFACTURING COMPANY
("Topps")
Master Uniforms
501 Main Street
Rochester, Indiana 46975 phone: 219-223-4311

Hours: Monday-Friday, 9 am-3 pm

Manufacturer of men's coveralls, shirts, trousers (sizes 28-52); men's and women's jumpsuits with long or short sleeves in a full range of sizes; men's counter coats; and women's smocks in orange, red, royal blue, yellow, and white.

Savings: From 20% and up on first quality service and work clothing for men and women.

Payment: Cash, check with identification, Master Charge, Visa.
Parking: Lot.

Seymour

EXCELLO FACTORY STORE
400 South Airport Road
Freeman Field
Seymour, Indiana 47274 phone: 812-522-1176

Hours: Monday-Saturday, 8:30 am-4:15 pm

Outlet for Excello Division of Kayser-Roth, manufacturers of men's dress and sport shirts and women's knit blouses in sizes 7 to 18.

Men's shirts in all sizes, long and short sleeved, in knits and blends, and some designer shirts.

Savings: 33⅓% to 50% on overruns, discontinueds, and some seconds.

Also: Ties and socks at some savings.

Payment: Cash, checks for exact amount with identification.
Parking: Lot.

Shipshewana

MASTERCRAFT, INC.
Indiana 5
Shipshewana, Indiana 46565 phone: 219-768-4101

Hours: Monday-Friday, 8 am-4:30 pm
Saturday, 8:30 am-11:30 am

Manufacturers of upholstery and bedding including the Heidelberg Collection of couches, chairs, and sofa sleepers; mattresses; box springs; and recreational van seating.
Savings: Up to 50% on upholstered pieces; 30% to 50% on mattresses.

Also: Large selection of 54" fabrics including tapestries, woven patterns, fake furs, velveteens, and tufted velvets. Bolt ends and remnants at excellent savings.

Payment: Cash, check for exact amount with identification.
Parking: Lot.

Sullivan

H. W. GOSSARD COMPANY FACTORY OUTLET STORE
312 Court Street
Sullivan, Indiana 47882 phone: 812-268-4460

Hours: Monday-Saturday, 9 am-5 pm
See: Batavia, Illinois, H. W. Gossard Company Factory Outlet Store.

Outlet for quality sleepwear and loungewear for women; hosiery and socks for men, women, and children; and boys' and men's sweaters. Two fitting rooms.
Savings: 30% to 70% on overstocks, discontinueds, and a few irregulars.

Payment: Cash, check for exact amount with identification, Master Charge, Visa.
Parking: Lot on south side of building.

Swayzee

SWAYZEE PACKING COMPANY, INC.
714 East Lyons Street
Swayzee, Indiana 46986   phone: 317-922-7996

Hours: Monday-Saturday, 8 am-5 pm

Packers and canners of diced tomatoes and tomato juice sold in case lots only. There are 24 cans of number 303 diced tomatoes to a case and 12 cans of 46 oz. tomato juice.
Savings: From 30% to 50% on first quality product, when available.

Payment: Cash, check for exact amount with identification.
Parking: In front.

Terre Haute

FACTORY STORE
General Housewares Corporation
3692 Dixie B Road
Terre Haute, Indiana 47804   phone: 812-232-8024
(½ mile south of Interstate 70 on US 41 in Towne South Plaza on east side of the road.)

Hours: Monday-Friday, 10 am-9 pm
          Saturday, 10 am-6 pm
          Sunday, 1 pm-5 pm

General Housewares Corporation manufactures cast aluminum, cast iron, porcelain on cast iron, graniteware, and enamel on steel cookware under the following names: Boutique, Classic, Columbian, Country Collection, Finesse, Graniteware, Griswold, and Magnalite.
Savings: At least 30% on first quality cookware and more on seconds, overruns, and discontinued.

Also: Candleholders and candles from Colonial Candles, another division of General Housewares, in standard shapes and sizes, 7½" to 12" scented and unscented, and in novelty shapes.
Savings: Average 30%.

Payment: Cash, check with identification, Master Charge, Visa.
Parking: Lot.

Vincennes

M. G. GRUNDMAN AND SONS, INC.
906 North 7th Street
Vincennes, Indiana 47591 phone: 812-882-2933

Hours: Monday-Saturday, 8 am-5 pm
Open Friday evenings until 8 pm

Manufacturers of Smooth Fit service oxfords, boots, orthopedic, and corrective shoes in black, brown, and white for men, women, and children. In babies' sizes 00 to size 16.

Tie or buckle styles. For a small additional charge, shoes can be specially ordered in other colors.

Savings: Average 33⅓% when compared with other all-leather, well-made shoes available in retail stores.

Payment: Cash, check for exact amount with identification.
Parking: Street.

Wabash

A. F. BILLINGS COMPANY
41 West Market Street
Wabash, Indiana 46992 phone: 219-563-4291

Hours: Monday-Friday, 8 am-5 pm
Saturday, 9 am-5 pm

Manufacturer of Christmas, seasonal, and party decorations. Sells decorations, ornaments, dried and artificial flowers, flower arrangements, candles, ribbons, and styrofoam.
Savings: 25% to 50%.

Payment: Cash, check for exact amount with identification, Master Charge.
Parking: In front.

Warsaw

BLUE BELL FACTORY OUTLET
120 South Buffalo Street
Warsaw, Indiana 46580 phone: 219-267-2258
(½ block south of courthouse.)

Hours: Monday-Saturday, 9:30 am-5:30 pm
See: Columbia City, Indiana, The Corral.

Savings: Up to 70% on overstocks, irregulars, seconds, and discontinueds.

Four fitting rooms.

Payment: Cash, check, Master Charge, Visa.
Parking: Street.

Whiting

KITCHENS OF SARA LEE THRIFT STORE
1749 Indianapolis Avenue
Whiting, Indiana 46394 phone: unlisted

Hours: Monday-Thursday, 8:30 am-5:30 pm
 Friday, 8:30 am-8:30 pm
 Saturday, 9 am-5 pm
See: Deerfield, Illinois, Kitchens of Sara Lee Thrift Store
Savings: 20% to 50% with greater savings on specials.

Best selection of products on Friday.

Payment: Cash only.
Parking: Lot.

MICHIGAN

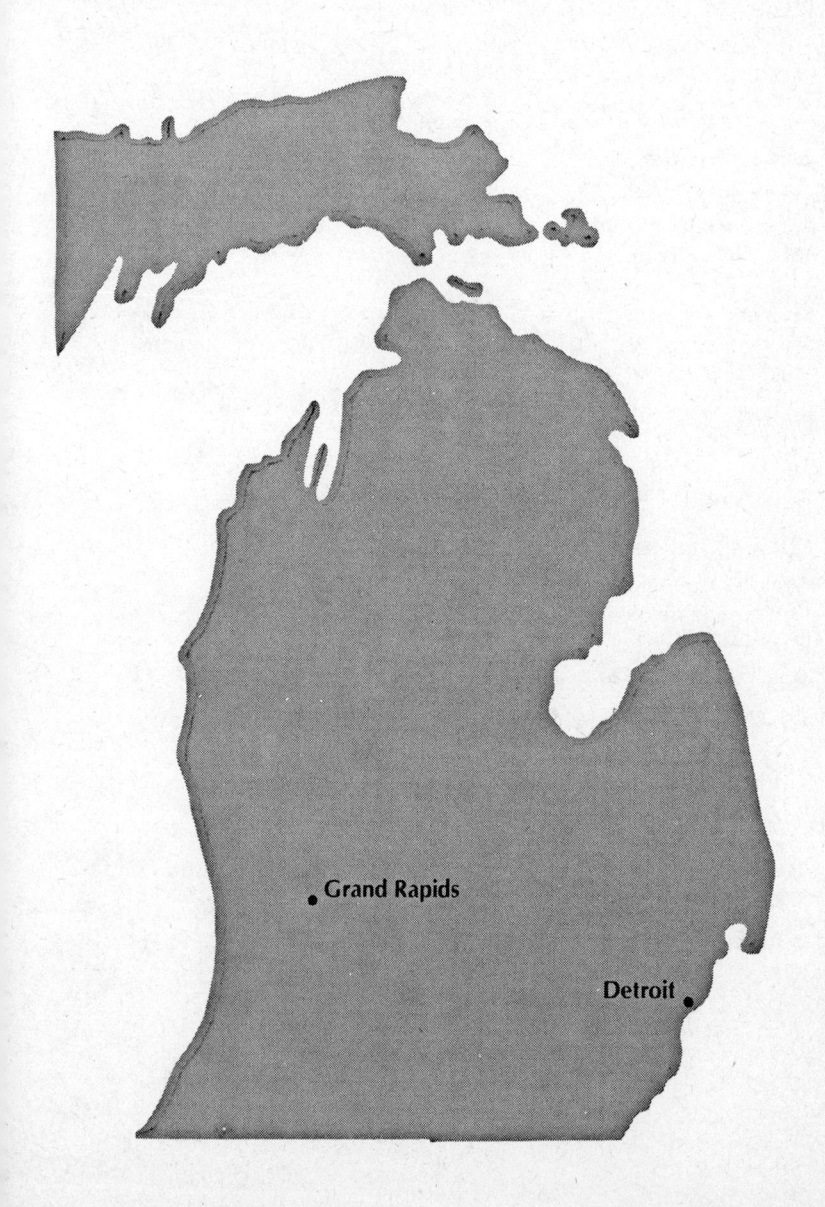

- Grand Rapids
- Detroit

Adrian

MERILLAT WAREHOUSE OUTLET
2075 West Beecher Street
Adrian, Michigan 49221   phone: 517-263-0771
(South side of town.)

Hours: Saturday morning only, 8 am-12 noon

Warehouse is at back of plant.

Merillat Industries, Inc. manufactures wood (and some formica laminate) stacking modular unit construction kitchen cabinets in six styles and several finishes. They also manufacture bathroom vanities (cabinets only—no tops.)
Savings: Up to 40% on first quality discontinueds; more on structurally sound, but slightly damaged, cabinets and vanities.

Payment: Cash, check for exact amount with identification.
Parking: Lot.

Ann Arbor

KURTIS KITCHEN AND BATH CENTERS
3666 South State Street
Ann Arbor, Michigan 48106   phone: 313-663-5575
(1 block south of Interstate 94.)

Hours: Monday-Friday, 9 am-6 pm
        Saturday, 9 am-5 pm
        Open Thursday evenings till 8 pm

Kurtis Manufacturing and Distributing Company manufactures custom kitchen and bathroom vanity cabinets and formica tops under the Adler Kay and Excel labels.
Savings: Up to 60% on kitchen cabinets, bathroom vanities, and formica tops in a wide range of styles.

Payment: Cash, check with identification, Master Charge, Visa.
Parking: Lot.

Battle Creek

AMERICAN BISCUIT COMPANY THRIFT STORE
Division of Interbake Foods, Inc.
Avenue C and 19th Street
Battle Creek, Michigan 49016 phone: 616-963-5575

Hours: Monday–Friday, 8 am–4:30 pm

Packaged oatmeal, iced oatmeal, French vanilla creme, duplex (chocolate and vanilla) creme, and tea biscuit cookies.
Savings: Up to 50% on packaged cookies that are considered irregular because of incorrect package weight or packaging misprints.

Payment: Cash, check for exact amount with identification.
Parking: In front.

SCHAFER BAKERIES, INC., THRIFT STORE
1290 East Columbia Avenue
Battle Creek, Michigan 49017 phone: 616-962-3444

Hours: Monday–Saturday, 9 am–5 pm

Bakery outlet store for day-old and overrun products including breads, lunch cakes, and angel food bars and cookies.
Savings: Average 40% on day-old and fresh overrun products, when available.

Payment: Cash only.
Parking: In front.

Belding

LU VAN, INC.
1129 South Bridge Street
Belding, Michigan 48809 phone: 616-794-1700

Hours: Monday–Friday, 8 am–5 pm

Lu Van manufactures enamel-finished metal-frame and wood-finished hardboard items including utility and typewriter tables, shelving and storage units, bookshelves, entertainment center tables and cabinets, file cabinets, desks, and desk chairs.
Savings: Average 40% for cash and carry on items that retail from about $25 to $350.

Payment: Cash only.
Parking: Lot.

ROYAL DOWN PRODUCTS, INC.
101 North Front Street
Belding, Michigan 48809   phone: 616-794-0510

Hours: Monday–Friday, 9 am–4 pm

Royal Down manufactures down-filled apparel for adults and children.
Savings: Up to 50% on factory overruns, samples, and some seconds.

Payment: Cash, check for exact amount with identification.
Parking: Lot.

Berrien Springs

COLLEGE WOOD PRODUCTS
Grove and Industry Streets
Andrews University
Berrien Springs, Michigan 49103   phone: 616-471-3355

Hours: Monday–Wednesday, 9 am–12 noon, 1 pm–5 pm
        Thursday, 9 am–12 noon, 1 pm–9 pm
        Sunday, 10 am–5 pm

College Wood Products is located on the Andrews University campus, and the furniture is made by university students.

The hardwood furniture line includes traditional and casual country styles in beds, bunk beds, and bookcase headboard beds; nightstands and mirrors; 3-, 4-, and 5-drawer chests, double dressers; bookcases and desks; dining room furniture; rockers; lamps and end tables.

Choice of dark pine or warm maple finish. All pieces are well constructed and are finished with antique brass-plated hardware.

Also: Mattresses and box springs.
Savings: 33⅓% to more than 50% on comparative pieces carried by leading catalog retailers.

Payment: Cash, check for exact amount with identification.
Parking: Lot.

Big Rapids

LITTLE RED SHOE HOUSE
Wolverine World Wide
804 North State Street
Big Rapids, Michigan 49307   phone: 616-796-5474

Hours: Monday-Saturday, 9 am-5 pm
       Open Friday evenings until 8 pm

Outlet for Wolverine World Wide shoes and Hush Puppy footwear for all members of the family.
Savings: 50% on discontinueds, seconds, and irregulars.

Note: This is one of several Hush Puppy outlets throughout Michigan.

Payment: Cash, check for exact amount with identification, Master Charge, Visa.
Parking: Lot behind store.

THE PINE SHOP STORE
826 North State Street
Big Rapids, Michigan 49037   phone: 616-796-6270

Hours: Monday-Saturday, 9 am-5 pm

Factory outlet for Pine Shops, Inc., manufacturers of oak dining room, occasional living room, and family room furniture. Quality styling and construction.
Savings: 33⅓% and up on first quality; greater savings on discontinueds, experimental samples, and sale specials.

Payment: Cash, check for exact amount with identification, Master Charge, Visa.
Parking: In back of store.

Birmingham

PEPPERIDGE FARM THRIFT STORE
1950 Southfield Road
Birmingham, Michigan 48009   phone: 313-642-4242

Hours: Monday-Friday, 10 am-6 pm
       Saturday, 9 am-5 pm

See: Downers Grove, Illinois, Pepperidge Farm Thrift Store.
Savings: 25% to 50%. Senior citizens receive an additional 10% discount on Thursdays, "Senior Citizen's Day."

Payment: Cash, check for exact amount with identification.
Parking: In front and at side of building.

Brighton

HARVARD OF HILLSDALE FACTORY OUTLET
9998 B East Grand River Avenue
Brighton, Michigan 48116　　　　　　phone: 313-227-1502
(Across from State Police Post.)

Hours: Tuesday-Saturday, 10 am-4 pm

See: Litchfield, Michigan, Harvard of Hillsdale, Inc.

Savings: Average 50% on first quality nylon fiberfill outerwear for all members of the family, from extra-small sizes to Triple X.

Payment: Cash, check for exact amount with identification.
Parking: Lot.

Cedar Springs

RED FLANNEL FACTORY
73 South Main Street
Cedar Springs, Michigan 49319　　　　phone: 616-696-9240

Hours: Monday-Thursday, 9 am-5 pm
　　　　Friday, 9 am-7 pm
　　　　Saturday, 9 am-5 pm

Red flannel pajamas, granny gowns and dust caps, muu muus, karate robes, and nighties in sizes small, medium, large, and extra large for girls and women; red flannel pajamas, knit long johns and union shirts, nightshirts and nite caps, and karate robes for men in small, medium, large, and extra large.
Savings: Almost 50% on irregulars.

Also: Red flannel dog coats and Christmas stockings.

Accept mail orders. Brochure available on request.

Payment: Cash, check, Master Charge, Visa.
Parking: Street.

Centreville

DENTON MILLS, INC.
North Clark Street
Centreville, Michigan 49032   phone: 616-467-9215

Hours: Wednesday-Friday, 10 am-4 pm
       Saturday, 9 am-12 noon

Manufacturer of children's pajamas (sometimes referred to as "Dr. Dentons"), blanket sleepers, robes, and sweaters for children. Also, sleepwear and sweaters for women and sweaters for men.
Savings: 50% and more on discontinueds and seconds.

Also: Excellent savings during the annual two-week sale, which begins the day after Thanksgiving, on Denton label items and men's pants, shirts, and jackets.

Payment: Cash, check for exact amount with identification.
Parking: Lot.

Clinton

HARVARD OF HILLSDALE FACTORY OUTLET STORE
1845 West Michigan Avenue
Clinton, Michigan 49326   phone: 517-456-7722
(1 mile west of Clinton on US 12.)

Hours: Tuesday-Saturday, 10 am-5 pm

See: Litchfield, Michigan, Harvard of Hillsdale, Inc.
Savings: Average 50% on nylon fiberfill outerwear for all members of the family.

Payment: Cash, check for exact amount with identification.
Parking: Lot.

Coldwater

SHAW SHOE STORE
40 West Chicago Street
Coldwater, Michigan 49036   phone: 517-278-8252

Hours: Monday-Saturday, 9 am-5:30 pm
       Open Friday evenings until 9 pm

Retail outlet for M. T. Shaw, Inc., manufacturers of nationally adver-

tised quality footwear for men. Shoes and boots in sizes 6 to 14 in B, C, D, E, and EEE widths.
Savings: 50% on seconds, closeouts, and discontinueds.

Payment: Cash, check, Master Charge, Visa.
Parking: Lot.

Decatur

HURON FARMS DECATUR STORAGE, INC.
201 South George Street
Decatur, Michigan 49045   phone: 616-423-7001

Hours: Monday-Friday, 8 am-4:30 pm

Big Valley quick frozen fruits including apples, cherries, blueberries, and strawberries and asparagus and green beans sold in 12-oz. and 20-oz. bags and larger packs of 20- and 30-lb. cartons.
Savings: Up to 50% on first quality frozen product bought in bulk.

Payment: Cash, check for exact amount with identification.
Parking: Lot.

Detroit

GREAT LAKES SPORTSWEAR INDUSTRIES, INC.
11371 East State Fair
Detroit, Michigan 48234   phone: 313-372-4500

Hours: Monday-Friday, 8 am-4 pm
       Closed for lunch from 12 noon-12:30 pm
       Saturday, 8 am-12 noon

Great Lakes designs and manufactures 100% Caprolan nylon, water repellent, front zippered all-weather jackets, lightweight jackets, and pile-lined jackets with trade mark, company name, or slogan emblems for premium and sales incentive programs.

Sizes include: Men's small (36-38), medium (40-42), large (44-46), X-large (48-50), and XX-large (52); women's and children's small (6-8), medium (10-12), and large (14-16).
Savings: Vary from 20% to 50% on first quality overruns and samples.

Payment: Cash only.
Parking: Lot.

HELIN TACKLE COMPANY
4099 Beaufait Street
Detroit, Michigan 48207   phone: 313-921-0888
(Corner of Beaufait Street and Gratiot Avenue.)

Hours: Monday-Friday, 8 am-4 pm

Manufacturer of Helin tackle and fishing accessories.
Savings: 40% on lure seconds.

Payment: Cash, check for exact amount with identification.
Parking: Street.

KURTIS KITCHEN AND BATH CENTERS
Kurtis Manufacturing and Distributing Company (Main Location)
20433 Livernois Street
Detroit, Michigan 48221   phone: 313-864-2300
(1 block south of 8 Mile Road.)

Hours: Monday-Friday, 8 am-6 pm
       Saturday, 8 am-4 pm

See: Ann Arbor, Michigan, Kurtis Kitchen and Bath Centers.

Savings: Up to 60% on kitchen cabinets, bathroom vanities, and formica tops in a wide range of styles.

Payment: Cash, check with identification, Master Charge, Visa.
Parking: Lot.

REGAL PACKING COMPANY
1445 East Kirby Avenue
Detroit, Michigan 48211   phone: 313-875-6777

Hours: Monday-Thursday, 7:30 am-6 pm
       Friday, Saturday, 7 am-7 pm

Restaurant quality fresh meat and fish including beef, pork, chicken, fish, and sausage products made by State Sausage Corporation.
Savings: 20% and up on top quality product. Greater savings on "super specials" for the freezer such as an assortment of six different items, each packaged in 5- to 10-lb. quantities.

Payment: Cash, checks only from local residents with identification.
Parking: Lot.

RUSSELL-PHINNEY PIES, INC., THRIFT BAKERY
Division of Ward Baking Company
5490 Missouri Avenue
Detroit, Michigan 48208   phone: 313-894-5038
(¼ block west of Grand River at Interstate 94.)

Hours: Monday–Saturday, 9 am–5:15 pm
Outlet for fresh and day-old pies including apple, blueberry, cherry, coconut and lemon meringue, and cream pies. Also 1- and 2-lb. loaves of white, wheat, and rye breads and assorted rolls.
Savings: 30% and up on day-old product and pie specials.

Payment: Cash only.
Parking: Street, metered.

SEARS CATALOG SURPLUS STORE
20425 Plymouth Road
Detroit, Michigan 48225   phone: 313-835-9700

Hours: Monday–Friday, 9:30 am–9 pm
       Saturday, 9:30 am–5:30 pm
       Sunday, 12 noon–5 pm
See: Chicago, Illinois, Sears Catalog Surplus Store.
Savings: 33⅓% to 80%.

Payment: Cash, check with identification, Sears charge card.
Parking: Lot behind store.

Eaton Rapids

DAVIDSON'S OLD MILL YARN OF EATON RAPIDS
109 Elizabeth Street
Eaton Rapids, Michigan 48827   phone: 517-663-2711

Hours: Monday–Friday, 1 pm–5 pm
       Saturday, 9:30 am–5 pm
Outlet for Old Mill Acrylic Yarns and wool, mohair, rayon loop, cotton, and blended yarns in a complete range of colors.
Also: Carpet warp and rug fillers and natural fibers including alpaca, cashmere, camel hair, and sheep's wool.
Yarns are sold by the skein, ounce, pound, tube, and cone. A large selection of yarns for knitters and fibers for spinners.
Savings: 50% and up on mill ends.

Davidson's ships mail and telephone orders and publishes a four-times-a-year "Odd Lot Bulletin" with exceptionally good buying values on closeouts and discontinueds.

Payment: Cash, check for exact amount with identification, Master Charge, Visa.
Parking: Lot.

Eau Claire

SILVER MILL FROZEN FOODS, INC.
Old Pipestone Road
Eau Claire, Michigan 49111   phone: 616-461-6931

Hours: Monday-Friday, 8 am-12 noon, 1 pm-5 pm

Processor of packaged frozen fruits and vegetables in institutional sizes. Strawberries in 12-lb. packs; dark sweet cherries in 12-lb. and 28-lb. packs; blueberries in 10- and 30-lb. packs; and black and red raspberries, red sour cherries, apricots, apples, rhubarb, and asparagus in large bulk packs.
Savings: Better than 75% for those who prefer to put up their own jellies, jams, and sauces.

Payment: Cash, check for exact amount with identification.
Parking: Lot.

Escanaba

H. W. GOSSARD COMPANY FACTORY OUTLET STORE
920 Ludington Street
Escanaba, Michigan 49829   phone: 906-786-9696

Hours: Monday-Saturday, 9:30 am-5 pm
        Open Friday evenings until 9 pm
See: Batavia, Illinois, H. W. Gossard Company Factory Outlet Store.

Outlet for quality sleepwear and loungewear for women; hosiery and socks for men, women, and children; and boys' and men's sweaters. Two fitting rooms.
Savings: 30% to 70% on overstocks, discontinueds, and a few irregulars.

Payment: Cash, check with identification, Master Charge, Visa.
Parking: Metered—pennies, nickels, dimes.

Farmington Hills

KURTIS KITCHEN AND BATH CENTERS
30835 West 10 Mile Road
Farmington Hills, Michigan 48924   phone: 313-478-8500
(East of Orchard Lake Road.)

Hours: Monday-Friday, 8 am-5 pm
       Saturday, 8 am-4 pm

See: Ann Arbor, Michigan, Kurtis Kitchen and Bath Centers.

Savings: Up to 60% on kitchen cabinets, bathroom vanities, and formica tops in a wide range of styles.

Payment: Cash, check with identification, Master Charge, Visa.
Parking: Lot.

Flint

SEARS CATALOG SURPLUS STORE
Small Mall
3775 South Dort Highway
Flint, Michigan 48507   phone: 313-742-1370

Hours: Monday-Friday, 10 am-9 pm
       Saturday, 10 am-6 pm
       Sunday, 12 noon-5 pm

See: Chicago, Illinois, Sears Catalog Surplus Store.

Savings: 20% to 80%.

Payment: Cash, check with identification, Sears charge card.
Parking: Lot.

Frankenmuth

FRANKENMUTH WOOLEN MILL COMPANY
570 South Main Street
Frankenmuth, Michigan 48734   phone: 517-652-8121

Hours: Summer and fall—Monday-Saturday, 9 am-8 pm
                        Sunday, 12 noon-8 pm
       Winter—Monday-Saturday, 9 am-5 pm
              Sunday, 12 noon-5 pm

Handmade and hand-tied lambs wool comforters, from crib to king size, and 45" fabrics and new wool batts for home quilt makers. Frankenmuth will process customers' own raw fleece into batting or for spinning.

Savings: 25% and up on new wool products not generally available in normal retail outlets.

Also: Large assortment of ladies' and men's sweaters in wool and orlon. Will take mail orders. Write for catalog sheet.

Payment: Cash, check with identification, Master Charge, Visa.
Parking: Lot.

Frankfort

SMELTZER ORCHARD COMPANY
Frozen Fruit Processors
6032 Joyfield Road
Frankfort, Michigan 49635   phone: 616-882-4421
(County Road 602)

Hours: Monday-Friday, 8 am-4:30 pm

Smeltzer freezer packs 30-lb. containers of apples, cherries (red tart and black sweet), blueberries, peaches, raspberries, and rhubarb.

During the packing season—when Smeltzer is processing apples, cherries, peaches, and strawberries at this plant—consumers can come in and buy the 30-lb. containers of fruit as they come off the line before freezing. At home, the can contents may be repackaged into smaller units for the home freezer.

Savings: Up to 75% when compared to prices of smaller unit packages of frozen fruit.

Note: Packing seasons are: strawberries, late June; cherries, from the middle to the end of July; and apples, September to January. Call first to determine which fresh products are being processed at a particular time.

Payment: Cash only.
Parking: Lot.

Fremont

GERBER PRODUCTS COMPANY OUTLET STORE
445 State Street
Fremont, Michigan 49412 phone: 616-928-2614

Hours: Monday–Saturday, 9 am–5 pm

Outlet for products made by Gerber subsidiaries including clothing for infants, from newly born to size 4, and bottles, vaporizers, baby toiletries, etc. Also, a Gerber Baby Sample kit containing feeding spoon, sample food items, and a book.

Stretch suits, pram suits, T-shirts in first quality, and baby plastic pants in first quality and seconds.

Savings: Anywhere from 10% to 50% on first quality product.

Payment: Cash, check for exact amount with identification.
Parking: Lot.

Grand Haven

PATCHWORK STORES
A Division of Glen of Michigan
First and Washington Street
Grand Haven, Michigan 49417 phone: 616-842-6290

Hours: Monday–Saturday, 10 am–5 pm
       Open Friday evenings until 9 pm

Outlet for Glen of Michigan, quality name women's ready-to-wear line in sizes 4 to 16.

Store also carries other lines, but savings are not as great. Five fitting rooms.

Savings: Up to 50% on first quality overruns and samples from Glen of Michigan. More than 75% on seconds.

Also: Fabric remnants and trims at excellent savings.

Payment: Cash, check, Master Charge, Visa.
Parking: Street.

Grand Rapids

BARGAIN CORNER OUTLET STORE
Corner of Ionia and Oaks Streets
Grand Rapids, Michigan 49502   phone: 616-459-1951

Hours: Monday-Friday, 9 am-5 pm
        First Saturday of each month, 10 am-4 pm

Outlet for H. Cutler and Company, manufacturers of infants' and children's wear.

Very large outlet with first quality merchandise on the first floor and seconds in the basement.

Savings: Average 50% on first quality overruns, discontinueds, samples, etc. Greater savings on seconds.

Payment: Cash, check for exact amount with identification.
Parking: Lot.

CAMEO FACTORY OUTLET
16 Ionia Street, S.W.
Grand Rapids, Michigan 49502   phone: 616-451-2759

Hours: Monday-Friday, 9 am-4 pm

Outlet for Cameo, manufacturer of dacron, feather, and decorative pillows; cushions; vinyl bean bag chairs; and dacron-filled quilted outerwear jackets for men, women, and children.

Savings: 25% to 60% on first quality, irregular, and overrun product.

Also: Savings on fabrics.

Payment: Cash, check for exact amount with identification.
Parking: Metered—dimes.

GRAND RAPIDS BRICK COMPANY
2730 44th Street, S.W.
Grand Rapids, Michigan 49509   phone: 616-538-9140

Hours: Monday-Friday, 7 am-4:30 pm

Manufacturer of smooth white and rock face brick.

Savings: Better than 30% on seconds. You pick them out from massive piles.

Payment: Cash, check for exact amount with identification.
Parking: Lot.

PATCHWORK STORES
A Division of Glen of Michigan
2887 28th Street, S.E.
Grand Rapids, Michigan 49506   phone: 616-942-8470
(Ridgemoor Center.)

Hours: Monday-Saturday, 10 am-5 pm
See: Grand Haven, Michigan, Patchwork Stores.
Savings: Up to 50% on first quality overruns and samples from Glen of Michigan. More than 75% on seconds.

Also: Fabrics, remnants, and trimmings at excellent savings.
Four fitting rooms.

Payment: Cash, check, Master Charge, Visa.
Parking: Lot.

UNITED BISCUIT COMPANY SURPLUS STORE
7780 Division Avenue South
Grand Rapids, Michigan 49508   phone: 616-455-3900

Hours: Monday-Friday, 8:30 am-5 pm
Packaged cookies including butter, chocolate chip, oatmeal, coconut chocolate chip, iced oatmeal, peanut butter, sugar, butter macaroon, coconut bars, and iced coconut bars.
Savings: Up to 50%.

Payment: Cash, check with identification for large orders only.
Parking: Lot.

Hillsdale

ANKE MANUFACTURING COMPANY
915 Steamburg Road
Hillsdale, Michigan 49242   phone: 517-254-4281
(8 miles south of Hillsdale.)

Hours: Monday-Friday, 8 am-4 pm
       Saturday, 8 am-12 noon
Manufacturers of dacron-filled snowmobile suits and jackets for men,

women, and children and dacron-filled sleeping bags.
Savings: Average 40% on first quality clothing.

Payment: Cash, check for exact amount with identification.
Parking: Lot.

Holland

BAKER FURNITURE COMPANY
573 Columbia Street
Holland, Michigan 49423   phone: 616-392-3181

Write to be placed on mailing list for annual factory sale held at another location.

Note: Factory is not open to the public at any time for regular sale of furniture.

Baker Furniture manufactures well-designed, superior quality classic furniture for the home and office including fine wood and upholstered pieces.

Savings: 50% and up at the scheduled annual factory sale during which old floor samples, discontinued styles, factory seconds, and freight-damaged merchandise and fabrics are sold at incredible prices.

Payment: Cash, check for exact amount with identification.
Parking: Lot.

SLIGH FURNITURE COMPANY AND TREND CLOCKS, INC.
174 East Eleventh Street
Holland, Michigan 49423   phone: 616-392-7101

Call to ask for date of warehouse sale usually held in early spring.

Sligh manufactures a quality line of classically styled desks, tables, chairs, commodes, bookcases; grandmother and grandfather clocks; and wall, mantle, and shelf clocks.

Savings: Average 50% and more on closeouts, seconds, slightly scratched, and one-of-a-kind during warehouse sale. (At other times, factory is not open to public.)

Payment: Cash, check for exact amount with identification.
Parking: Lot.

Howard City

OLSEN KNIFE COMPANY, INC.
Retail Store—Corner of Factory
Old US Highway 31
Howard City, Michigan 49329   phone: 616-937-4373

Hours: Monday-Saturday, 9 am-5:30 pm

Swedish hard carbon steel and stainless steel knives with rosewood handles, in all sizes from small paring to large chef's knives, sold at regular retail prices. Also hunting knives, carving sets, and sharpeners.
Savings: Up to 50% on Olsen Knife seconds in the bargain barrel.

Payment: Cash, check for exact amount with identification.
Parking: Lot.

Ishpeming

H. W. GOSSARD COMPANY FACTORY OUTLET STORE
308 Cleveland Avenue
Ishpeming, Michigan 49849   phone: 906-486-6475

Hours: Monday-Saturday, 9 am-4 pm
         Open Thursday evenings until 8:30 pm

See: Batavia, Illinois, H. W. Gossard Company Factory Outlet Store.
Savings: 30% to 70%.

Fitting rooms.

Payment: Cash, check for exact amount with Michigan identification.
Parking: Street.

Keeler

BURNETTE FARMS PACKING COMPANY
Keeler Road
Keeler, Michigan 49057   phone: 616-621-3181

Hours: Monday-Friday, 8 am-3 pm
Canners of quality fruits and vegetables including applesauce, cher-

ries, asparagus, tomato, and apple juice, sold in case lots only.
Savings: Average 25% on first quality products to 50% on "dents" (first quality product in dented cans), when available.

Payment: Cash, check with identification.
Parking: Lot.

Lansing

KWAST BAKERY
1825 South Washington Avenue
Lansing, Michigan, 48910   phone: 517-484-1317
(Thrift department for day-old is located in downstairs area of store.)

Hours: Daily, 7 am–5:30 pm

Kwast is "Lansing's cake baker." Products include fried rolls and fried cakes, Danish and doughnuts, bread, rolls, and other bakery items.
Savings: Up to 50% on day-old product packaged in units of four (i.e., four doughnuts, four Danish, etc.), when available. Sold in the downstairs area of the store.

Payment: Cash, check for exact amount with identification.
Parking: Lot.

UNITED GLAZED PRODUCTS, INC.
4500 Aurelius Road
Lansing, Michigan 48910   phone: 517-882-2463

Hours: Monday–Friday, 8 am–5 pm

Concrete block with glazed face in a spectrum of 48 colors. Some blocks glazed on two sides, some with textured or design patterns. Glazed surface looks like ceramic tile.
Savings: 33⅓% to 50% on seconds, sold by the yard.

Tiles make attractive bases for benches, home planter units, or bookshelf supporters.

Payment: Cash, check for exact amount with identification.
Parking: Lot.

Lawton

HONEE BEAR
Division of Packer's Canning Company, Inc.
Highway Michigan 40
Lawton, Michigan 49065   phone: 616-624-4681
(1 mile south of Lawton.)

Hours: Monday-Friday, 8 am-4:30 pm

Packers of asparagus, sweet and sour cherries, blueberries, and plums, sold in case lots only.

Savings: Up to 50% on first quality canned goods sold by the case. Greater savings on "dents" (first quality product in dented cans), which are generally unlabeled, when available.

Payment: Cash, check for exact amount with identification.
Parking: Lot.

Lincoln Park

KURTIS KITCHEN AND BATH CENTERS
1491 Southfield Road
Lincoln Park, Michigan 48146   phone: 313-388-1900
(Between Interstate 75 and Fort Street.)

Hours: Monday-Friday, 9 am-6 pm
       Saturday, 9 am-4 pm
       Open Thursday evenings until 8 pm

See: Ann Arbor, Michigan, Kurtis Kitchen and Bath Centers.

Savings: Up to 60% on kitchen cabinets, bathroom vanities, and formica tops in a wide range of styles.

Payment: Cash, check with identification, Master Charge, Visa.
Parking: Street.

Litchfield

HARVARD OF HILLSDALE, INC.
Michigan 99 North
Litchfield, Michigan 49252   phone: 517-456-7722

Hours: Monday-Friday, 9 am-12 noon, 1 pm-4:30 pm

In-plant outlet store for Harvard of Hillsdale, manufacturers of nylon fiberfill coats, jackets, vests, and snowmobile suits for men, women,

and children. Also water repellent or waterproof windbreakers, jackets, coats, and bib overalls.
Savings: Average 50% on first quality outerwear for all the family.

Also: Good savings on quilted nylon, waterproof nylon, and nylon taffeta by the yard.

Send for Factory Outlet Price Sheets for mail orders.

Payment: Cash, check for exact amount with identification.
Parking: Lot.

Livonia

BROWNBERRY NATURAL BREADS
31221 West Five Mile Road
Livonia, Michigan 48154   phone: 313-425-1260

Hours: Monday-Friday, 9 am-9 pm
       Saturday, 9 am-5 pm
       Sunday, 10 am-5 pm

See: LaGrange Park, Illinois, Brownberry Ovens Thrift Store.

Savings: 33⅓% and up on day-old and seconds. Extra 10% savings on Tuesdays and Sundays.

Payment: Cash, check for exact amount with identification.
Parking: Lot.

PEPPERIDGE FARM THRIFT STORE
29115 Eight Mile Road
Livonia, Michigan 48152   phone: 313-477-2046

Hours: Monday-Friday, 9:30 am-5:30 pm
       Saturday, 9 am-5 pm

See: Downers Grove, Illinois, Pepperidge Farm Thrift Store.

Savings: 25% to 50%. For best selection, shop early in the morning.

Payment: Cash, check for exact amount with identification.
Parking: Lot.

Ludington

WOLVERINE SPORTSWEAR COMPANY
801 North Rowe Street
Ludington, Michigan 49431   phone: 616-845-6580

Hours: Monday-Friday, 10 am-12 noon, 1:30 pm-5 pm
          Saturday, 10 am-12 noon

Outlet for Wolverine Sportswear; men's, women's, and boys' winter, spring, and rain coats; and women's coats in sizes 6 to 24½.
Savings: Up to 50% on first quality overruns and discontinueds.

Also: Fabrics, linings, buttons, and sewing accessories at savings.

Payment: Cash, check for exact amount with identification.
Parking: Street.

Manistee

LITTLE RED SHOE HOUSE
537 Cypress Street
Manistee, Michigan 49660   phone: 616-723-7274

Hours: Monday-Saturday, 9:30 am-5 pm
          Open Friday evenings until 9 pm

See: Big Rapids, Michigan, Little Red Shoe House.

Savings: 50% on discontinueds, seconds, and irregulars.

Payment: Cash, check for exact amount with identification.
Parking: Street.

PATCHWORK STORES
A Division of Glen of Michigan
77 Hancock Street
Manistee, Michigan 49660   phone: 616-723-4462

Hours: Monday-Saturday, 10 am-5 pm

See: Grand Haven, Michigan, Patchwork Stores.

Savings: Up to 50% on first quality; more than 75% on seconds.

Fitting rooms.

Payment: Cash, check, Master Charge, Visa.
Parking: Street.

Middleville

BABY BLISS, INC., OUTLET STORE
314 Arlington Avenue
Middleville, Michigan 49333　　　　　　phone: 616-795-9523
(On Michigan 37—2 blocks north of the traffic light.)

Hours: Monday-Friday, 8:30 am-5 pm
　　　　Saturday, 9 am-3 pm

Baby dresses, sleepers, warm-up suits, rompers, and blue jeans in small, medium, and large sizes. Also sales representatives' samples from other manufacturers. Samples include girls' sweaters, jeans, and snowsuits in sizes up to 14 on some items.
Savings: Up to 50% on Baby Bliss discontinueds, irregulars, and samples. Greater savings on sales representatives' samples from other manufacturers, when available.

Also: Fabrics, trims, buttons, and appliques at good savings.

Payment: Cash, check for exact amount with identification.
Parking: Street.

Muskegon

LITTLE RED SHOE HOUSE
1630 Apple Avenue
Beltline Plaza
Muskegon, Michigan 49442　　　　　　phone: 616-777-1066

Hours: Monday-Thursday, Saturday, 9:30 am-6 pm
　　　　Friday, 9:30 am-9 pm

See: Big Rapids, Michigan, Little Red Shoe House.
Savings: 50% on discontinueds, seconds, and irregulars in shoes, boots, and Hush Puppy footwear.

Payment: Cash, check for exact amount with identification, Master Charge, Visa.
Parking: Lot.

Niles

MICHIGAN MUSHROOM GROWERS, LTD.
1400 South Third Street
Niles, Michigan 49120 phone: 616-683-5100

Hours: Monday-Friday, 8:30 am-12 noon

Top quality mushrooms picked fresh daily.
Savings: About 50% on second-grade mushrooms, which are not perfectly shaped. Smaller savings on fresh A-1 quality.

Payment: Cash, check for exact amount with identification.
Parking: Lot.

North Muskegon

LITTLE RED SHOE HOUSE
Plumb's Supermarket
1834 Holton Road (Michigan 120)
North Muskegon, Michigan 49445 phone: 616-744-9503
(Shoe department is in back of store.)

Hours: Monday-Saturday, 9 am-9 pm

See: Big Rapids, Michigan, Little Red Shoe House.

Savings: 50% on discontinueds, seconds, and irregulars in shoes, boots, and Hush Puppy footwear.

Payment: Cash, check for exact amount with identification, Master Charge, Visa.
Parking: Lot.

Oak Park

PAPER AND GRAPHIC SUPPLIES CENTER
Division of Seaman-Patrick Paper Company
13331 Cloverdale Road
Oak Park, Michigan 48237 phone: 313-546-2080

Hours: Monday-Friday, 7:30 am-4:30 pm

The Supplies Center sells Linweave, Velvetsheen, and Fox River papers, envelopes, and graphic art supplies.
Savings: Average 30% on all supplies.

Payment: Cash, check for exact amount with identification.
Parking: Lot.

Pittsford

HARVARD TROUSER COMPANY, INC.
Factory and Salesroom
Pittsford, Michigan 49271 phone: 517-523-2167
(Michigan 34, 1 block south of blinker light.)

Hours: Monday-Saturday, 8:30 am-4:30 pm
       April to August—Monday-Friday, 8:30 am-3:30 pm

Outlet store for H.T.C., manufacturers of nylon fiberfill jackets and outerwear for all members of the family: car coats, jackets, vests, snowmobile suits, and bib overalls. Women's sizes: 8 to 34 in jackets; 8 to 22 in coats. Men's sizes: small to XXX large. Children's sizes: 4 to 18.
Savings: Average 30% and up on machine washable outerwear.

Write for mail order brochure to P.O. Box 317, Pittsford, Michigan 49271.

Payment: Cash, check for exact amount with identification.
Parking: Lot.

Portland

LITTLE RED SHOE HOUSE
C & B Discount Store
1465 East Grand River Avenue
Portland, Michigan 48875   phone: 517-647-7945

Hours: Monday-Thursday, 9 am-8 pm
  Friday, 9 am-9 pm
  Saturday, 9 am-6 pm
  Sunday, 10 am-6 pm

See: Big Rapids, Michigan, Little Red Shoe House.

Savings: 50% on discontinueds, seconds, and irregulars in shoes, boots, and Hush Puppy footwear.

Payment: Cash, check for exact amount with identification, Master Charge, Visa.
Parking: Lot.

Rockford

LITTLE RED SHOE HOUSE
Wolverine World Wide Factory Shoe Outlet
Squires Street Square
Rockford, Michigan 49341   phone: 616-866-9316
(North of Grand Rapids just off US 131. Exit at 10 Mile Road.)

Hours: Monday-Friday, 10 am-8 pm
  Saturday, 10 am-5:30 pm
  Sunday, 1 pm-5 pm

See: Big Rapids, Michigan, Little Red Shoe House.

Savings: 50% on discontinueds, seconds, and irregulars in Wolverine World Wide and Hush Puppy footwear.

Payment: Cash, check for exact amount with identification, Master Charge, Visa.
Parking: Lot.

RED FLANNEL FACTORY OUTLET STORE
Squires Street Square
Rockford, Michigan 49341   phone: 616-866-4968

Hours: Monday-Saturday, 10 am-5 pm
       Open Saturday evenings until 6 pm

See: Cedar Springs, Michigan, Red Flannel Factory.

Savings: Up to 50% on irregulars.

Payment: Cash, check, Master Charge, Visa.
Parking: Lot.

Royal Oak

MALAGA BRIAR PIPE COMPANY
1406 East 11 Mile Road
Royal Oak, Michigan 48067   phone: 313-542-5000

Hours: Monday-Friday, 9 am-6 pm
       Saturday, 9 am-4 pm

Malaga, manufacturer of better-priced briar pipes, sells pipe "seconds with small defects" throughout the year, with the exception of the month of December.

The best selection of shapes and seconds will be found during Malaga's big annual sale, which begins at 9 am on December 26th and runs through the month of January.

Savings: 50% and up on pipe seconds.

Malaga also sells tobacco, fine pipes, and accessories.

Payment: Cash, check, Master Charge, Visa.
Parking: Lot in rear.

Saugatuck

GALLERIE LA BARGE
322 Butler Street
Saugatuck, Michigan 49453   phone: 616-857-4660

Hours: April 1-June 15 (weekends only)—Saturday, Sunday, 10 am-5 pm
June 15-Labor Day—Tuesday-Sunday, 10 am-5 pm
Open by appointment only during the winter months

Outlet for La Barge Mirrors, Inc., exclusive decorator line of mirrors, tables, and glass and brass accessories. Shop items, often one-of-a-kind, retail for $125 to $650 for accessories that might normally retail for up to $2,000.
Savings: Up to 50% on La Barge discontinueds. Very small savings on special order La Barge accessories from the current lines.

Also: This shop carries antique accessories imported from China by La Barge at some savings over normal retail or decorator prices.

Payment: Cash, check for exact amount with identification.
Parking: Street.

Sault Ste. Marie

H. W. GOSSARD COMPANY FACTORY OUTLET STORE
210 Ashmun Street
Sault Ste. Marie, Michigan 49783   phone: 906-635-1443

Hours: Monday-Saturday, 9 am-5 pm
Open Friday evenings until 9 pm

See: Batavia, Illinois, H. W. Gossard Company Factory Outlet Store.

Outlet for quality sleepwear and loungewear for women; hosiery and socks for men, women, and children; and boys' and men's sweaters. One fitting room.
Savings: 30% to 70% on overstocks, discontinueds, and a few irregulars.

Payment: Cash, check for exact amount with identification, Master Charge, Visa.
Parking: Lot across the street.

South Haven

LITTLE RED SHOE HOUSE
Factory Outlet Shoes
Lagrange at Aylworth Avenues
South Haven, Michigan 49090   phone: 616-637-1307
(Located in Harding's Friendly Market.)

Hours: Monday-Saturday, 8 am-9 pm
       Sunday, 9 am-4 pm
See: Big Rapids, Michigan, Little Red Shoe House.
Savings: 50% on discontinueds, seconds, and irregulars for all members of the family.

Payment: Cash, check for exact amount with identification, Master Charge, Visa.
Parking: Lot.

Spring Lake

MARÜSHKA FABRIC OUTLET STORE
Marüshka, Inc., Richard Sweet Designs
17771 West Spring Lake Road
Spring Lake, Michigan 49456   phone: 616-846-3510

Hours: Monday-Saturday, 10 am-5 pm
Marüshka Graphics and Field Prints, designed by Richard Sweet, are hand-screened designs on imported natural linen fabric. They can be used for stretch pictures (fabric is stretched on a lightweight frame, which can then be hung on a nail), wall hangings, banners, pillows, and other home decorative projects. The finely detailed designs are based on natural objects: leaves, trees, flowers, vegetables, shells, Indian design motifs, and contemporary designs. Fabric is sold by the yard—$5 to $15; stretched pictures, which range in size from 8" × 10" to 24" × 36", are sold by the individual unit—$1 to $40.
Savings: Up to 50% on seconds and discontinued designs.

Factory tours are available.

Payment: Cash, check, American Express, Master Charge, Visa.
Parking: Lot.

Traverse City

BURWOOD PRODUCTS COMPANY FACTORY OUTLET
807 Airport Access Road
Traverse City, Michigan 49684   phone: 616-946-4950
(1 block south of Fox Haus.)

Hours: Tuesday-Saturday, 12 noon-5 pm

Burwood manufactures wall accessories such as clocks, mirrors, sconces, shelves, pull-up tables, and decorative accents for the home. **Savings: 50% and more on overruns, discontinueds, and some seconds.**

Payment: Cash, checks from local residents only.
Parking: Lot.

PATCHWORK STORES
A Division of Glen of Michigan
122 Cass Street
Traverse City, Michigan 49684   phone: 616-946-0260

Hours: Monday-Saturday, 10 am-5:30 pm
       Open Friday evenings until 9 pm

See: Grand Haven, Michigan, Patchwork Stores.

Savings: Up to 50% on first quality; 75% on seconds.

Also: Fabrics, remnants, and trimmings at excellent savings.
Fitting rooms.

Payment: Cash, check, Master Charge, Visa.
Parking: Street.

Warren

KURTIS KITCHEN AND BATH CENTERS
5751 Thirteen Mile Road
Warren, Michigan 48089   phone: 313-939-1500
(At Mound, Green Acres Plaza.)

Hours: Monday, Tuesday, Wednesday, Friday, 9 am-6 pm
       Thursday, 9 am-8 pm
       Saturday, 9 am-4 pm

See: Ann Arbor, Michigan, Kurtis Kitchen and Bath Centers.
Savings: Up to 60% on kitchen cabinets and bathroom vanity cabinets.

Payment: Cash, check with identification, Master Charge, Visa.
Parking: Lot.

PAPER AND GRAPHIC SUPPLIES CENTER
13845 Nine Mile Road
Warren, Michigan 48089   phone: 313-771-7130

Hours: Monday-Friday, 8 am-5 pm
See: Oak Park, Michigan, Paper and Graphic Supplies Center.
Savings: Average 30% on all paper supplies.

Payment: Cash, check for exact amount with identification.
Parking: Lot.

Wayland

KESSLER, INC., FACTORY OUTLET
801 South Main Street
Wayland, Michigan 49348   phone: 616-792-2222

Hours: Monday-Saturday, 10 am-4 pm

Factory outlet store sells Kessler infantwear products including diapers, undershirts, blankets, blanket sleepers (up to size 12), sleepers (up to extra large, which will fit a 26-lb. infant), and shirts and pants (up to size 7).

Also: Knit, double knit, and cotton fabrics sold by the piece or off the bolt by the yard.
Savings: Up to 50% on first quality items; higher savings on irregulars or seconds.

Payment: Cash, check with identification.
Parking: Lot.

MINNESOTA

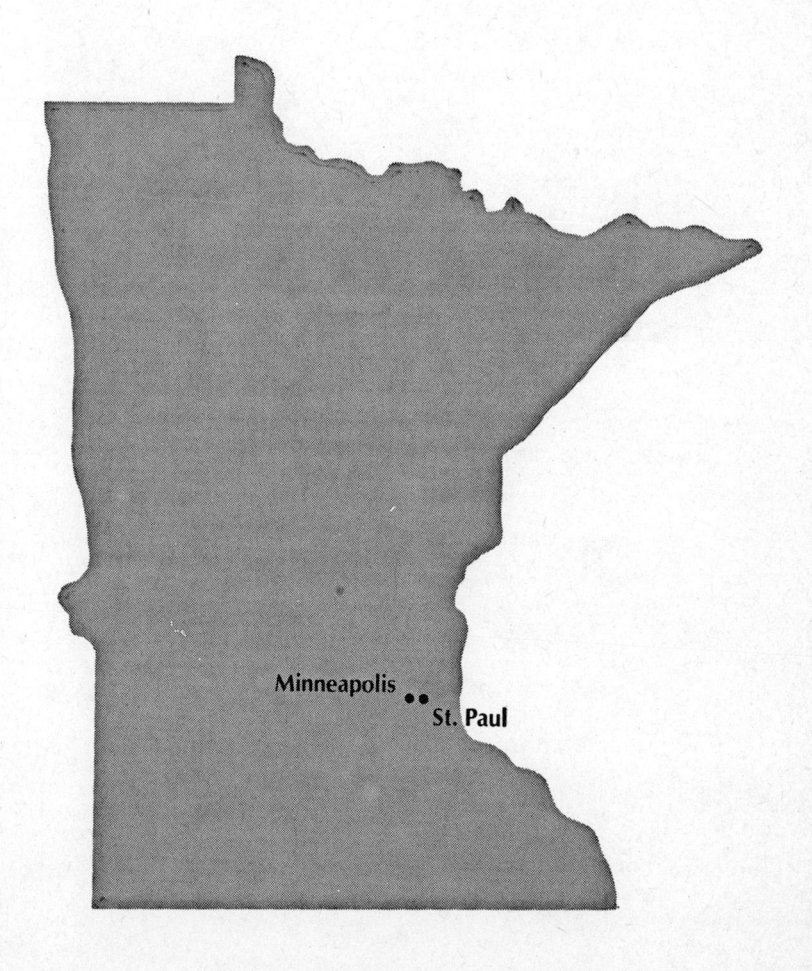

150   Minnesota • Arlington

Arlington

BIG STONE, INC.
300 Third Avenue, S.W.
Arlington, Minnesota 55307   phone: 612-964-2204

Hours: Wednesday only, 7:30 am-4:30 pm

Big Stone packs green beans, kidney beans, peas, and whole kernel corn in #303 cans (24 cans to a case) and #10 cans (6 cans to a case).
Savings: Up to 50% on cases of dented, mislabeled, or unlabeled cans. Call first, as not all product is always available.

Payment: Cash, check for exact amount with identification.
Parking: Lot.

Bemidji

BEMIDJI BOAT COMPANY, INC.
Core-Craft Lifetime Canoes
US 2 West
Bemidji, Minnesota 56601   phone: 218-751-2254
(Industrial Park, just east of Bemidji.)

Hours: Monday-Friday, 8 am-5 pm
Inquire at office in mobile trailer.

Bemidji Boat manufactures Core-Craft fiberglass Lifetime Canoes in several sizes and in six color options. They also manufacture Snow Wonders, a snow-removal scoop made of molded fiberglass.
Savings: Up to 80% on canoe seconds, functionally perfect canoes with blemishes or wrinkles in the gel coat finishing process.

Payment: Cash, check with identification, Master Charge, Visa.
Parking: Lot.

BEMIDJI WOOLEN MILLS
Mill Retail Store
3rd and Irvine Street
Bemidji, Minnesota 56601   phone: 218-751-5166

Hours: Monday-Saturday, 8 am-5:30 pm
Send for mail-order catalog.

Bemidji manufactures the famous Hudson Bay point blanket made from tightly woven 100% virgin wool in two sizes: 72" × 90" and 90" ×

Bloomington • Minnesota

100". The mills also manufacture wool and nylon blend blankets and throws, wool socks, and blended wool and nylon shirts.

The store also sells hats, mittens, scarves, dickies, sweaters, deerskin gloves and shoes, wool blend pants, and men's, women's, and children's jac shirts and coats.

Savings: Up to 30% on first quality; 50% on seconds or irregulars in socks and on factory closeouts.

Also: Good savings on natural, unbleached yarn homespun in natural color or grey, 100% new wool batting covered in cheesecloth, and 100% dacron-polyester wool batting.

Payment: Cash, check for exact amount with identification, Master Charge, Visa.
Parking: Street.

Bloomington

BROWNBERRY OVENS THRIFT STORE
9412 Lyndale South
Bloomington, Minnesota 55420   phone: 612-884-6836

Hours: Monday, Wednesday, Thursday, Friday, 9 am-7 pm
    Tuesday, 9 am-9 pm
    Saturday, 9 am-6 pm
    Sunday, 11 am-5 pm

See: LaGrange Park, Illinois, Brownberry Ovens Thrift Store.

Savings: 33⅓% and up on day-old and seconds. Extra 10% savings on Tuesdays and Sundays.

Payment: Cash, check for exact amount with identification.
Parking: Lot.

GOTTLIEB FURNITURE AND CARPET COMPANY
8940 Lyndale Avenue South
Bloomington, Minnesota 55320   phone: 612-884-7799

Hours: Monday-Friday, 9 am-5:30 pm

Gottlieb sells Berne, Burlington, Davis, Hekman, Monitor, Peters, Revington, and Virginia House furniture lines for 10% over cost, F.O.B. their stores. They will special order direct from the factories

with delivery in eight to fourteen weeks. Also, Stiffel and Tyndale lamps at 40% less than retail.
Savings: 40% and more on lamps and furniture ordered directly from the factories.

Also: Carpeting at excellent savings.

Payment: Cash or check for merchandise upon delivery.
Parking: Street.

SEARS CATALOG SURPLUS STORE
9056 Penn Avenue South
Bloomington, Minnesota 55431   phone: 612-884-5317

Hours: Monday-Friday, 9 am-9 pm
        Saturday, 9 am-6 pm
        Sunday, 12 noon-5 pm

See: Chicago, Illinois, Sears Catalog Surplus Store.
Savings: 20% to 80%.

Payment: Cash, check with identification, Sears charge card.
Parking: Lot.

Burnsville

ABDALLAH CANDY STORE
12220 12th Avenue South
Burnsville, Minnesota 55337   phone: 612-890-4770

Hours: Monday, 8 am-4:30 pm
        Tuesday-Friday, 8 am-5 pm
        Saturday, 9 am-1 pm
        Closed Saturdays from June-August

Store is located in front of factory. Abdallah makes a full line of light and dark chocolates including caramels, cordials, assorted creams, nougats, chocolate bark and crunch, and chocolate covered fruits and nuts. Also, hard candies.
Savings: Average 30% on imperfect candies which may be misshapen, not completely covered by chocolate, or "leakers" (small holes in chocolate covering).

Payment: Cash, check with identification.
Parking: Lot.

Cannon Falls

GRANDMOTHER'S ATTIC
Main Street
Cannon Falls, Minnesota 55009   phone: 507-263-4325

Hours: Monday, Wednesday, Friday, 9 am-5:30 pm
       Thursday, 9 am-9 pm
       Saturday, 9 am-5 pm

Outlet for Kid Duds made by Lees Manufacturing Company including brushed cotton nightgowns and pajamas in sizes from infants' to girls' size 14.
Savings: About 50% on sleepwear irregulars.

Also: Clothing from other manufacturers at small savings.

Payment: Cash, check for exact amount with identification, Master Charge, Visa.
Parking: Street.

POINT OF SALES, INC.
324 West Washington Avenue
Cannon Falls, Minnesota 55009   phone: 507-263-4231

Hours: Monday-Friday, 8 am-4:30 pm

Point of Sales, Inc. manufactures display hooks, racks, clips, card holders, and wire bins for in-store promotional uses. They also sell Ready Flo pen sets and inks for making posters, signs, and banners.

Several products such as the handy steel hooks backed with Tuff two-way tape and the high tech wire dump bin displays can be easily converted from commercial use to in-home or workshop space and storage aids.
Savings: 30% and up on products which can be adapted from commercial to in-home use.

Payment: Cash, check.
Parking: Lot.

Chanhassen

ANIMAL FAIR SECONDS STORE
581 West 78th Street
Chanhassen, Minnesota 55317   phone: 612-474-0444

Hours: Tuesday-Friday, 9 am-4 pm
        Saturday, 9 am-1 pm

Animal Fair makes soft, washable (and fire retardant) stuffed animals of all sizes and varieties including a teddy bear.
Savings: 33⅓% to 50% on overstocks, factory rejects, discontinueds, and seconds.

Payment: Cash, check for exact amount with identification.
Parking: Lot.

Clarkfield

ASSOCIATED MILK PRODUCERS, INC.
1204 Tenth Avenue
Clarkfield, Minnesota 56223   phone: 612-669-4411
(Stock room at west end of plant.)

Hours: Monday-Friday, 8 am-5 pm

Producers of State Brand Cheese including American, colby, colby longhorn, mild and sharp cheddar, Monterrey Jack, and Swiss. Also AMPI butter.
Savings: Average 20% and more on fresh cheese and butter products.

Payment: Cash only.
Parking: Lot.

Crystal

BROWNBERRY OVENS THRIFT STORE
6200 Bass Lake Road
Crystal, Minnesota 55429   phone: 612-537-2225

Hours: Monday, Wednesday, Thursday, Friday, 9 am-7 pm
        Tuesday, 9 am-9 pm
        Saturday, 9 am-6 pm
        Sunday, 11 am-5 pm

See: LaGrange Park, Illinois, Brownberry Ovens Thrift Store.
Savings: 33⅓% and up on day-old and seconds. Extra 10% savings on Tuesdays and Sundays.

Payment: Cash, check for exact amount with identification.
Parking: Lot.

Eveleth

CLUETT FACTORY OUTLET
Cluett Peabody Corporation
409 Grant Street
Eveleth, Minnesota 55734   phone: 218-744-4871

Hours: Monday-Saturday, 9 am-5 pm
       Open Monday evenings until 8:30 pm

Outlet for several divisions of Cluett Peabody Manufacturing Corporation including Arrow and Lady Arrow shirts, Duo-Fold underwear, and Donmoor and Dobie's children's wear.

Women's shirts in sizes 6 to 18 and men's shirts in 14½" to 17½" neck sizes in cotton and cotton and polyester blend fabrics.

Also: Girls' blouses and boys' shirts and corduroy slacks, men's and women's slacks, pajamas, underwear, and men's sweaters.
Savings: Up to 50% on seconds. Smaller savings on first quality.

Payment: Cash, check for exact amount with identification.
Parking: Street.

Faribault

THE FARIBAULT CANNING COMPANY
128 N. W. 15th Street
Faribault, Minnesota 55021   phone: 507-345-5520

Hours: Monday-Friday, 8 am-4:30 pm

Faribault packs vegetables under the following brand names: Butter Kernel, Cannon Valley, Dainty Miss, Fleetfoot, Top Value, Vandever.
Savings: About 50% on cases of dented or unlabeled cans of peas and corn, when available. Call first to be sure plant has "dent" product on hand.

Payment: Cash, check for exact amount with identification.
Parking: Lot.

FARIBO MANUFACTURING COMPANY
Division of Plastics, Inc.
820 N. W. 20th Street
Faribault, Minnesota 55021 phone: 507-334-4376

Hours: Monday-Friday, 8 am-5 pm

Faribo manufactures plastic Microware, for use in microwave ovens, in sets of 5, 9, and 11 pieces.
Savings: 30% to 50% on Microware seconds sets.

Payment: Cash, check for exact amount with identification.
Parking: Lot.

FARIBO WOOLENS, INC.
1500 Second Avenue, N.W.
Faribault, Minnesota 55021 phone: 507-334-6444

Hours: Monday-Saturday, 9 am-5:30 pm
       Sunday, 1 pm-5 pm

Faribo manufactures blankets (single, double, queen, and king size), robes, pak-a-robes, and afghan throws (50" × 60" and 50" × 70") in all wool and wool blends.
Savings: 35% to 50% on blanket and pak-a-robe irregulars, available at the store or through mail order.

Also: Excellent savings on 100% wool remnants (in regular and thermal weaves), wool blend remnants, and wool rug strips (3" to 10" wide, 66" to 80" long, sold by the lb.).

Send for mail-order price list of irregular products.

Payment: Cash, check with identification, American Express, Master Charge, Visa.
Parking: Lot.

TREASURE CAVE, INC., RETAIL STORE
222 N. E. 3rd Street
Faribault, Minnesota 55021 phone: 507-334-4123

Hours: Monday-Friday, 8 am-12 noon
                     1 pm-5 pm

Treasure Cave Blue Cheese may be purchased in the shipping receiving area (last door by the parking lot) in quantities that include a 5-lb. carton of wedges (one 5-lb. carton contains 8 individually wrapped

10-oz. wedges); 4-oz. squares, which may be purchased individually; 2½-lb. wedges; and 1¼-lb. bags of crumbled cheese.
Savings: Up to 35% on branded blue cheese.

Payment: Cash, check for exact amount with identification.
Parking: Lot.

Fergus Falls

D. B. ROSENBLATT, INC.
409 Roberts Street
Fergus Falls, Minnesota 56537 phone: 218-736-5872

Two-day plant sales held twice a year in the spring and fall.

Call or write for exact dates of next sale.

D. B. Rosenblatt manufactures quality classically tailored sports clothes for men and women under the Burnbrae label. For men, you will find coats, slacks, and 3- and 4-piece suits in wool, wool blends, and polyester fabrics. For women, there are camel hair coats and coordinated blazers and skirts in wool and wool blends.

Burnbrae 3-piece men's suits normally retail for up to $175 and sport jackets for about $125. Burnbrae skirts for women normally retail for up to $90 and blazers for $175.

Savings: 35% to 50% on first quality overruns during the twice yearly plant sale.

Also: Excellent fabric remnant values.

Payment: Cash, check with identification, Master Charge, Visa.
Parking: Lot.

MEDALLION OUTLET STORE
Medallion Kitchens, Inc.
302 East Washington Street
Fergus Falls, Minnesota 56537 phone: 218-736-5645

Hours: Saturday, 8 am-2 pm

Medallion manufactures quality oak kitchen cabinets in three finishes—butternut, chestnut, and nutmeg—and in several different door styles.

Savings: Up to 75% on structurally sound cabinets with nicked, scratched, or slightly blemished finishes.

Payment: Cash, check with identification.
Parking: Lot.

Fridley

SEARS CATALOG SURPLUS STORE
6199 Minnesota 65, N.E.
Fridley, Minnesota 55421   phone: 612-571-8010

Hours: Monday-Friday, 9 am-9 pm
       Saturday, 9 am-6 pm
       Sunday, 12 noon-5 pm

See: Chicago, Illinois, Sears Catalog Surplus Store.

Savings: 20% to 80%.

Payment: Cash, check with identification, Sears charge card.
Parking: Lot.

Jackson

VILLAGER FOODS, INC., FACTORY DISCOUNT STORE
Blum's of San Francisco
Industrial Parkway
Jackson, Minnesota 56143   phone: 507-847-3800

Hours: Monday-Friday, 8 am-5 pm

Factory where famous Blum's of San Francisco, Inc. candies are made. Products include dark chocolate: buttercreams, cherry cordials, molasses chips, vanilla caramel squares, peanut and raisin clusters, and honey nougats. They also include milk chocolate: buttercreams, almond caramels, chocolate fudge, cherry cordials, cream caramel chews, cashew and almond nut clusters, peanut and raisin clusters, and honey nougats.

Also: San Francisco mints, square mints, and mint chips and Christmas, Halloween, Valentine, and other seasonal specialties.
Savings: About 25% on over-production purchased at plant factory discount store.

Payment: Cash, check for exact amount with identification.
Parking: Lot.

Kenyon

THE GALLERY
648 2nd Street
Kenyon, Minnesota 55946 phone: 507-789-5222

Hours: Monday-Saturday, 10 am-5 pm

Outlet for Foldcraft library tables, adjustable folding tables with leaves, and folding chairs. Formica laminated table surfaces.
Savings: Up to 60% on first quality discontinued styles.

Payment: Cash, check only with local identification.
Parking: Street.

Lakeville

MERILLAT INDUSTRIES, INC.
21755 Cedar Avenue South
Lakeville, Minnesota 55044 phone: 612-469-5444

Hours: Open every other Saturday morning, 8 am-12 noon
Call to check exact dates.

Merillat manufactures stacking, modular unit construction kitchen cabinets made of wood in six styles and several finishes. (Cabinets only—no counter tops.)
Savings: Up to 40% on first quality discontinueds; 60% on structurally sound but slightly damaged cabinets.

Payment: Cash, check for exact amount with identification.
Parking: Lot.

La Salle

LA SALLE FOOD PROCESSING ASSOCIATION
Main Street
La Salle, Minnesota 56056   phone: 507-375-3408

Hours: Monday-Friday, 8 am-12 noon
                    1 pm-5:30 pm
       Saturday, 8 am-12 noon

La Salle makes all-meat summer sausages and bologna products and pork links.
Savings: Average 25% on fresh beef and pork products.

Payment: Cash, check for exact amount with identification.
Parking: Street.

Mankato

CHIP STEAK AND PROVISION COMPANY
Dewey and Linder Streets
Mankato, Minnesota 56001   phone: 507-388-6277

Hours: Monday-Friday, 8 am-5 pm

Chip packages portion control products for institutions and home freezers in bulk pack. These include beef patties, floured beef cubes, and ground beef; club, rib, sirloin, T-bone, and tenderloin steaks; pork chops and ribs; breaded shrimp, fish, and seafood; corned beef, ham, and bacon; meat balls and meat loaf; lunch meats and sausages; turkey rolls and breaded chicken halves; and more.
Savings: Up to 30% on bulk pack purchases of portion control meats.

Payment: Cash, check for exact amount with identification.
Parking: Lot.

Milaca

MILACA MILLS, INC., STORE
US 169
Milaca, Minnesota 56353   phone: 612-983-6635
(Just past the center of town.)

Hours: Monday-Friday, 8 am-4:30 pm

Milaca Mills manufactures women's nightgowns, pajamas (winter

pajamas with feet), and robes in sizes petite, small, medium, and large. Also, women's underpants.
Savings: 20% to 50% on discontinueds, irregulars, and some samples.

Also: Good savings on cotton and cotton blend fabric remnants, ribbons, and trims.

Payment: Cash, check for exact amount with identification.
Parking: Lot.

Minneapolis

ABDALLAH CANDY STORE
3805 Cedar Avenue South
Minneapolis, Minnesota 55400   phone: 612-722-1312

Hours: Tuesday-Saturday, 10 am-5 pm
See: Burnsville, Minnesota, Abdallah Candy Store.
Savings: Average 30% on imperfect candies, which may be misshapen, not completely covered by chocolate, or "leakers" (small holes in chocolate covering).

Payment: Cash, check for exact amount with identification.
Parking: Lot.

ARVEY PAPER AND SUPPLIES CENTER
A Division of Arvey Corporation
1401 West River Road
Minneapolis, Minnesota 55411   phone: 612-529-9133

Hours: Monday-Friday, 8:30 am-5:30 pm
          Saturday, 9 am-1 pm
See: Chicago, Illinois, Arvey Paper and Supplies Center.
Savings: At least 33⅓% on mimeo and bond paper bought by the ream (500 sheets) and envelopes bought by the box (500 envelopes); greater savings on the monthly specials featured in the "salesmailers."

Payment: Cash, check for exact amount with identification.
Parking: Lot.

BEST MAID COOKIE COMPANY
3964 Minnehaha Avenue
Minneapolis, Minnesota 55401   phone: 612-722-7234

Hours: Monday-Friday, 8 am-4:30 pm

Best Maid bakes cookies for the larger, local supermarket chain stores. Flavors include butterscotch chip, chocolate chip, coconut, fudge nut, molasses, nut crunch, oatmeal, peanut butter, and sugar.
Savings: 50% on cookie overruns and imperfects sold in bags of 30 cookies of assorted flavors.

Payment: Cash only.
Parking: Street.

THE BOX SHOP
Cedar Box Factory Outlet
1413 Washington Avenue South
Minneapolis, Minnesota 55454   phone: 612-338-7092

Hours: Monday-Friday, 12 noon-5 pm
       Saturday, 10 am-5 pm

Aspen, northern white, and ponderosa pine, "crate-like" boxes in a variety of sizes (from a 14¾" × 5½" × 6" spice box up to a double record storage box size, 32" × 13½" × 13"). The boxes can be painted or stained and used as furniture storage units.
Also: toy boxes, toy chests, slotted utility racks, and box sofa and ottoman frames.
Savings: 20% and up on unfinished boxes, which can be painted and stained for use as mobile furniture units.

Payment: Cash, check for exact amount with identification.
Parking: Lot.

DAISY THRIFT STORE
Metz Baking Company
2900 Park Avenue
Minneapolis, Minnesota 55407   phone: 612-832-6244

Hours: Monday-Saturday, 9 am-5 pm

Day-old baked goods and some fresh products including sliced sandwich breads, pumpernickel, Roman Meal, and Old Home breads;

brown and serve, hamburger, and hot dog rolls; sweet rolls; snack and cup cakes; bread crumbs; cakes and cookies; and snack items.
Savings: Up to 40% on day-old bakery products.

Payment: Cash.
Parking: Street.

D. B. ROSENBLATT, INC.
Outlet Sale Location
10th Street at 1st Avenue North
Minneapolis, Minnesota 55403   phone: 612-336-2601
(Across from Greyhound Bus Depot.)

Annual fall and spring "Outlet Sales," usually scheduled over three consecutive weekends (Thursday evening, Friday, and Saturday).

Call or write D. B. Rosenblatt, Inc., 912 Currie Ave., Minneapolis, Minnesota 55403, to be placed on mailing list for notification of future sales.

See: Fergus Falls, Minnesota, D. B. Rosenblatt, Inc.

Savings: 35% to 50% on Burnbrae label overruns and first quality garments including men's sport coats and slacks, and women's coats, blazers, and skirts during the special "Outlet Sales."

Also: All-wool, wool blend, and polyester fabric remnants at excellent savings.

Payment: Cash, check, Master Charge, Visa.
Parking: Street.

DOUG'S FACTORY OUTLET STORE
5400 Wayzata Boulevard
Minneapolis, Minnesota 55416   phone: 612-545-2488

Hours: Monday-Friday, 10:30 am-4:30 pm
        Saturday, 11:30 am-2 pm

See: Milaca, Minnesota, Milaca Mills, Inc., Store.

Savings: 20% to 50% on discontinueds, irregulars, and some samples in women's sleepwear and underpants made by Milaca Mills.

Fitting rooms.

Payment: Cash, check.
Parking: Lot.

EGEKVIST THRIFT SHOP
922 East 24th Street
Minneapolis, Minnesota 54404   phone: 612-871-2961, ext. 126

Hours: Monday-Friday, 9 am-5 pm
       Saturday, 9 am-3 pm

Bakers of commercial and specialty breads including English muffin loaf, farm bread, French bread, garlic, Italian, Jewish, peasant pumpernickel, sourdough, and Vienna breads. Also kaiser, graham, potato, and wheat rolls; croutons; cookies; doughnuts; and fresh and frozen party cakes.
Savings: Up to 50% on day-old and some fresh products.

Payment: Cash only.
Parking: Large lot.

THE FACTORY STORE
Sharpee Manufacturing Company
1015 South Sixth Street
Minneapolis, Minnesota 55400   phone: 612-333-6536

Hours: Monday-Friday, 9:30 am-3:30 pm
       Saturday, 9 am-1 pm

Outlet store in factory building carries coats for women in sizes 6 to 20 and 8 to 52 including raincoats, storm coats, ski jackets, and some items from the Designer Collection of all-wool coats.

Also: Boys' and girls' ski jackets in sizes 6 to 20, fabric remnants, linings, buttons, and zippers.
Savings: Up to 50% on samples, overstocks, discontinueds, and some seconds.

Payment: Cash, check for exact amount with identification.
Parking: Lot next to building.

GOTTLIEB FURNITURE AND CARPET COMPANY
2750 Johnson Street, N.E.
Minneapolis, Minnesota 55401   phone: 612-781-1313
(Corner of 28th Street.)

Hours: Monday-Friday, 9 am-5:30 pm

See: Bloomington, Minnesota, Gottlieb Furniture and Carpet Company.

Savings: 40% and more on lamps and furniture ordered directly from the factory.

Also: Carpeting at excellent savings.

Payment: Cash, check for exact amount with identification.
Parking: Street.

HANS ROSACHER ROSE ACRES
1850 Stinson Boulevard
Minneapolis, Minnesota 55418   phone: 612-789-3577

Hours: Monday-Friday, 8 am-5:15 pm
       Saturday, 8 am-5 pm

In addition to green plants and other seasonal specialties, Hans Rosacher grows red, pink, and rose red azaleas; lavender, pink, yellow, and white mums; orange kalanchoes; and cinerarias.
Savings: As compared to plants available through other retail sources, about 20% on 6" potted cinerarias, kalanchoes, and mums with robust flowering and healthy bud development.

Payment: Cash, check with identification, Master Charge, Visa.
Parking: Lot.

HOME BEAUTIFUL ENTERPRISES, INC.
115 Washington Avenue North
Minneapolis, Minnesota 55401   phone: 612-336-8941

Annual Warehouse Fabric Sale.

Write to be placed on mailing list for notice of once-a-year sale.

Home Beautiful Enterprises makes custom and special order draperies. Once a year, they hold a warehouse fabric sale.
Savings: Up to 50% on drapery remnants or fabrics by the yard.

Payment: Cash, check for exact amount.
Parking: Lot.

THE KRAMARCZAK SAUSAGE COMPANY DELI AND BAKERY
215 East Hennepin Avenue
Minneapolis, Minnesota 55414   phone: 612-379-3018

Hours: Monday-Thursday, 9 am-6 pm
       Friday, 8 am-8 pm
       Saturday, 8 am-6 pm

Hungarian, Italian, Polish, and Portuguese sausages; bologna, bratwurst, salami, summer sausage, thuringer, franks, etc. Room beyond sausage counter is a cafeteria-style sandwich shop with "big" sandwiches and Polish specialties and desserts to eat on the spot or take out.

Savings: 25% and up on bologna, salami, bacon, and ham ends.

Payment: Cash.
Parking: Lot.

LAKESIDE GAMES
A Division of Leisure Dynamics, Inc.
4400 West 78th Street
Minneapolis, Minnesota 55435   phone: 612-835-3000
                                      Customer
                                      Service

A one-day, once-a-year warehouse sale, scheduled right after Thanksgiving.

Note: Factory is not open to the public except on this one day.

This is an "insider's warehouse sale" (no public notice), which is held once a year from 5 pm until midnight or until merchandise is sold out.

Savings: Average 50% on seconds, overruns, and discontinueds in board games, computer games, pens, flashlights, and items from the previous year's line.

Payment: Cash only.
Parking: Lot.

LERNER PUBLICATIONS, INC., "HURT BOOKS" ROOM
241 First Avenue North
Minneapolis, Minnesota 55401   phone: 612-332-3345

Hours: Monday-Friday, 9 am-5 pm

Lerner publishes educational books for school systems under the East-West Learning Corporation, Carol Rhodi Books, and Book Blocks

of America imprints. Subjects covered include careers, science, social studies, and the "First Fact" series.
Savings: Up to 80% on "hurt" books (books returned for imperfect bindings) and overruns.

Payment: Cash, check for exact amount with identification.
Parking: Street.

LITIN PAPER COMPANY
701 North Washington Street
Minneapolis, Minnesota 55401   phone: 612-333-4331

Hours: Monday-Friday, 8 am-5 pm
Saturday, 9 am-12 noon

Litin services schools, churches, and institutions with paper products including napkins, placemats, coasters, cold and hot drink cups, plates, toilet paper, facial tissue, paper and envelopes, and limited cleaning supplies (like Joy and Comet).
Savings: Up to 50% on products bought by the case (such as toilet paper and facial tissue) and on broken cases and odd lot, clear-out merchandise, sold in smaller quantities (such as packages of placemats, cups, napkins, and envelopes).

Payment: Cash, check.
Parking: Lot at side of building.

MATERNITY FACTORY OUTLET
Dan Howard Maternity Clothes
Southtown Center
Interstate 494 and Pennsylvania Avenue South
Minneapolis, Minnesota 55431   phone: 612-881-1734

Hours: Monday-Friday, 10 am-9 pm
Saturday, 10 am-6 pm
Sunday, 12 noon-5 pm

See: Chicago, Illinois, Maternity Factory Outlet.
Savings: 20% to 50% on first quality production overruns, overcuts, and samples.

Payment: Cash, check with identification, Master Charge, Visa.
Parking: Lot.

MATERNITY FACTORY OUTLET
Dan Howard Maternity Clothes
Central Avenue and 125th Street
Pioneer Village Shopping Center
Minneapolis, Minnesota 55434   phone: 612-755-9344

Hours: Monday-Friday, 10 am-9 pm
       Saturday, 10 am-6 pm
       Sunday, 12 noon-5 pm

See: Chicago, Illinois, Maternity Factory Outlet

Savings: 20% to 50% on first quality production overruns, overcuts, and samples.

Payment: Cash, check with identification, Master Charge, Visa.
Parking: Lot.

MIDWEST NORTHERN NUT COMPANY, INC.
3105 Columbia Avenue, N.E.
Minneapolis, Minnesota 55418   phone: 612-781-6596

Hours: Monday-Friday, 8 am-5 pm
       Open the Saturday before Christmas

Midwest roasts quality sized nuts every other day. These include whole natural or blanched and slivered almonds; whole Brazil nuts; jumbo cashews and splits and butts; cocktail filberts; Spanish, redskin, Virginia, garlic, and onion redskins; sweet and salty tavern and salted in the shell peanuts; large pecan halves or baking pieces; salted in the shell or red pistachios; hulled and roasted or salted in the shell sunflower seeds; macadamia nuts; walnut halves and pieces; and natural or trail (with fruit) snax. Also candy items that include jelly beans and chocolate kisses and miniatures.

Savings: Up to 30% on top quality, deluxe size freshly roasted nuts.

Payment: Cash, check for exact amount with identification.
Parking: Lot.

MILL END FABRICS
S. R. Harris Industries
173 Glenwood Avenue North
Minneapolis, Minnesota 55405   phone: 612-332-6020

Hours: Monday-Friday, 8:30 am-4:30 pm
Saturday, 9 am-4 pm
Sunday, 12 noon-4 pm

Knit and woven fabrics sold by the yard including brushed knits; sweater, swimwear, thermal, and T-shirt knits; and double knits. Also: cotton velour, flannel and fleece fabrics, and denims.
Savings: 50% to 80% on fabric irregulars and remnants.

Note: There is a playroom for children in the back of the store.

Payment: Cash, check for exact amount with identification, Master Charge, Shoppers Charge, Visa.
Parking: Lot at left side of building.

MUNSINGWEAR REMNANT ROOM
718 Glenwood Avenue
Minneapolis, Minnesota 55404   phone: 612-340-4757

Hours: Monday-Friday, 7:30 am-3 pm

Munsingwear, manufacturer of sleepwear and underwear, has a fabric outlet store at the main plant where they sell by the yard: stretch and polyester blend fabrics, sheers, laces, and lace trims.
Also: zippers, neckers (ribbed remnants), appliques, threads, etc.
Savings: About 50% and more on fabrics and sewing notions.

Payment: Cash, check with identification.
Parking: Lot.

NATIONAL PURITY SOAP AND CHEMICAL COMPANY
Sales Desk
110 Fifth Street, S.E.
Minneapolis, Minnesota 55414   phone: 612-378-1465

Hours: Monday-Friday, 8:30 am-5 pm

National sells detergent, and soap and washing compounds in bulk quantities. Rex Low Suds detergent is sold in 25-lb. packages and 3V all-purpose liquid detergent concentrate is available in gallon containers.
Savings: 20% and up on cleaning compounds purchased in bulk.

Payment: Cash, check for exact amount with identification.
Parking: Street.

NORTHLAND ALUMINUM PRODUCTS, INC.
5120 County Road 16 (Cedar Lake Road)
Minneapolis, Minnesota 55416
(West of Minnesota 100 behind
Winn Stephens Buick.)

phone: 612-920-2888
Consumer
Service

Monthly sales of Nordic Ware are held at this location.

Telephone for the exact date of sales, usually held the first weekend of each month.

Sale Hours: Friday, 12 noon–9 pm
Saturday, 9 am–5 pm
Sunday, 10 am–5 pm

Northland manufactures a complete line of Nordic Ware cookware including Bundt pans, electric woks, griddles and pizza ovens, baking pans, saucepans, and skillets in graduated sizes.
Savings: Up to 40% on first quality discontinueds and some seconds during the scheduled weekend sales.

Payment: Cash, check with identification, American Express, Master Charge, Shoppers Charge, Visa.
Parking: Lot.

PICTURE FRAME SUPPLY COMPANY
2828 University Avenue, S.E.
Minneapolis, Minnesota 55401

phone: 612-379-0552

Hours: Monday–Friday, 10 am–6 pm
Saturday, 10 am–5 pm

Retail outlet store for Twin City Framing Company.

Ready-made frames in all sizes from 5"×7" to 14"×18"; discontinued moldings in oak, pine, and walnut (both finished and unfinished); picture framing hardware; cut-to-size glass; and wood finishing agents.
Savings: Up to 50% on discontinued moldings sold by the foot.

Payment: Cash, check with identification, Master Charge, Visa.
Parking: Street—one hour.

SEARS RETAIL STORE OUTLET
2700 Winter Street, N.E.
Minneapolis, Minnesota 55401

phone: 612-874-3636

Hours: Monday-Friday, 9 am-9 pm
Saturday, 9 am-5:30 pm

Outlet for furniture and for Sears appliances that have been damaged in deliveries or warehousing or appliances that have been reconditioned. All appliances are covered by Sears warranty.
Savings: 35% to 50%.

Payment: Cash, check with identification, Sears charge card.
Parking: Lot.

THE UNPAINTED PLACE
Cedar Lake Unpainted Furniture Company, Inc.
1601 Hennepin Avenue
Minneapolis, Minnesota 55403   phone: 612-339-1500
                                             612-336-5200

Hours: Monday and Thursday, 8:30 am-8 pm
Tuesday, Wednesday, Friday, 8:30 am-6 pm
Saturday, 9 am-4 pm

Retail store for Cedar Lake Unpainted Furniture Company, Inc., manufacturers of pine, birch, and particleboard unfinished furniture. Units sold in the store are made by Cedar Lake and other manufacturers and include bookcases, chairs, chests, desks, rocking chairs, stereo cabinets, stools, and tables.
Savings: Up to 33⅓% and 40% on some items.

Payment: Cash, check, Master Charge, Visa.
Parking: Street or behind building.

Minnetonka

MARCEAU SPORTS, INC.
3740 Williston Road
Minnetonka, Minnesota 55343   phone: 612-933-6144
(Industrial Complex.)

Hours: Monday-Friday, 9 am-5 pm

Marceau manufactures a very attractive, well designed line of knitwear that features Nordic motifs for men, women, and children. Included

are all-wool ski sweaters, mittens, hats, scarves, and neckgators (neck warmers).
Savings: Up to 50% on seconds, when available, in hats, scarves, neckgators, and some sweaters.

Payment: Cash, check for exact amount with identification.
Parking: In front of building.

Olivia

OLIVIA CANNING COMPANY WAREHOUSE
301 North 11th Street
Olivia, Minnesota 56277   phone: 612-523-1702

Hours: Monday-Friday, 7:30 am-4 pm
Telephone first to be sure "dent" product is available.
Olivia cans cream style corn in #303 cans, sold by the case only (24 cans to a case).
Savings: Up to 50% on cases of cream style corn "dents," first quality product in dented cans, when available.

Payment: Cash.
Parking: Lot.

Owatonna

UBER GLOVE COMPANY
308 Adams Street
Owatonna, Minnesota 55060   phone: 507-451-1990

Hours: Monday-Friday, 8 am-4 pm
       Saturday, 8 am-3 pm
Uber manufactures pile-lined mittens for men, women, and children, and men's (sizes 8½ to 11½) and women's (sizes 7 to 8½) leather semi-dress gloves. They also make deluxe snowmobile mittens with deerskin palms, deerskin work and all-purpose gloves, chopper mittens, and deerskin pants, shirts, jackets, and vests.
Savings: Up to 50% on deerskin work glove seconds and unlined chopper mittens.

Uber will fill mail orders. Request catalog and current price list.

Payment: Cash, check for exact amount with identification.
Parking: Lot.

Park Rapids

H. W. CARTER AND SONS, INC.
Ringer Division
420 West Second Street
Park Rapids, Minnesota 56470   phone: 218-732-3316
(Sales Room Office—North Entrance.)

Hours: Monday-Friday, 7 am-3:30 pm
       Closed first two weeks of July

Manufacturer of Ringer fiber-filled coats and vests for boys.
Savings: 40% on seconds, irregulars, and closeouts in boys' outerwear.

Payment: Cash, check for exact amount with identification.
Parking: Lot.

Princeton

WIMAN CORPORATION
106 North 6th Avenue
Princeton, Minnesota 55371   phone: 612-389-1144

Hours: Monday-Friday, 8:30 am-4:30 pm

Wiman manufactures sturdy ranch-style outerwear, which retails for under $50, for men and women.
Savings: About 50% on factory seconds.

Payment: Cash, check for exact amount with identification.
Parking: Lot.

Red Wing

WALT'S SHOE SERVICE
312 Fourth Street
Red Wing, Minnesota 55066   phone: 612-388-5510
(Across from City Hall.)

Hours: Monday-Saturday, 8 am-5 pm
       Open Thursday evenings until 9 pm

Outlet for Red Wing Shoe Company. Men's work shoes, boots, lei-

sure, and sport shoes in sizes 5½ to 18 and some ladies' boots.
Savings: About 33⅓% and up on Red Wing factory damaged shoes.

Payment: Cash, check for exact amount with identification.
Parking: Street.

WINONA KNITTING MILLS OUTLET STORE
1902 West Main Street
Red Wing, Minnesota 55066   phone: 612-388-5738

Hours: Monday-Saturday, 8:30 am-5:30 pm
       Sunday, 9 am-6 pm

See: Downers Grove, Illinois, Winona Knitting Mills, Inc., Outlet Store.

Savings: Up to 50% on firsts and overruns in Winona labeled sweaters and knitwear accessories; more on seconds and irregulars.

This store also carries clothing from other manufacturers.

Payment: Cash, check with identification, Master Charge, Visa.
Parking: Lot.

St. Anthony

HAPPY'S POTATO CHIP COMPANY
3900 Chandler Drive
St. Anthony, Minnesota 55421   phone: 617-781-3121
(Thrift racks for sale of overrun product are against left wall of office.)

Hours: Monday-Friday, 9 am-4 pm

Savings: 10% to 20% on Happy Potato Chip overrun and route rotation product including bulk potato chips, popcorn, cheese snacks, boxed pretzels, potato ripples, and beer nuts.

Payment: Cash only.
Parking: Lot.

St. Cloud

THE HOLES WEBWAY COMPANY
28150 Clearwater Road
St. Cloud, Minnesota 56301   phone: 612-251-3822
(Off Interstate 94.)

Hours: Monday-Friday, 8 am-4:30 pm

Holes Webway manufactures photo albums from purse size to 11"x14", memory books, and desk accessories in simulated leather materials.
Savings: 20% to 50% on samples, discontinued colors and styles, and overruns.

Payment: Cash, check, American Express, Master Charge, Visa.
Parking: Lot.

St. Paul

BRO-TEX COMPANY
Fibers Division
800 Hampden Avenue
St. Paul, Minnesota 55114   phone: 612-645-5721

Hours: Monday-Friday, 9 am-4 pm
       Saturday, 9 am-3 pm

Fabric outlet selling materials by the piece, by the pound, and by the yard. Available here are unbleached cotton terry toweling and denim (sold by the pound); tablecloths and napkins (sold by the pound); bath towels; felt squares; ½-yard quilting pieces (sold by the piece); and shipping drums of fibers, trims, and cones of yarn (sold by the pound). Also, discontinued patterns.
Savings: 50% and up on fabrics and odds and ends of all kinds.

Payment: Cash, check for exact amount with identification.
Parking: Next to building.

CAPTAIN KEN'S FIREHOUSE BEANS, INC.
Food Processors
344 South Robert Street
St. Paul, Minnesota 55107
(Old Peters Meat Building.)

phone: 612-646-0750

Hours: Monday–Friday, 9:30 am–5:30 pm
         Saturday, 10 am–12 noon

Regular old-fashioned oven-baked beans sold in 6-lb., 20-lb., 30-lb., and 48-lb. containers, fresh and frozen.
Savings: Up to 50% on beans purchased in 6-lb. container.

Payment: Cash, check for exact amount with identification.
Parking: Street.

THE COAT STORE
M. Liman Company
230 East 5th Street
St. Paul, Minnesota 55101

phone: 612-222-0579

Hours: Monday–Friday, 9 am–4 pm
         Saturday, 9 am–11 am

Outlet is in factory.

Liman manufactures a classic, casual coat line that normally retails at $50 to $160. Styles include car coats, full length all-wool coats—some with reversible linings and matching scarves, and poplin storm coats—some pile lined. Sizes run from 6 to 22½, depending on the styles.

Also: Quality 100% wool and wool blend fabrics and buttons.
Savings: 50% on samples, seconds, and overruns. More on fabrics.

Payment: Cash, check for exact amount with identification.
Parking: Street, metered.

DAISY THRIFT STORE
Metz Baking Company
1090 Prosperity Avenue
Phalen Shopping Center
St. Paul, Minnesota 55106

phone: 612-771-4137

Hours: Monday-Saturday, 9 am-6 pm
See: Minneapolis, Minnesota, Daisy Thrift Store.
Savings: Up to 40% on day-old bakery products.

Payment: Cash only.
Parking: Lot.

DAISY THRIFT STORE
Metz Baking Company
97 Sherburne Avenue
St. Paul, Minnesota 55101   phone: 612-293-0688

Hours: Monday-Friday, 9 am-5 pm
       Saturday, 8 am-5 pm
See: Minneapolis, Minnesota, Daisy Thrift Store.
Savings: Up to 40% on day-old bakery products. Extra 10% savings on total bill on Wednesdays and Saturdays.

Note: Hamburger and hot dog rolls are baked in this plant.

Payment: Cash only.
Parking: Street or lot.

DAISY THRIFT STORE
Metz Baking Company
Eagan Store
3207 Sibley Avenue
St. Paul, Minnesota 55121   phone: 612-454-7978

Hours: Monday-Friday, 9 am-6 pm
       Saturday, 8 am-5 pm
       Sunday, 11 am-5 pm
See: Minneapolis, Minnesota, Daisy Thrift Store.
Savings: Up to 40% on day-old bakery products.

Payment: Cash only.
Parking: Lot.

EASTERN WOOLEN COMPANY FABRICS PLUS
6th Floor
230 East 5th Street
St. Paul, Minnesota 55101 phone: 612-222-2737

Hours: Monday-Friday, 10 am-3 pm
Saturday, 9 am-12 noon

Lingerie fabrics, laces, net fabric, and a large selection of lace trim in all colors from 1/8" wide to 6" wide.

Also: elastic in all widths and colors, felt squares, thread, some poly-fill by the bag, and wooden hangers for crocheters.
Savings: 35% and up on fabrics and lace remainders from manufacturing production runs.

Payment: Cash only.
Parking: Street, metered.

GLASS HOUSE STUDIO, INC.
457 South Wabash Avenue
St. Paul, Minnesota 55107 phone: 612-222-1114

Hours: Monday and Thursday, 10 am-9 pm
Tuesday-Saturday, 10 am-5 pm

Glass House makes leaded art glass home accessories including "suncatchers" and sells materials and patterns for making leaded art glass.
Savings: Up to 50% on glass scrap including opalescent and antique glass and mixed nuggets, sold by the pound.

Payment: Cash, check for exact amount with identification, Master Charge, Visa.
Parking: Street.

J C PENNEY OUTLET STORE
1441 East Magnolia Street
Phalen Shopping Center
St. Paul, Minnesota 55101 phone: 612-744-0371

Hours: Monday-Friday, 9:30 am-9 pm
Saturday, 9:30 am-5:30 pm
Sunday, 12 noon-5 pm

See: Villa Park, Illinois, J C Penney Catalog Outlet Store.

Savings: 30% and up on Penney catalog surplus and returned merchandise including clothing, housewares, and sporting goods equipment. Greater savings on seasonal specials.

Payment: Cash, check with identification, J C Penney charge card.
Parking: Lot.

KURYSCH MANUFACTURING COMPANY OUTLET STORE
508 4th Street
White Bear Lake
St. Paul, Minnesota 55110   phone: 612-429-7719
Hours: Monday-Friday, 8 am-4 pm

Kurysch manufactures nylon shells, poplin jackets, insulated vests, and snowmobile suits for women (sizes 8 to 20) and men (34 to extra large).
Savings: About 50% on production overruns and samples.

Payment: Cash, check for exact amount with identification.
Parking: Lot.

LEHMANN'S MUSHROOMS
Hudson Boulevard
Lake Almo
St. Paul, Minnesota 55119   phone: 612-739-0686

Hours: Monday-Friday, 7 am-4 pm

Mushroom canners and processors of pickled mushrooms in 8-oz. to 22-oz. containers. Also fresh mushrooms, large and mixed, sold in 5-lb. boxes.
Savings: Average 20% on the 1-lb. cans of whole mushrooms.

Fresh mushrooms are retail priced, but the quality and size are better than that found in most supermarket mushrooms.

Payment: Cash, check for exact amount with identification.
Parking: Lot.

MIDDLE EAST BREAD
Middle East Bakery
555 North Snelling Avenue
St. Paul, Minnesota 55104   phone: 612-644-4409

Hours: Monday-Friday, 9 am-6 pm
Saturday, 9 am-4 pm

The Middle East Bakery bakes the 5,000-year-old pita bread in large and mini sizes, using regular white flour or 100% stone ground whole wheat flour. The larger "pocket" breads are sold by the dozen; mini-sized pita breads are sold 8 to a package or in bags of 20.
Savings: 20% to 50% on pita bread, baked fresh each morning.

Payment: Cash only.
Parking: Street.

MILBERN MEN'S CLOTHING
Griggs Midway Building
St. Paul, Minnesota 55104   phone: 612-645-2922
(Corner of University and Fairview Avenues.)

Hours: Monday and Thursday, 9 am-9 pm
Tuesday, Wednesday, Friday, Saturday, 9 am-5 pm

Retail outlet (one of two in the St. Paul area) for Milbern of St. Paul, manufacturer of private label men's suits and sport coats for leading department stores.

The store carries a good selection of sizes and traditionally styled menswear including suits that normally retail for up to $200.
Savings: From 25% to 45% on first quality men's suits and sport coats.

Payment: Cash, check with identification, Master Charge, Visa.
Parking: Lot.

MILTON CLOTHING
242 East 5th Street
St. Paul, Minnesota 55101   phone: 612-224-6443

Hours: Monday-Friday, 9 am-5 pm
Saturday, 9 am-4 pm

See: St. Paul, Minnesota, Milbern Men's Clothing.

One of two retail stores for Milbern of St. Paul, manufacturer of private label men's suits and sport coats for leading department stores.

Savings: From 25% to 45% on first quality men's suits and sport coats.

Payment: Cash, check with identification, Master Charge, Visa.
Parking: Street, metered—nickels, dimes.

MONTGOMERY WARD CATALOG SURPLUS STORE
1425 South Robert Street
St. Paul, Minnesota 55118   phone: 612-647-2595

Hours: Monday-Friday, 9:30 am-9 pm
        Saturday, 9:30 am-5:30 pm
        Sunday, 12 noon-5 pm

See: Chicago, Illinois, Montgomery Ward Catalog Liquidation Center.

Savings: 20% to 50% on surplus and catalog merchandise return items.

Payment: Cash, check with identification, Montgomery Ward Charge-All.
Parking: Lot.

MONTGOMERY WARD CATALOG SURPLUS STORE
1400 University Avenue
Midway
St. Paul, Minnesota 55104   phone: 612-647-2100

Hours: Monday-Friday, 9:30 am-9 pm
        Saturday, 9:30 am-5:30 pm
        Sunday, 12 noon-5 pm

See: Chicago, Illinois, Montgomery Ward Catalog Liquidation Center.

Savings: 20% to 50% on surplus and catalog merchandise return items.

Payment: Cash, check with identification, Montgomery Ward Charge-All.
Parking: Lot.

MUNSINGWEAR REMNANT ROOM
1253 South Robert Street
St. Paul, Minnesota 55123   phone: 612-457-3046

Hours: Monday-Friday, 9 am-9 pm
        Saturday, 9 am-5 pm

See: Minneapolis, Minnesota, Munsingwear Remnant Room.

In addition to fabrics and trims, this outlet sells irregulars and close-

outs from other Munsingwear divisions including men's and boys' boxer shorts; boys', girls', and men's T-shirts; and women's velour robes.
Savings: 30% and up on irregulars and closeouts; more on fabrics.

Payment: Cash, check with identification, Master Charge, Visa.
Parking: Lot.

PEDRO'S OF ST. PAUL
501 North Robert Street
St. Paul, Minnesota 55101 phone: 612-224-2388

Hours: Monday and Thursday, 9:30 am-8 pm
Tuesday, Wednesday, Friday, 9:30 am-5:30 pm
Saturday, 9:30 am-5 pm

Pedro's manufactures custom cases including instrument cases; artists' portfolios; briefcases; tool, slide, and salespersons' cases; and luggage accessories, such as tote bags, in leather, vinyl, and fabric.

Also: They sell and service a large inventory of top brand leather goods and leather accessories.
Savings: Up to 50% on factory seconds. (Each second is marked with a description of the flaw on the price tag.)

Payment: Cash, check for exact amount with identification, American Express, Diners, Master Charge, Shoppers Charge, Visa.
Parking: In front of building.

PIONEER SAUSAGE COMPANY
616 Rice Street
St. Paul, Minnesota 55101 phone: 612-224-0484
612-224-0634

Hours: Monday, 11 am-5:30 pm
Tuesday, Wednesday, Thursday, 9 am-5:30 pm
Friday and Saturday, 8 am-5:30 pm

Pioneer custom cures and smokes sausages and "home-makes" sausages and lunch meats including four kinds of bologna; summer sausage with or without garlic or double-smoked; smoked and regular bratwurst and bockwurst; blood sausage; ham, tongue, and turkey

loaf; Swedish and fresh Italian sausage; German style thuringer; and franks, wieners, bacon, ham, and pork. The store also sells fresh meat and pork.
Savings: Up to 20% on ham, bacon, and sausage ends, and seconds in franks, wieners, and Polish sausage.

Payment: Cash, check for exact amount with identification.
Parking: Street.

SEARS CATALOG SURPLUS STORE
1907 Suburban Avenue
St. Paul, Minnesota 55119   phone: 612-739-4330

Hours: Monday-Friday, 9 am-9 pm
        Saturday, 9 am-6 pm
        Sunday, 12 noon-5 pm
See: Chicago, Illinois, Sears Catalog Surplus Store.
Savings: 20% to 80%.
Payment: Cash, check with identification, Sears charge card.
Parking: Lot.

WARD'S WAREHOUSE
Montgomery Ward Bargain Outlet Store
1700 Wynne Avenue
St. Paul, Minnesota 55100   phone: 612-647-2275
(Near State Fairgrounds.)

Hours: Monday-Friday, 9 am-9 pm
        Saturday, 9 am-5 pm
See: Chicago, Illinois, Montgomery Ward Catalog Liquidation Center.
Outlet for Montgomery Ward surplus and catalog furniture and appliances including ranges, refrigerators, washing machines, dryers, televisions, vacuums, etc.
Savings: Average 50% on returns, nicked and scratched, and surplus merchandise.

Payment: Cash, check with identification, Montgomery Ward Charge-All.
Parking: Lot.

Staples

H. W. CARTER AND SONS, INC.
Ringer Division
US 10—East of Staples
Staples, Minnesota 56479   phone: 218-894-2602

Hours: Monday-Friday, 7 am-3 pm
See: Park Rapids, Minnesota, H. W. Carter and Sons, Inc.
Savings: Average 40% on seconds, irregulars, and closeouts in boys' fiber-filled coats and vests.

Payment: Cash, check for exact amount with identification.
Parking: Lot.

Stillwater

GOGGIN PARTY SHOP
Grand Garage and Gallery Building
324 South Main Street
Stillwater, Minnesota 55082   phone: 612-439-3981

Hours: Monday-Thursday, 10 am-6 pm
       Friday, 10 am-9 pm
       Saturday, 10 am-6 pm
       Sunday, 12 noon-5 pm

Goggin makes chocolate and milk chocolate candies including miniatures, creams, patties, mints, and chocolate covered nuts; hard candies; and candy bars.
Savings: Up to 50% on candy bar specials sold 10 to a bag; up to 25% on store specials.

Payment: Cash, check for exact amount with identification.
Parking: Lot.

J. A. GOGGIN CANDY COMPANY
Plant Store
902 South Fourth Street
Stillwater, Minnesota 55082   phone: 612-439-1516

Hours: Monday-Friday, 8:30 am-5 pm
       Saturday, 10:15 am-5 pm

Savings: Up to 50% on candy bar specials sold 10 to a bag; up to 25% on store specials.

Payment: Cash, check for exact amount with identification.
Parking: Lot.

Waldorf

EISEN SAUSAGE, INC.
Main Street
Waldorf, Minnesota 56091   phone: 507-239-2241

Hours: Tuesday-Friday, 9 am-5 pm
       Saturday, 9 am-12 noon

Eisen has a small counter in the plant from which they sell Grand Beef ground beef, beef steak patties, steaks, summer, Polish, and link sausages, skinless wieners, and bolognas in 10-lb. boxed quantities.
Savings: Up to 20% on Grand Beef products bought in 10-lb. boxed quantities.

Payment: Cash, check for exact amount with identification.
Parking: Lot.

Willmar

WILLMAR COOKIE COMPANY, INC., OUTLET STORE
East US 12
Willmar, Minnesota 56201   phone: 612-235-0600
(Front of factory.)

Hours: Monday-Friday, 8 am-12 noon
                     1 pm-5 pm

Willmar makes a variety of cookies including vanilla, chocolate chip, apple-filled, cashew, pecan, and iced oatmeal. Call first to see which flavors are available on a particular day.
Savings: Up to 40% on cookies purchased at the 2-bag special price. (Each bag contains 1¼ lb. of cookies—anywhere from 2 to 3 dozen.)

Payment: Cash only.
Parking: Lot.

Winona

BOLAND MANUFACTURING COMPANY
400 West Third Street
Winona, Minnesota 55987 phone: 507-454-1830
(Store is located in west end of building.)

Hours: Open March-December—Friday and Saturday, 10 am-1 pm

Boland manufactures heavy gauge plastic closet, garment, and storage bags; small and large appliance covers; and stadium cushions.
Savings: Up to 50% on production overruns.

Also: Plastic fabrics by the yard for do-it-yourself projects at good savings.

Payment: Cash, check for exact amount with identification.
Parking: Lot.

WINONA KNITTING MILLS, INC., SALES ROOM
902 East 2nd Street
Winona, Minnesota 55987 phone: 507-454-4381

Hours: Monday-Sunday, 9 am-5 pm

See: Downers Grove, Illinois, Winona Knitting Mills, Inc., Outlet Store.

Savings: Up to 50% on firsts and overruns; more on seconds and irregulars.

This store has the largest selection of the three Winona Outlet stores.

Payment: Cash, check with identification, Master Charge, Visa.
Parking: Lot.

OHIO

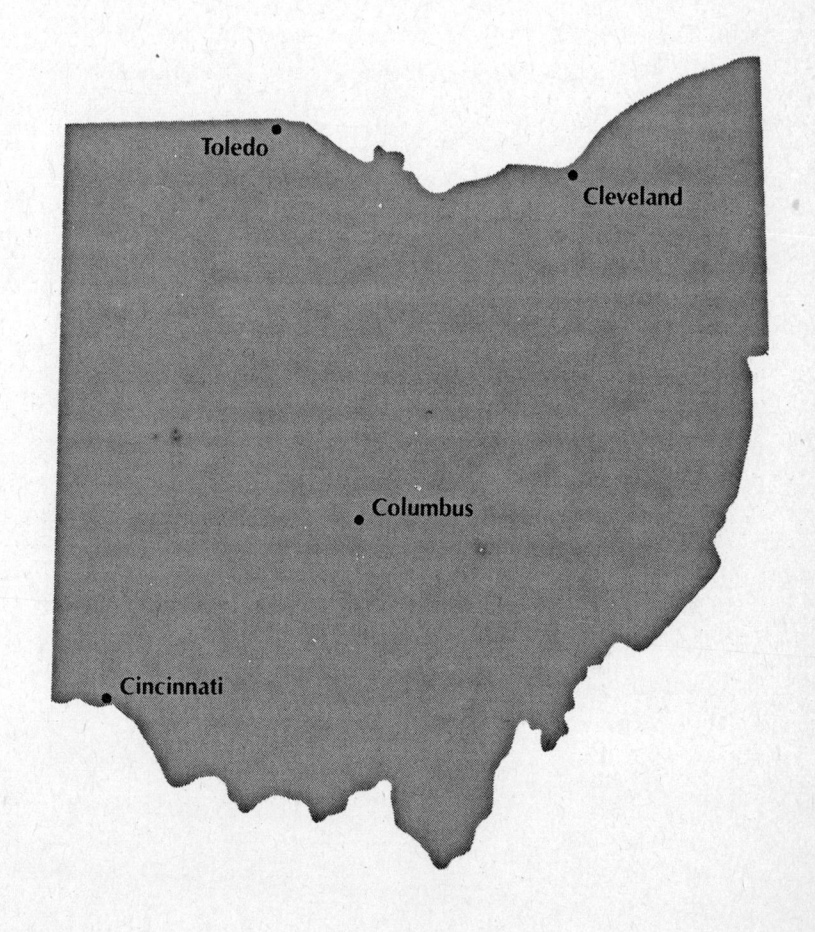

Akron

BROWNBERRY OVENS THRIFT STORE
1889 Triplett Boulevard
Akron, Ohio 44318   phone: 216-784-4889

Hours: Monday-Saturday, 8 am-6 pm

See: LaGrange Park, Illinois, Brownberry Ovens Thrift Store.

Savings: 33⅓% and up on day-old and seconds. Extra 10% savings on Tuesdays.

Payment: Cash, check for exact amount with identification.
Parking: Lot.

Alliance

BRESSAN SHOES FACTORY OUTLET
1548 South Linden Avenue
Alliance, Ohio 44601   phone: 216-821-3942

Hours: Monday-Saturday, 10 am-5 pm

Outlet for women's all-leather shoes and boots, designed to order for an American wholesaler and made in Italy in sizes 4 to 10 in narrow and medium widths. Some men's after-ski and hunting boots.

Labels might include Amalfi, Andrew Geller, Famolare, 9 West, and Nickels.

Savings: 30% to 60% on quality leather shoes and boots.

Payment: Cash, check.
Parking: Lot.

Ashtabula

TANNERY HILL FURNITURE MANUFACTURING COMPANY, INC.
3906 Tannery Hill Road
Ashtabula, Ohio 44004   phone: 216-998-1238

Hours: Monday-Friday, 9 am-5:30 pm
       Saturday, 9 am-2:30 pm

Factory showroom for Debra Joy, manufacturer of living room furni-

ture, including upholstered couches and chairs, retailing in the $200 to $500 range.
Savings: 25% on showroom inventory. Greater savings on fabric remnants and upholstery supplies.

Payment: Cash, check for exact amount with identification.
Parking: Lot.

Barnesville

THE GLASS CORNER
Lotus Glass Company Outlet Store
East Main Street
Barnesville, Ohio 43713   phone: 614-425-1996

Hours: Monday–Saturday, 10 am–5 pm
        Open Friday evenings until 7 pm from June through September only

Outlet for Lotus Glass Company, manufacturers of cut and etched glass and silk-screened glass. This store is manned by volunteers from the Barnesville Emergency Squad and senior citizens who donate their time. All profits go to the purchase of Emergency Squad equipment.

Inventory usually includes glasses, tumblers, bud vases, candy dishes, candy jars, figurines, small miniature animals, and lamps. Other manufacturers represented include Westmoreland, L. S. Smith, and Scio Pottery.
Savings: Average 50% on first quality discontinueds and seconds.

Payment: Cash, check for exact amount with identification.
Parking: Village lot in rear of store.

Bedford

DALTON FACTORY OUTLET
665 Broadway Street
Bedford, Ohio 44014   phone: 216-232-3360

Hours: Tuesday, Wednesday, Thursday, 10 am–4 pm
        Friday, Saturday, 10 am–5 pm

Outlet for Dalton and James Kenrob, quality names in women's fash-

ionable clothing. Sportswear, dresses, cashmere sweaters, coordinated separates in sizes 6 to 18. Fitting rooms.
Savings: 50% on first quality, but styles are one season behind retail stores.

Payment: Cash, check for exact amount with identification, Master Charge, Visa.
Parking: Community parking lot off Tarbell Street.

LAMRITE
565 Broadway
Bedford, Ohio 44146   phone: 216-232-9300

Hours: Monday, Thursday, Friday, 9 am-8:30 pm
        Tuesday, Wednesday, 9 am-5:30 pm
        Saturday, 10 am-5:30 pm

Lamrite manufactures craft materials and kits, and imports, distributes, and sells seasonal decorations and materials for making decorative accessories. Stock includes plastic and silk flowers, plastic foliage, ribbons, raffia, straw, wicker, baskets, and Christmas ornaments.
Savings: Up to 25%.

Lamrite also offers craft classes ($1 instruction fee per session). Class registration can be made in person or by mail.

Payment: Cash, check for exact amount with identification, Visa.
Parking: Lot.

S. E. MIGHTON COMPANY
150 Northfield Road
Bedford, Ohio 44146   phone: 216-232-3880
(Look for the large "Doggie Dinner" sign.)

Hours: Monday-Friday, 8:30 am-4:30 pm

Mighton packs dog and cat food for large food chains under other labels and under their own labels, Doggie Dinner and Ocean Fish.

The pet food products are sold here by the case, 48 cans to a case.
Savings: 25% on first quality; 35% to 40% on mixed flavor cases, cases with soiled labels, and cases of dented cans.

Payment: Cash only.
Parking: Lot.

Bellaire

IMPERIAL GLASS HAY SHED
29th Street—Ohio 7
Bellaire, Ohio 43906   phone: 614-676-3511

Hours: Monday-Saturday, 9 am-5 pm
Sunday, 12 noon-5 pm
Closed only on national holidays

Imperial handcrafted glass tableware, stemware, and giftware in both clear and colored crystal and in a variety of styles and shapes. Stock includes punchbowls, candy dishes, serving pieces, Lenox candles, etc.

Savings: 50% on discontinueds and seconds in Old Hay Shed Gift Shop.

Plant tours at scheduled times, Monday through Friday.

Payment: Cash, Master Charge, Visa.
Parking: Lot.

Brunswick

CARTER'S FACTORY OUTLET
1077 Pearl Road
Conley's Plaza
Brunswick, Ohio 44212   phone: 216-225-0900

Hours: Monday-Saturday, 10 am-5 pm
Sunday, 1 pm-5 pm

See: Franklin, Indiana, Carter's Factory Outlet.

Savings: 30% to 60% on Carter samples, closeouts, and irregulars.

Payment: Cash, check for exact amount with identification.
Parking: Lot.

HOLLO'S PAPERCRAFT
1878 Pearl Road
Brunswick, Ohio 44212   phone: 216-225-0911
(US 42.)

Hours: Monday-Friday, 9 am-8 pm
        Saturday, 9 am-6 pm
        Sunday, 12 noon-6 pm

Hollo supplies paper, teaching aids, and a full line of paint and art supplies to schools and businesses. Paper can be purchased here in quantities from one sheet to one million sheets, by the package, the pound, or in cut-to-size dimensions.

Savings: 50% to 80% on packaged units of multi-sized and multi-colored note pads in an assortment of sizes ranging from 2" × 3½" to 8½" × 11¼".

Good savings on art and hobby inventory closeout items.

Payment: Cash, check with identification, Master Charge, Visa.
Parking: Lot.

Bucyrus

SCHRIER LUNCH AND DAIRY BAR
Schrier Cheese Factory, Inc.
1820 East Mansfield Street
Bucyrus, Ohio 44820   phone: 419-562-8946
(Old US 30N.)

Hours: Monday-Friday, 6 am-7 pm

Schrier makes an excellent rindless colby cheese which is sold whole in a 12- to 14-lb. piece or by the pound. They also sell Swiss and cheddar cheeses. (The cheese counter is to the right of the lunch counter.)

Savings: Up to 50% on colby cheese.

Payment: Cash only.
Parking: In front.

Cambridge

GUERNSEY GLASS COMPANY, INC.
609 South 8th Street
Cambridge, Ohio 43725   phone: 614-439-2397
(Small garage next to factory houses the outlet store.)

Hours: Monday-Friday, 10 am-5 pm

Manufacturers of fine, handmade glassware. Blown and pressed glass novelty items selling from under one dollar.
Savings: 40% to 50% on novelty items.

Payment: Cash only.
Parking: Lot.

Canton

DALTON FACTORY STORE
401 Second Avenue, S.E.
Canton, Ohio 44301   phone: 216-454-8300

Hours: Monday, Wednesday, Saturday, 10 am-3 pm

See: Bedford, Ohio, Dalton Factory Outlet.

Savings: 50% on first quality; greater savings on seconds.

Also: Excellent savings on polyesters, wools, and knits, sold by the yard.

No fitting rooms. You may try on blouses or sweaters that button in front. Bring along a tape measure or old pair of slacks to compare pant sizes.

Payment: Cash, personal check with identification, traveler's checks.
Parking: Lot.

Chillicothe

WEAREVER ALUMINUM FACTORY OUTLET
North Fork Shopping Center
US 50 West
Chillicothe, Ohio 45601　　　　　　　　phone: 614-775-9150

Hours:　Monday-Thursday, 12 noon-6 pm
　　　　Friday, 12 noon-8 pm
　　　　Saturday, 9 am-5 pm

Outlet for Wearever, manufacturers of bakeware and cookware in lightweight and heavyweight aluminum, including frying pans (8″ to 12″), sauce pans (1 quart to 5 quarts), covered pots, and cookware sets.
Savings: Average 50% on seconds and returns.

Payment: Cash, check with identification, Master Charge, Visa.
Parking: Lot.

Cincinnati

BENJAMIN HEY COMPANY
4124 Airport Road
Cincinnati, Ohio 45226　　　　　　　　phone: 513-321-3343
(200 yards west of Lunken Airport Terminal Building.)

Hours:　Monday, Tuesday, Wednesday, Saturday, 10 am-5 pm
　　　　Thursday, Friday, 10 am-8:30 pm

Outlet for orlon factory hanks of 2-, 3-, and 4-ply yarns for knitting, crocheting, macrame, and rug making. Also, a very large inventory of drapery, upholstery, and dress fabrics and sewing accessories.
Savings: 20% to 80% on discontinueds, overruns, and specials in yarn. Good savings on fabrics.

Payment: Cash, check with identification, Master Charge, Visa.
Parking: Side or rear of building.

BROWNBERRY OVENS THRIFT STORE
3100 Galbraith Road
Cincinnati, Ohio 45239　　　　　　　　phone: 513-521-3195

Hours: Monday, Wednesday, Thursday, 9 am-7 pm
Tuesday, Friday, Saturday, 9 am-9 pm
Sunday, 11 am-5 pm

See: LaGrange Park, Illinois, Brownberry Ovens Thrift Store.

Savings: 33⅓% and up on day-olds and seconds.

Payment: Cash, check for exact amount with identification.
Parking: Lot.

CAMBRIDGE TILE CENTER
90 Novner Drive
Cincinnati, Ohio 45215   phone: 513-771-3232
(West off Springfield.)

Hours: Monday-Friday, 8 am-4:30 pm
Saturday, 8 am-12 noon

Ceramic wall and floor tiles, 4¼" × 4¼", in a range of colors in both standard or first quality and "bengals"—second quality.
Savings: Up to 20% less than cost of comparable tiles in other retail sources; greater savings on second quality "bengals."

Payment: Cash only.
Parking: Lot.

CANDLE TREE FACTORY OUTLET
4212 Airport Road
Cincinnati, Ohio 45202   phone: 513-321-4066
(2 doors west of Wilmer Road and Lunken Airport Terminal.)

Hours: Monday-Friday, 9 am-6 pm
(Call first. Hours are not always strictly observed.)

Decorative candles formed in tree bark and basket shapes and candles created to simulate ice cream sodas, banana splits, ice cream cones, and cupcakes.
Savings: 50% on first quality product.

Payment: Cash, check for exact amount with identification.
Parking: Street or lot.

CAROLINA FACTORY OUTLET
4351 Montgomery Road
Norwood
Cincinnati, Ohio 45212   phone: 513-631-0078

Hours: Monday-Saturday, 10 am-6 pm
Sunday, 12 noon-5 pm

Outlet for a Carolina manufacturer of casual wear and jeans for men, women, and children. Also an outlet for other companies with whom the manufacturer does business.

All labels are removed on samples, regulars, and "third quality" (jeans with holes in fabric, broken zippers, etc.) merchandise including blouses, shirts, jeans, slacks, etc. Some of the removed labels might include Levi's, Country Set, Hathaway, Farah, and Rob Roy.
Savings: Up to 65% on samples; more on irregulars (all marked) and "third quality." (Note: "Third quality" goods are sold with patches for holes and new zippers, if zipper is broken.)

Payment: Cash, Master Charge, Visa.
Parking: Lot.

COTTON MILL STORE
4351 Montgomery Road
Norwood
Cincinnati, Ohio 45212   phone: 513-631-4464
(Enter through the Carolina Factory Outlet.)

Hours: Tuesday, Wednesday, Saturday, 10 am-6 pm
Monday, Thursday, Friday, 10 am-8 pm
Sunday, 12 noon-5 pm

Factory outlet for the Leshner Corporation, manufacturers of sheets, towels, blankets, and bedspreads under the Leshner, St. Mary's, Penney, Pacific, Wamsutta, and Fieldcrest labels.

Sheets, pillowcases, and bedspreads; tablecloths; stadium and thermal blankets; kitchen and bath towels in mix or match combinations; bathroom rugs and mats; potholders; and aprons.

Also: Bolt fabrics, remnants, and bags of quilt squares.
Savings: 35% to 80% on firsts, discontinueds, overruns, seconds, and irregulars.

Payment: Cash, Master Charge, Visa.
Parking: Metered—pennies, nickels, dimes.

COTTON MILL STORE
Leshner Corporation Outlet
2201 Spring Grove Avenue
Cincinnati, Ohio 45214   phone: 513-241-3021
(Bottom floor of factory.)

Hours: Monday-Saturday, 10 am-6 pm

Savings: 35% to 80% on firsts, discontinueds, overruns, seconds, and irregulars in sheets, towels, and fabrics.

Payment: Cash, Master Charge, Visa.
Parking: Side of building.

COTTON MILL STORE
Leshner Corporation Outlet
7386 Reading Road
Roselawn
Cincinnati, Ohio 45237   phone: 513-731-5114
(Corner of Section Road and Reading Road.)

Hours: Monday-Saturday, 10 am-6 pm

Savings: 35% to 80% on first, discontinueds, overruns, seconds, and irregulars in sheets, towels, and fabrics.

Payment: Cash, Master Charge, Visa.
Parking: Large lot in back of building.

DOWN-LITE PRODUCTS
1910 South Street at Gest Street
Sharonville
Cincinnati, Ohio 45241   phone: 513-921-3355
(In Ohio Feather Company Building.)

Hours: Monday-Friday, 9 am-5 pm

Down-Lite manufactures down-filled comforters and pillows for quality catalog retailers and custom makes comforters on individual order.

They also stock and sell—in October and November only—down-filled jackets and vests in red, blue, and yellow rip-stop nylon, which

are made by one of their overseas suppliers. Prices for jackets and vests are incredibly low.
Savings: Up to 75% on down-filled jackets and vests, when available.

Payment: Cash, Master Charge, Visa.
Parking: Lot.

FECHEIMER BROTHERS COMPANY
4545 Malsbary Road
C.I.C. Industrial Park
Blue Ash
Cincinnati, Ohio 45242   phone: 513-793-5400
(Outlet entrance is at front of factory.)

Hours: Monday-Friday, 8 am-12 noon
                       1 pm-4:30 pm

Fecheimer manufactures uniforms for postal workers, bus drivers, police personnel, clerical workers, etc. Women's sizes; 8 to 24 and 14½ to 24½. Men's sizes: 28 to 50 in trousers; 34 to 50 in jackets and coats. Two fitting rooms.
Savings: Up to 75% in closeouts of discontinued styles, overruns, and seconds in pants, shirts, jackets, and blazers. Call first if you are looking for a specific item, since all items are not available at all times.

Payment: Cash only.
Parking: Lot.

IBOLD CIGAR COMPANY, INC.
420 Plum Street
Cincinnati, Ohio 45202   phone: 513-721-3135

Hours: Monday-Friday, 8:30 am-4:30 pm
Savings: Up to 40% on Ibold Cigar seconds (crooked wrappings, off-center hole, or no holes) sold in boxes of 50 cigars.

Payment: Cash, check for exact amount with identification.
Parking: Metered.

J C PENNEY CATALOG OUTLET STORE
8770 Colerain Avenue
Cincinnati, Ohio 45200   phone: 513-385-9700

Hours: Monday-Saturday, 9:30 am-9:30 pm
Sunday, 11 am-7 pm
See: Villa Park, Illinois, J C Penney Catalog Outlet Store.

Savings: 40% and up on returned merchandise including clothing, housewares, and some "scratch" and "dent" bigger ticket items. Big savings on seasonal specials.

Payment: Cash, check with identification, J C Penney charge card, Master Charge, Visa.
Parking: Lot.

J & H CLASGENS COMPANY
10861 Sharondale Road
Sharonville
Cincinnati, Ohio 45241   phone: 513-563-9486
(Off Glendale/Milford Road.)

Hours: Monday-Friday, 10 am-5:30 pm
Saturday, 10 am-4 pm
Closed Thursday and Sunday

Outlet store for J & H Clasgens Mills. Sells knitting, weaving, rug, and crewel yarns in 100% wool and 100% orlon. Wide range of colors and weights.
Savings: 50% and up on first quality wool yarns, discontinueds, samples, and closeouts.

Also: Polyester stuffing by the pound.

Payment: Cash, check with identification, Master Charge, Visa.
Parking: Lot.

J & H CLASGENS COMPANY
7529 Colerain Avenue
Cincinnati, Ohio 45239   phone: 513-931-1132
(The white house in back of the Airy Meat Market building.)

Hours: Monday-Friday, 9:30 am-5:30 pm
Saturday, 9:30 am-3:30 pm
Savings: 50% and up.

Payment: Cash, check with identification, Visa.
Parking: Lot.

KING BAG AND MANUFACTURING COMPANY
1500 Spring Lawn Avenue
Cincinnati, Ohio 45223   phone: 513-541-5440

Hours: Monday-Friday, 8:30 am-5 pm
        Saturday, 9 am-1 pm
        Open Tuesday evenings until 9 pm

King, manufacturers of burlap bags, also does custom work for consumers in draperies, slipcovers, and reupholstering. They stock and sell drapery and slipcover fabrics by the yard or bolt including crewels; damasks; osnaburg; satins and sheers in prints and textures; and colored burlaps and trim. Also: drapery rods, window shades, and woven wood shades.

Savings: 20% to 50% on first quality fabrics, rods, and shades.

Payment: Cash, check for exact amount with identification.
Parking: Lot.

LOVE-FORE OUTLET
8935 Rossah Road
Blue Ash
Cincinnati, Ohio 45236   phone: 513-793-2100
(At Plainfield and Cross Country Highways.)

Hours: Monday-Friday, 10 am-4 pm

Love-Fore appliques and hand paints golf and tennis motifs on polyester and cotton blend shirts, skirts, shorts, tennis dresses, and rain slickers for women only in sizes 6 to 16.

Savings: Up to 50% on samples and overstocks. Not all sizes always available.

Payment: Cash, check for exact amount with identification.
Parking: Lot.

MILL SAMPLE STORE
10600 Chester Road
Woodlawn
Cincinnati, Ohio 45215   phone: 513-771-5798

Hours: Monday-Saturday, 10 am-5 pm

Outlet for Jerk's hose and hosiery in all sizes and styles for men, women, and children. Also J.S.I. sportswear for men including tennis

separates, T-shirts, woven sports shirts, and turtlenecks; ladies' tennis clothes, sweaters, jackets, designer blouses, pants, and some skirts in sizes 6 to 18; and children's sweaters.
Savings: Average 50% on overruns, discontinueds, and seconds.

Payment: Cash, Master Charge, Shopper's Charge, Visa.
Parking: Lot.

MONTGOMERY WARD DISTRIBUTION CENTER BUDGET STORE
East Kemper Road
Sharonville
Cincinnati, Ohio 45241　　　　　　　　phone: 513-782-5451

Hours:　Monday-Thursday, Saturday, 10 am-6 pm
　　　　Friday, 10 am-9 pm
　　　　Sunday, 12 noon-5 pm
See: Chicago, Illinois, Montgomery Ward Catalog Liquidation Center.
Savings: 30% to 80% on overruns, discontinueds, and catalog returns.

Payment: Cash, check for exact amount with identification, Montgomery Ward Charge-All.
Parking: Lot.

MULLANE TAFFY COMPANY
4108 Spring Grove Avenue
Cincinnati, Ohio 45223　　　　　　　　phone: 513-542-4573
(Small 1-story building next to American Motors.)

Hours:　Monday-Saturday, 8 am-1 pm
Mullane Candy Kitchens has a retail counter in the Spring Grove plant, where they sell taffy kisses, taffy slenders, assorted chocolates, and seasonal specialties.
Savings: 20% to 33⅓% on candy specials offered four times a year. 50% and more on chocolate irregulars (odd sized pieces), when available.

Payment: Cash, check for exact amount with identification.
Parking: Street.

POLLY FLINDERS GIRLS DRESSES
The Baylis Brothers Company
A U.S. Industries Company
234 East 8th Street
Cincinnati, Ohio 45202 phone: 513-621-3222
(Between Main Street and Sycamore Street.)

Hours: Monday-Saturday, 9:30 am-5 pm

Manufacturer of girls' hand-smocked "best dresses" in cottons, cotton combinations, and velvets from infants' sizes through size 12. Fine fabrics and quality detailing rarely seen in manufactured ready-to-wear today.

Savings: 50% to 80% on designer samples, overruns, and seconds.

Also: Fabrics by the yard, in remnants, and boxed quilt pieces at excellent savings.

Put name on mailing list for special sales.

Payment: Cash, check for exact amount with identification.
Parking: Street.

SEARS CATALOG SURPLUS STORE
6340 North Glenway Avenue
Cincinnati, Ohio 45211 phone: 513-662-8900
(Near Western Woods—go into driveway.)

Hours: Monday-Friday, 10 am-9 pm
       Saturday, 10 am-5 pm
       Sunday, 12 noon-5 pm

See: Chicago, Illinois, Sears Catalog Surplus Store.

Savings: 20% to 80%.

Payment: Cash, check with identification, Sears charge card.
Parking: Lot.

SECTION FACTORY OUTLET
Mack Shirt Corporation
4817 Section Avenue
Norwood
Cincinnati, Ohio 45212 phone: 513-351-1332
(Next to Norwood Lateral, 4 blocks behind Quality Inn on Montgomery Road.)

Hours: Monday-Wednesday, Saturday, 10 am-5 pm
Thursday, Friday, 10 am-8 pm
Sunday, 12 noon-5 pm

Direct outlet for Shapely Blouses for women in sizes 5/6 to 17/18—all current styles. Also fabrics and sewing notions. Fitting rooms.
Savings: 50% to 70% on samples, overstocks, seconds, and irregulars. Greater savings during monthly sale specials.

Payment: Cash, Master Charge, Visa.
Parking: Lot.

THE SHOE MARKET
Outlet for the United States Shoe Corporation
11439 Princeton Road
Cincinnati, Ohio 45246 phone: 513-772-6757
(Near Tri-County Mall.)

Hours: Monday-Friday, 10 am-9 pm
Saturday, 10 am-7 pm
Sunday, 12 noon-5 pm

Outlet for first quality name-brand shoes including such well-known labels as Etienne Aigner, Amalfi, Pappagallo, Red Cross, Bally, Birmingham, Freeman, and Pierre Cardin. Women's sizes: 5 to 11; men's sizes 6 to 16; and children's sizes up to 6.
Savings: Up to 50% on first quality men's, women's, and children's name-brand shoes.

Payment: Cash, local checks only with identification, Master Charge, Visa.
Parking: Lot.

THE SHOE MARKET
Beechmont Avenue
Cherry Grove Plaza
Cincinnati, Ohio 45230　　　　　　　　phone: 513-752-8961

Hours: Monday-Friday, 10 am-9 pm
　　　　Saturday, 10 am-8 pm
　　　　Sunday, 12 noon-5 pm

Savings: Up to 50% on first quality men's, women's, and children's name-brand shoes.

Payment: Cash, local checks only with identification, Master Charge, Visa.
Parking: Lot.

THE SHOE MARKET
7613 Reading Road
Roselawn
Cincinnati, Ohio 45237　　　　　　　　phone: 513-761-7644
(In Valley Theatre Centre.)

Hours: Monday-Friday, 10 am-9 pm
　　　　Saturday, 10 am-6 pm
　　　　Sunday, 12 noon-6 pm

Savings: Up to 50% on first quality men's, women's, and children's name-brand shoes.

Payment: Cash, local checks only with identification, Master Charge, Visa.
Parking: Lot.

THE SHOE MARKET
9890 Colerain Avenue
Northgate
Cincinnati, Ohio 45239　　　　　　　　phone: 513-385-9566
(Central Plaza—north of Northgate Mall.)

Hours: Monday-Friday, 10 am-9 pm
Saturday, 10 am-8 pm
Sunday, 12 noon-5 pm

Savings: Up to 50% on first quality men's, women's, and children's name-brand shoes.

Payment: Cash, local checks only with identification, Master Charge, Visa.
Parking: Lot.

SPRING WATER COOKIE COMPANY
9730 Montgomery Road
Cincinnati, Ohio 45242   phone: 513-984-8301

Hours: Monday-Saturday, 9:30 am-5:30 pm

Each Spring Water chocolate chip and oatmeal raisin cookie is about 5" in diameter and weighs 5 ounces.
Savings: About 50% on fresh broken cookies, when available. Call before you go to be sure they're baking fresh cookies that day.

Payment: Cash only.
Parking: Lot.

VALLEY KITCHENS TRI-COUNTY FACTORY OUTLET
Ohio 747 at Dues Drive
Cincinnati, Ohio 45200   phone: 513-874-8400
(1 mile north of Tri-County Shopping Center.)

Hours: Monday-Thursday, Saturday, 10 am-5 pm
Friday, 10 am-8 pm
Sunday, 12 noon-5 pm

Manufacturers of Valley Kitchens cabinets and bathroom vanities.
Savings: 20% on first quality overruns and "oops, we goofed" (measurement mistakes); more on "scratch" and "dent" vanities and kitchen cabinets.

Payment: Cash, check with identification, Master Charge, Visa.
Parking: Lot.

VELVA SHEEN MISPRINT STORE
24 Cemetery Road
Milford Shopping Center
Cincinnati, Ohio 45150   phone: 513-831-7382

Hours: Monday, Tuesday, Thursday, 10 am-6 pm
Wednesday, Friday, 10 am-8 pm
Saturday, 9 am-5 pm

Velva Sheen silk screens T-shirts, sweat shirts, ski jackets, insulated vests, jackets, nylon windbreakers, sweaters, warm-up robes, and nightshirts for schools, universities, athletic teams, and consumer companies. The four Cincinnati outlets sell all the misprints, smudges, and poor color-register items. (Each outlet also has a heat transfer machine for personalizing decals on any item.)

Great buys in fun shirts for today's teens.
Savings: 20% to 50% on misprints, mistakes, and overruns.

Payment: Cash, Master Charge, Visa.
Parking: Lot.

VELVA SHEEN MISPRINT STORE
7323 Vine Street
Carthage
Cincinnati, Ohio 45216   phone: 513-821-7526

Hours: Monday, Tuesday, Thursday, 10 am-6 pm
Wednesday, Friday, 10 am-8 pm
Saturday, 9 am-5 pm

Savings: 20% to 50% on misprints, mistakes, and overruns.

Payment: Cash, Master Charge, Visa.
Parking: Lot.

VELVA SHEEN MISPRINT STORE
3710 Paxton Avenue
Cincinnati, Ohio 45209   phone: 513-631-7460
(Near Hyde Park Plaza.)

Hours: Monday, Tuesday, Thursday, 10 am-6 pm
Wednesday, Friday, 10 am-8 pm
Saturday, 9 am-5 pm

Savings: 20% to 50% on misprints, mistakes, and overruns.

Payment: Cash, Master Charge, Visa.
Parking: Lot.

VELVA SHEEN MISPRINT STORE
3621 Glenmore Avenue
Western Hills
Cincinnati, Ohio 45211   phone: 513-662-5403

Hours: Monday, Tuesday, Thursday, 10 am-6 pm
Wednesday, Friday, 10 am-8 pm
Saturday, 9 am-5 pm

Savings: 20% to 50% on misprints, mistakes, and overruns.

Payment: Cash, Master Charge, Visa.
Parking: Lot.

WHITING MANUFACTURING COMPANY, INC.
Outlet Store
9999 Carver Road
Blue Ash
Cincinnati, Ohio 45242   phone: 513-791-9100
(Exit Pfeiffer Road off Interstate 171. On west side of Reed Hartman Highway.)

Hours: Monday-Friday, 10 am-5 pm

Whiting manufactures quality bedspreads, comforters, pillows, bed ruffles, and coordinated draperies. Also tablecloths, napkins, and placemats.

Savings: 30% to 80% on overruns, discontinueds, some samples, and irregulars.

Also: Excellent savings on fabrics by the yard and on bags of fabric scraps for quilting and trimmings.

Payment: Cash, Master Charge, Visa.
Parking: Lot.

Newport, Kentucky (Cincinnati area)

MILL OUTLET
Palm Beach/Austin Hill
Fifth and Washington Street
Newport, Kentucky 41071 phone: 606-581-7666
(From Cincinnati, take Interstate 75 south. Use 5th Street Covington Exit.)

Hours: Monday, Thursday, Friday, Saturday, 9 am–5 pm
Tuesday, Wednesday, 9 am–6 pm
Sunday, 11 am–5 pm

Five minutes from downtown Cincinnati, this is the Palm Beach/Austin Hill direct factory outlet for top quality clothes for men, women, and boys.

Men's executive suits, sports coats, pants, and formalwear in sizes 36 to 56; boy's sports coats in sizes 8 to 20. Women's Austin Hill, Dudley, Evan Picone, and Craig Craely suits, skirts, pants, blouses, jackets, and dresses in sizes 6 to 18. Also: Joseph Picone tailor's line for larger women, up to size 44. 18 fitting rooms.
Savings: 33⅓% to 50% on overruns, discontinueds, and some samples. All current styles.

Also: Fabrics sold by the yard.

Payment: Cash, Master Charge, Visa.
Parking: Street.

Cleveland

BLACK AND DECKER MANUFACTURING COMPANY
3901 Detroit Avenue
Cleveland, Ohio 44113 phone: 216-651-4243

Hours: Monday–Friday, 8 am–5 pm

Black and Decker manufactures a full line of home workshop tools including drills, drill bits, sanders, saws, circular saws, sharpeners, etc.
Savings: Average 20% and more on reconditioned and discontinued tools—all sold with a one-year guarantee.

Payment: Cash, check with identification, Master Charge, Visa.
Parking: Lot.

CAPCO NUTS
The Peterson Nut Company
917 Carnegie Avenue
Cleveland, Ohio 44115 phone: 216-861-4353

Hours: Monday-Friday, 8:15 am-5 pm
Saturday, 9 am-12 noon

Processors of shelled and salted nuts including Spanish, redskin, blanched, and fancy peanuts in the shell; whole, sliced, and slivered almonds; filberts; pecans; pistachios; walnuts; and fancy, imperial, or broken nut mixes.

Also: Jelly beans, peanut brittle, caramel corn, pecan logs, and chocolate mint sticks.

Savings: 20% and up on quality processed nuts; 50% on broken nut mixes and broken cashew butts.

Payment: Cash only.
Parking: Lot.

CAROLINA MILL WHOLESALE FABRICS
2498 Superior Avenue
Cleveland, Ohio 44114 phone: 216-861-1166
(Corner of East 25th Street.)

Hours: Monday-Friday, 9:30 am-4 pm

Fabric outlet selling first- and second-quality fabrics for 25¢ to $5 per yard.

Also: Trims, buttons, appliques, and sewing supplies at some savings and patterns.

Savings: Up to 70%.

Payment: Cash, check with identification, Master Charge, Visa.
Parking: Lot.

Ohio • Cleveland

DALTON FACTORY STORE
6116 Broadway
Cleveland, Ohio 44127   phone: 216-271-7978

Hours: Monday-Thursday, 9:30 am-4 pm
              Friday, Saturday, 9:30 am-5 pm
See: Bedford, Ohio, Dalton Factory Outlet.
Savings: 50% on first quality; greater savings on seconds.

Also: Excellent savings on polyesters, wools, and knits, sold by the yard.
This is one of the larger Dalton stores in the area. Fitting rooms.

Payment: Cash, personal check with identification, traveler's checks.
Parking: Lot.

HILLSON NUT COMPANY, INC.
3225 West 71st Street
Cleveland, Ohio 44102   phone: 216-961-4477
(Corner of Dearborn and 71st.)

Hours: Monday-Friday, 8 am-5 pm
Factory counter. Fancy salted nuts in 1-lb. plastic bags including super deluxe mix (no peanuts); whole jumbo cashews; mammoth pecan halves; jumbo red pistachios; large, whole, blanched peanuts; and Spanish peanuts.
Savings: 25% to 50% on top quality fresh processed nuts, when bought in plastic bags.

Payment: Cash, check for exact amount with identification.
Parking: Lot.

HOUGH BAKERIES, INC., THRIFT STORE
12513 Euclid Avenue
Cleveland, Ohio 44112   phone: 216-795-0600

Hours: Monday-Saturday, 9 am-6 pm
One of Cleveland's finest bakeries. Fresh and day-old baked products include such specialties as whole wheat, rye, and banana nut breads;

coffee and dessert cakes; doughnuts; sweet rolls; English muffins; blueberry muffins; and pies.
Savings: 40% to 60% on day-old bread and pastry seconds.

Payment: Cash, check for exact amount with identification, food stamps.
Parking: Lot behind store.

HOUSE OF PLASTICS
1859 Prospect Street
Cleveland, Ohio 44115   phone: 216-621-0986
(Between East 18th and East 22nd.)

Hours: Monday-Friday, 8:30 am-5 pm
       Saturday, 9 am-5 pm

Clear, white, and colored scrap plastic varying in size from a 5" × 5" square to a 20" × 30" piece. Sold by the pound.
Savings: 80% and more on scrap plastic pieces remaining from the custom fabricating process.

Payment: Cash only.
Parking: Metered—nickels, dimes. Lot is across the street.

IMPERIAL SPORTSWEAR "NAME BRAND" STORE
1660 East 40th Street
Cleveland, Ohio 44103   phone: 216-361-8050
(Between Payne and Superior Streets—2 blocks from May Company Warehouse. Store is located on the first floor.)

Hours: Monday-Saturday, 9 am-4:15 pm

Imperial Sportswear manufactures women's sportswear and dresses in sizes 7 to 15 and 8 to 18 under Lisa Linn and Dede Lynn labels. Blouses, skirts, slacks, shorts, and shirts usually retail in the $20 to $50 range.

Also: Men's sweaters and knit shirts in small, medium, large, and extra large (Andrew MacRae label).
Savings: 50% to 80% on first quality overruns, "as is" samples, and seconds. Greater savings during the end-of-season sales.

Payment: Cash, check for exact amount with identification, Master Charge, Visa.
Parking: Lot across the street.

JERRIE LURIE FACTORY FABRIC OUTLET STORE
4516 Superior Avenue
Cleveland, Ohio 44103   phone: 216-431-6600

Hours: Monday-Friday, 9 am-3 pm
       Saturday, 9 am-1 pm

Located across the street from the factory, this outlet sells a large variety of fabrics including double knit and knit polyesters, metallics, satins, cottons, and trims.

Also: Women's ready-to-wear including long and short dresses, slacks, sweaters, and blouses in junior sizes, regular sizes, and half-sizes.

Savings: 50% and up on overruns, discontinueds, and some seconds.

Payment: Cash only.
Parking: Street.

LAMP FACTORY OUTLET STORE
Philmar Lamps
1100 East 222nd Street
Cleveland, Ohio 44123   phone: 216-531-8805

Hours: Tuesday-Friday, 10 am-5 pm
       Saturday, 9:30 am-3:30 pm

Philmar makes chandeliers and lamps in brass, ceramic, marble, wood, and Tiffany glass and in a wide variety of styles including hanging lamps, floor, table, and tray lamps, which sell here for about $10 to $75.

Savings: Up to 50% on overruns, discontinueds, samples; greater savings on bases that can be used to make your own lamps.

Payment: Cash, check, Master Charge, Visa.
Parking: Lot.

LAMP FACTORY OUTLET STORE
Philmar Lamps
33623 Aurora Road
Solon Square
Cleveland, Ohio 44139   phone: 216-248-9366

Hours: Monday, Thursday, Friday, 10 am-9 pm
   Tuesday, Wednesday, Saturday, 10 am-6 pm
Savings: Up to 50% on overruns, discontinueds, and samples.

Payment: Cash, check for exact amount with identification, Master Charge, Visa.
Parking: Lot.

LAMP FACTORY OUTLET STORE
Philmar Lamps
Southland Shopping Center
US 42
Cleveland, Ohio 44101   phone: 216-888-6591
(Exit from Interstate 71 at Bagley Road.)

Hours: Monday, Thursday, Friday, 10 am-9 pm
   Tuesday, Wednesday, Saturday, 10 am-6 pm
Savings: Up to 50% on overruns, discontinueds, and samples.

Payment: Cash, check for exact amount with identification, Master Charge, Visa.
Parking: Lot.

LION KNITTING MILLS COMPANY
3256 West 25th Street
Cleveland, Ohio 44109   phone: 216-351-5137
(2 blocks south of Clark Avenue.)

The Lion warehouse on Meyer Avenue is open to the public once a year for a clearance sale, usually held on the two weekends following Thanksgiving. Call or write to this address to request placement on mailing list for notice of sale.

Lion manufactures men's and women's sweaters including cardigans and pullovers, men's sleeveless sweaters and short-sleeved knit shirts, and afghans.
Savings: At least 50% to 75% on closeouts, overruns, and irregulars in sweaters during the once-a-year sale.

Payment: Cash only.
Parking: Lot. Enter off Meyer Avenue.

MARKS AND SONS COMPANY
3160 West 68th Street
Cleveland, Ohio 44102   phone: 216-631-1140
(Off Clark Avenue, near the end of the road.)

Hours: Monday–Friday, 9 am–3 pm
       Saturday, 9 am–12 noon

Sells sausage products from the plant in minimum-sized packs of 5 lbs. and 10 lbs. Whole bolognas, whole salamis, knockwurst, pork sausage, and a variety of quality, all-beef wieners (no cereals or fillers used.)
Savings: 25% and up on bulk purchases.

Payment: Cash, check for exact amount with identification.
Parking: Lot.

MATTHEWS MEATS, INC.
Processors of Prince Royal Products
7611 Jones Road
Cleveland, Ohio 44105   phone: 216-441-2222

Hours: Monday–Friday, 8 am–4:30 pm

Matthews processes Prince Royal frozen fish and meat products for restaurants, institutions, and home freezers. Portion-controlled units, sold in bulk and by the box, include T-bone, rib-eye, strip, sandwich, and loin steaks; chopped beef, sirloin cubes, and Swiss steak; veal cutlets, veal patties, and veal parmigiana; pork chops, pork patties, and sausage links; bacon and ham; sandwich meats; bar-b-que beef in tubs; chili with beans; breaded cod, shrimp, scallops, oysters, perch, and flounder; salamis and wieners; stuffed cabbage; corned and roast beef; breaded chicken and chicken and turkey rolls.
Savings: 25% and up on restaurant quality products, with additional discounts on bulk purchases.

Payment: Cash, check for exact amount with identification.
Parking: Lot in back of building.

MISTER SIRLOIN
50 Alpha Park
Highland Heights
Cleveland, Ohio 44143 phone: 216-449-2294

Hours: Monday-Friday, 9 am-5 pm

Mister Sirloin packs portion-controlled meats and fast freezes them at 40 degrees below zero. All meats, which are cut by Sugardale, are wrapped in individual portions but sold in bulk. For instance, ground beef patties are sold 40 to the box.

Also: Seafood (lobster and shrimp); cold cuts; and boned, skinless, pre-browned Chicken Kiev and Cordon Bleu, which are sold in 12-portion quantities.
Savings: About 20% for quality, trimmed, frozen meat, fish, and chicken specialties.

Payment: Cash only.
Parking: Lot.

NATIONAL POTTERS OUTLET STORE
26201 Richmond Road
Cleveland, Ohio 44143 phone: 216-292-6161
(Back of plant.)

Hours: Wednesday-Friday, 11:30 am-4:30 pm

Manufacturer of decorative glazed containers for flowers and plants, ceramic figurines, artificial and silk flowers, and a wide variety of gift items. Supplier of flower arrangement accessories to florists.
Savings: Up to 50% on seconds (slightly defective pottery items), discontinueds, and overruns.

Payment: Cash only.
Parking: Lot.

OHIO MILL FACTORY FASHIONS
4735 West 150th Street
Cleveland, Ohio 44100 phone: 216-267-1295
(Between Purtias and Brookpark.)

Hours: Thursday, Friday, Saturday, 10 am-4 pm

Outlet for Ohio Knitting Mills knit goods and outerwear including

women's sweaters, slacks, skirts, blouses, and dresses (sizes 3 to 46). Fitting room.
Savings: 25% to 50% on first quality knitwear and up to 80% on seconds. Excellent savings during annual sale in January.

Payment: Cash, check with identification, Master Charge, Visa.
Parking: Lot at side of building.

SAFETY FOOTWEAR, INC.
2030 West 65th Street
Cleveland, Ohio 44102   phone: 216-281-9055

Hours: Monday-Friday, 8:30 am-5 pm
        Saturday, 8:30 am-12 noon

Factory outlet for Lehigh's Safety Shoes, steel-toed and laced styles in leather and suede. Colors include black, brown, tan, beige, blue, loden, and white. Women's sizes are 4½ to 11 in medium and wide widths; men's sizes are 5½ to 15 in A-EEE widths.
Savings: 20% to 30% on first quality shoes.

Payment: Cash, check for exact amount with identification.
Parking: Street.

SCHWEBEL'S THRIFT BAKERY
13112 Broadway
Cleveland, Ohio 44101   phone: 216-587-4400

Hours: Monday-Saturday, 8 am-5 pm

Bakery outlet for fresh and day-old product including breads, rolls, layer and lunch cakes, cookies, and snacks.
Savings: Up to 50% on day-old product and fresh product overruns. Extra 10% savings on Wednesday.

Payment: Cash only.
Parking: Lot.

SCHWEBEL'S THRIFT BAKERY
9701 Walford Avenue
Cleveland, Ohio 44101   phone: 216-651-6200
(Off West Boulevard.)

Hours: Monday-Saturday, 8 am-5 pm

Savings: Up to 50% on day-old product and fresh product overruns. Extra 10% savings on Wednesday.

Payment: Cash only.
Parking: Lot.

SKIL PRODUCT SERVICE CENTER
9000 Bank Street
Valley View
Cleveland, Ohio 44125   phone: 216-447-0250
(Off Canal Road.)

Hours: Monday-Friday, 8 am-5 pm

Skil manufactures power tools for the home owner and do-it-yourselfer: power and band saws, high speed sanders, routers, cordless drills, drill kits, and Skil's Xtra tool.
Savings: 10% to 40% on seconds, Skil reconditioned power tools with full, new-product guarantee.

Also: Accessories available at regular retail price.

Payment: Cash, check for exact amount with identification.
Parking: Metered.

STATE FISH, INC.
1600 Merwin Avenue
Cleveland, Ohio 44113   phone: 216-696-0080
(In the flats.)

Hours: Monday-Friday, 7 am-5 pm
       Saturday, 7 am-12 noon

"Fish Center of Ohio" sells fresh, frozen, and packaged fish and seafoods including raw, cooked, breaded, and stuffed shrimp; cold-water and warm-water lobster tails; scallops, oysters, and clams; cod, haddock, perch, snapper, turbot, flounder, and white fish fillets; frog legs and turtlemeat; pickled fish; and other fish specialties.
Savings: 20% and up on a wide variety of fish and sea food, sold in bulk quantities. Bigger savings on advertised specials.

Payment: Cash, check for exact amount with identification.
Parking: Lot.

STORK BABY FURNITURE AND TOY COMPANY
3203 Lorain Avenue
Cleveland, Ohio 44113   phone: 216-631-2900

Hours: Monday, Thursday, Friday, 9 am-9 pm
Tuesday, Wednesday, Saturday, 9 am-6 pm

Retail outlet carrying Cleveland-made Century Juvenile Furniture. Also, Simmons, Child Craft, Bassett, etc., in a large inventory of carriages and strollers; high chairs; cribs and junior beds; table and chair sets and rockers; toys and toy chests; tricycles and wagons.

Also: Infants' and toddlers' clothing.
Savings: 20% to 40% on top-name juvenile products.

Payment: Cash, check with identification, Master Charge, Visa.
Parking: Lot behind store on West 32nd Street.

TRAIT TEX INDUSTRIES
Division of Colonial Woolen Mills, Inc.
5611 Hough Avenue
Cleveland, Ohio 44103   phone: 216-391-0234

Mail order only. Send $1 (refundable with first order) for samples and a current price list.

Yarn manufacturers, selling direct to the consumer by mail order only. Weaving yarns and macrame cords, mainly in synthetic fibers. Minimum order: $20.
Savings: 20% to 50% on first quality yarns.

Payment: Payment must accompany each order.

WORK SMART STORE—FACTORY OUTLET
12414 Lorain Avenue
Cleveland, Ohio 44111   phone: 216-941-9603

Hours: Monday-Thursday, 10 am-6 pm
Friday, 10 am-8 pm
Saturday, 10 am-6 pm

Work Smart manufactures gabardine and blended fabric men's work

pants (sizes 28 to 52) and work, flannel, and sweat shirts (sizes small to extra large).
Savings: 40% to 60% on men's work clothing overruns, closeouts, and irregulars.

Payment: Cash only.
Parking: Across the street just beyond the Convenient Store.

Columbus

ARVEY PAPER AND SUPPLIES CENTER
431 East Livingston Avenue
Columbus, Ohio 43515   phone: 614-221-0153

Hours: Monday-Friday, 8:30 am-5 pm
       Saturday, 9 am-1 pm
See: Chicago, Illinois, Arvey Paper and Supplies Center.
Savings: At least 33⅓% on mimeo and bond paper bought by the ream (500 sheets) and envelopes bought by the box (500 envelopes); greater savings on the monthly specials featured in the "salesmailers."

Payment: Cash, check for exact amount with identification.
Parking: Lot.

BROOKS SHOES FACTORY OUTLET STORE
11th and High Streets
Columbus, Ohio 43210   phone: 614-291-6747
(Ohio State University Campus area.)

Hours: Monday-Saturday, 10 am-8 pm
       Sunday, 12 noon-5 pm
This outlet store has hiking, work, and western boots made by William Brooks Shoe Company for men (sizes 7 to 13) and boots for women (sizes 5 to 10).
Savings: 33⅓% to 50% on factory overruns, discontinueds, and blemished boots.

Also: Factory defects and overstocks in Levi's jeans and shirts.
Savings: Average 33⅓%.

Payment: Cash, check for exact amount with identification, Master Charge, Visa.
Parking: Difficult. Metered parking—nickels, dimes—on 11th Street.

BROOKS SHOES FACTORY OUTLET STORE
1619 West Fifth Street
Columbus, Ohio 43200 phone: 614-486-6260

Hours: Monday-Saturday, 10 am-8 pm
Sunday, 12 noon-5 pm

Factory outlet store for William Brooks Shoe Company, manufacturers of men's and boys' work shoes and boots and of women's oxfords and dress shoes. William Brooks shoes and boots retail for about $36 to $60.

Savings: 40% and up on factory overruns and discontinued shoes and on blemished shoes and boots for men in sizes 6 to 13 and for women in sizes 5 to 10.

Payment: Cash, Master Charge, Visa.
Parking: Lot.

BROWNBERRY OVENS THRIFT STORE
1855 North West Boulevard
Columbus, Ohio 43212 phone: 614-488-3189

Hours: Monday-Friday, 9 am-7 pm
Saturday, 9 am-6 pm
Open Tuesday evenings until 9 pm

See: LaGrange Park, Illinois, Brownberry Ovens Thrift Store.

Savings: 33⅓% and up on day-old and seconds. Extra 10% savings on Tuesdays.

Payment: Cash, check for exact amount with identification.
Parking: Lot.

FRANKLIN ART GLASS STUDIOS, INC.
222 East Sycamore Street
Columbus, Ohio 43206 phone: 614-221-2972
(In Germantown area.)

Hours: Monday-Friday, 8 am-4:30 pm
Saturday, 8 am-12 noon

Franklin designs and constructs stained-glass windows. They sell faceted and stained glass, leading supplies, hand-spun glass roundels,

large pieces and small chunks of glass.
Savings: About 50% on glass scraps, pieces, and chunks in a variety of colors, sold by the pound.

Note: Mail orders accepted for specialty sizes and glass by the foot.

Payment: Cash, check for exact amount with identification.
Parking: Lot.

H. C. CECUTTI BAKERY COMPANY
Home of Bread Sticks
1490 Clara Avenue
Columbus, Ohio 43211   phone: 614-294-5461
(1st street west of Freeway—right off 11th Street.)

Hours: Monday-Friday, 7:30 am-7:30 pm
        Saturday, Sunday, 7:30 am-5:30 pm

Bakers of pumpernickel, rye, and French breads; bread sticks; Jewish rye; cheese bread; club rolls; doughnuts; cookies; and pizza crusts sold in packages of ten in 10", 12", and 15" sizes. Bread is baked three times daily.
Savings: Average 20%, with up to 50% on specials.

Also: Railroad salvage canned goods and paper goods at savings.

Payment: Cash, check for exact amount with identification, food stamps.
Parking: In front.

HERCULES OUTLET STORE
2025 Corvair Boulevard
Columbus, Ohio 43207   phone: 614-445-8101
(Located in Southeast Industrial Park.)

Hours: Monday-Friday, 10 am-6 pm
        Saturday, 9 am-5 pm
        Sunday, 11 am-5 pm

Factory outlet open to the public. This large warehouse facility carries a complete line of men's dress suits, sport coats, and slacks in wools, dacron and wool, and polyesters under the Hercules and Reston labels. Eleven fitting rooms.
Savings: Average 50% on first quality clothing.

Payment: Cash, check for exact amount, Master Charge, Visa.
Parking: Large lot.

J C PENNEY CATALOG OUTLET STORE
Scarborough Boulevard
Columbus, Ohio 43216 phone: 614-868-0250
(Brice Road exit off Interstate routes 270 and 70 east.)

Hours: Monday-Saturday, 10 am-9 pm
       Sunday, 12 noon-6 pm

See: Villa Park, Illinois, J C Penney Catalog Outlet Store.

Savings: 40% and up on catalog surplus and returned merchandise, with extra savings on seasonal specials.

Payment: Cash, check with identification, J C Penney charge card, Visa.
Parking: Lot.

KREMA PRODUCTS
996 Goodale Boulevard
Columbus, Ohio 43216 phone: 614-229-4131

Hours: Monday-Friday, 8 am-5 pm
       Saturday, 8 am-2 pm

Processors and roasters of nuts and nut products including fancy white cashews; salted, redskin, Spanish, and jumbo peanuts; black walnuts; raw and roasted sunflower seeds; pistachios; slivered, natural, blanched, and ground almonds; pecans; and Brazil nuts.

Savings: 25% and up on freshly roasted, top quality nuts.

Also: Krema peanut oil and bulk-packed pure peanut old-fashioned peanut butter.

Payment: Cash, check with identification.
Parking: In front.

MID-AMERICAN TEXTILES, INC.
The Sample Room
1950 North Fourth Street
Indianola Shopping Center
Columbus, Ohio 43201 phone: 614-294-5284

Hours: Monday-Friday, 8 am-4:30 pm

Mid-American manufactures top quality stretch nylon athletic wear under the Cambridge label. These include warm-up suits and pants, wrestling wear, dance costumes, jerseys, shirts, uniforms, leotards, and men's swimwear.
Savings: 50% and up on factory overruns, discontinueds, samples, seconds, and closeouts of catalog items sold in the factory sample room.

Also: Excellent savings on discontinued knits by the yard and on zippers and dance materials.

Payment: Cash, Master Charge, Visa.
Parking: Lot.

OHIO STEAK AND BARBECUE COMPANY
Temptaste Brand Meats
281 North Grant Avenue
Columbus, Ohio 43215   phone: 614-221-3245
(Entrance is on Natton Street.)

Hours: Monday-Friday, 8 am-4:30 pm
Saturday, 8 am-12 noon

Portion-controlled meats, fish, and chicken are sold in bulk pack for institutions and the home freezer. Products include 8-lb. packs of T-bone, strip, and rib-eye steaks; hamburger and chopped sirloin; beef patties in 5-lb. and 6-lb. packs; breaded veal; oysters; and institutional sized 6-lb. packs of tuna and noodles, beef stew, macaroni and cheese, etc.

Also: Bulk packs of vegetables, bean and chicken soup, chili, and other prepared main dishes.
Savings: 20% and up on ready to cook and serve products packaged in bulk. Greater savings on weekly specials.

Payment: Cash, check with identification, food stamps.
Parking: Lot.

PEPPERIDGE FARM THRIFT STORE
1174 Kenny Centre
Columbus, Ohio 43220   phone: 614-457-4800
(Kenny and Old Henderson Road.)

Hours: Monday-Friday, 9:30 am-5 pm
        Saturday, 9 am-5 pm

See: Downers Grove, Illinois, Pepperidge Farm Thrift Store.

Savings: 25% to 50%. For best bread selection, shop early in the morning.

Payment: Cash, check for exact amount with identification.
Parking: Lot.

QUALITY BAKERY COMPANY
Mountain Top Frozen Pies
50 North Glenwood Avenue
Columbus, Ohio 43222   phone: 614-224-1424

Hours: Monday-Friday, 8 am-11 am

Bakers of frozen apple, peach, cherry, blackberry, and rhubarb pies and pumpkin, strawberry, and mince pies in season. Each 9" pie contains 1 lb. of fruit and no preservatives.

Savings: 30% to 75% on overweight, underweight, or damaged pies. Savings depend upon pie condition.

Enter small room and be seated. Someone will tell you what pies are available that morning. You make your selection and pay the cashier.

Payment: Cash only. Company requests that you have exact change ready when paying for pies.
Parking: Side of building.

SEARS CATALOG SURPLUS STORE
University City Shopping Center
2855 Olentangy River Road
Columbus, Ohio 43202   phone: 614-268-8437

Hours: Monday-Friday, 10 am-9 pm
        Saturday, 10 am-6 pm
        Sunday, 12 noon-5 pm

See: Chicago, Illinois, Sears Catalog Surplus Store.
Savings: 33⅓% to 80%.

Payment: Cash, check with identification, Sears charge card.
Parking: Lot.

SEARS CATALOG SURPLUS STORE DISTRIBUTION CENTER
4545 Fisher Road
Columbus, Ohio 43228   phone: 614-272-3000

Hours: Monday-Friday, 10 am-9 pm
       Saturday, 10 am-6 pm
       Sunday, 12 noon-5 pm
See: Chicago, Illinois, Sears Catalog Surplus Store.
Savings: 33⅓% to 80%.

Payment: Cash, check with identification, Sears charge card.
Parking: Lot.

SHOE FACTORY STORE
R. G. Barry Corporation
2068 Integrity Drive
Columbus, Ohio 43216   phone: 614-443-1008

Hours: Monday-Saturday, 10 am-5:30 pm
       Sunday, 12 noon-5 pm

Outlet for Bernardo Footwear, a subsidiary of R. G. Barry Corporation, manufacturers of women's highly styled leather shoes, sandals, and slippers and of Mushrooms, Quoddy Moccasins, and Apres Ski boots. Outlet also carries tennis shoes.

Women's sizes: 5 to 10, narrow and medium widths. Men's sizes: 7 to 13, up to D width.

Savings: 25% to 80% on overruns, samples—when available—and "factory defective" shoes (small flaws that may have been corrected, but shoe cannot be considered first quality).

Note: This is the largest of the four outlet stores in the Columbus area.

Payment: Cash, check with identification, Master Charge, Visa.
Parking: Lot.

SHOE FACTORY STORE
R. G. Barry Corporation
5763 Karl Road
Columbus, Ohio 43216   phone: 614-846-3380

Hours: Monday-Friday, 10 am-9 pm
        Saturday, 10 am-6 pm
        Sunday, 12 noon-5 pm

Savings: 25% to 80% on overruns, samples—when available—and "factory defective" shoes.

Payment: Cash, check with identification, Master Charge, Visa.
Parking: Lot.

SHOE FACTORY STORE
R. G. Barry Corporation
6097 Maughten Center
Columbus, Ohio 43216   phone: 614-861-3138
(Corner of Main Street and Maughten Road.)

Hours: Monday-Friday, 10 am-9 pm
        Saturday, 10 am-6 pm
        Sunday, 12 noon-5 pm

Savings: 25% to 80% on overruns, samples—when available—and "factory defective" shoes.

Payment: Cash, check with identification, Master Charge, Visa.
Parking: Lot.

SHOE FACTORY STORE
R. G. Barry Corporation
2025 West Henderson Road
Green Tree Shopping Center
Columbus, Ohio 43216   phone: 614-451-7890

Hours: Monday-Friday, 10 am-9 pm
        Saturday, 10 am-6 pm
        Sunday, 12 noon-5 pm

Savings: 25% to 80% on overruns, samples—when available—and "factory defective" shoes.

Payment: Cash, check with identification, Master Charge, Visa.
Parking: Lot.

Dayton • Ohio

TEDESCHI'S BAKERY, INC.
1210 West Third Avenue
Columbus, Ohio 43212   phone: 614-294-3278
(Corner of Third and Doton Street. Enter through back door.)

Hours: Monday-Friday, 8 am-5 pm
        Saturday, 8 am-12 noon

Bread, submarine buns, dinner rolls, and pizza crusts sold 10 to a package in 10", 12", and 14" sizes. All baked here.
Savings: Average 50%.

Payment: Cash, check for exact amount with identification.
Parking: Back of building.

Dayton

BROWNBERRY OVENS THRIFT STORE
4600 Salem Avenue
Dayton, Ohio 45416   phone: 513-278-8746

Hours: Monday, Wednesday, Thursday, Saturday, 9 am-6 pm
        Tuesday, Friday, 9 am-9 pm
        Sunday, 11 am-5 pm

See: LaGrange Park, Illinois, Brownberry Ovens Thrift Store.

Savings: 33⅓% and up on day-old and seconds. Extra 10% savings on Tuesdays.

Payment: Cash, check for exact amount with identification.
Parking: Lot.

COTTON MILL STORE
3940 Linden Avenue
Eastown Shopping Center
Dayton, Ohio 45432   phone: 513-254-3891

Hours: Monday-Wednesday, Saturday, 10 am-6 pm
        Open Thursday and Friday evenings until 8 pm

See: Cincinnati, Ohio, Cotton Mill Store.

Savings: 35% to 80% on firsts, discontinueds, overruns, seconds, and irregulars in sheets, towels, and fabrics including quilted remnants.

Payment: Cash, Master Charge, Visa.
Parking: Lot.

COTTON MILL STORE
4211 North Main Street
Northtown Shopping Center
Dayton, Ohio 45405 phone: 513-274-4344

Hours: Monday-Saturday, 10 am-5:30 pm
   Open Thursday and Friday evenings until 8 pm
See: Cincinnati, Ohio, Cotton Mill Store.
Savings: 35% to 80% on firsts, discontinueds, overruns, seconds, and irregulars in sheets, towels, and fabrics including quilted remnants.

Payment: Cash, Master Charge, Visa.
Parking: Lot.

DAYTON NUT SPECIALTIES, INC.
919 North Main Street
Dayton, Ohio 45405 phone: 513-223-3225

Hours: Monday-Friday, 8:30 am-5 pm
Complete line of raw and roasted nut meats in 1-lb., 5-lb., and 20-lb. packs: almonds, pecans, pistachios, peanuts, cashews, sunflower seeds. Also dried fruits, fruit and nut mixes, and specialty gift packs.
Savings: Up to 50% on bulk packs of 5 lbs. and larger.

Also: Pure peanut butter in 1-lb. and 5-lb. tubs and peanut oil by the gallon.

Payment: Cash, check for exact amount with identification.
Parking: Street (1 hour limit).

MEHAFFIE PIE COMPANY
3013 Linden Avenue
Dayton, Ohio 45410 phone: 513-253-1163

Hours: Monday-Saturday, 8 am-6 pm
   Sunday, 8 am-3 pm
Bakers of 9″ pies including apple, Dutch apple, cherry, mince, peach, pecan, pineapple, pumpkin, raisin, and rhubarb; blackberry,

blueberry, gooseberry, and strawberry; banana, butterscotch, chocolate, coconut, and lemon; custard; and blueberry cream, Boston cream, cherry cream, strawberry cream, and pineapple cream.
Savings: 50% on damaged and day-old pies, when available.

Also: 35¢ to 50¢ savings on each pie on purchases of 10 or more fresh pies (good buys for home freezers), except the day before Thanksgiving and the day before Christmas.

Payment: Cash, checks from local residents.
Parking: Lot.

OHIO STEAK AND BARBECUE COMPANY
3610 Linden Avenue
Dayton, Ohio 45401   phone: 513-253-9221
(Across from Color Tile.)

Hours: Monday-Friday, 4 pm-6 pm
Call first to place order.
See: Columbus, Ohio, Ohio Steak and Barbecue Company.
Savings: 20% and up on ready-to-cook-and-serve products packaged in bulk for institutional use and home freezers.

Payment: Cash only.
Parking: Lot.

PEPPERIDGE FARM THRIFT STORE
5843 Far Hills Drive
Dayton, Ohio 45429   phone: 513-434-7680

Hours: Monday-Friday, 9:30 am-5:30 pm
       Saturday, 9:30 am-5 pm
See: Downers Grove, Illinois, Pepperidge Farm Thrift Store.
Savings: 25% to 50%. For best bread selection shop right after store opens.

Payment: Cash, check for exact amount with identification.
Parking: Lot.

THE SHOE MARKET
Rike's Kettering Shopping Center
2068 Dorothy Lane
Dayton, Ohio 45439   phone: 513-293-4748

Hours: Monday-Friday, 10 am-9 pm
 Saturday, 10 am-9 pm
 Sunday, 12 noon-5 pm

See: Cincinnati, Ohio, The Shoe Market.

Savings: Up to 50% on first-quality name-brand men's, women's, and children's shoes.

Payment: Cash, check with identification, Master Charge, Visa.
Parking: Lot.

Deerfield

THE FACTORY OUTLET STORE
State Route 14-A
Deerfield, Ohio 44411   phone: 216-584-2571
(1 mile south of Deerfield.)

Hours: Monday-Sunday, 10 am-5 pm

Salem China dinnerware sets in firsts and some seconds and open stock and serving pieces. Also, seconds in Royal China, Taylor, Smith and Taylor, Hall, and Scio dinnerware and first quality Salem items imported from England, Japan, Portugal, and New Zealand.
Savings: Up to 50% on imperfects or seconds.

Payment: Cash, Master Charge, Visa, traveler's checks.
Parking: Lot.

Delaware

HENRY H. BEAVER PACKING COMPANY, INC.
Route 1175 South
Delaware, Ohio 43105   phone: 614-363-6561
(US 42.)

Hours: Monday-Thursday, 7 am-5:30 pm
         Friday, 8 am-5 pm
         Saturday, 8 am-12 noon

Beaver Company meat, from local corn- and grain-fed cattle, is aged and tenderized naturally and sold by the side or quarter. Beaver also sells ground beef in 5-lb. packs and ribs, bacon, sausage, and steaks by the pound.
Savings: About 20% and up on bulk purchases of top quality meat.

Payment: Cash, check for exact amount with identification.
Parking: Lot.

WORLDWIDE GAMES, INC.
3527 West State Route 37
Delaware, Ohio 43015   phone: 614-369-9631
(About 4 miles out of Delaware.)

Hours: Monday-Friday, 8 am-5 pm
         Open Saturdays during November and December, 9 am-5 pm

Manufacturer of quality wood games and toys including skittles, shoot the moon, backgammon, cribbage, tick-tack-toe, Chinese checkers, black walnut dancing dolls, and an assortment of challenging wood puzzles.
Savings: 20% to 40% on discontinueds, overruns, and seconds.

Also: 10% cash and carry on all games bought here at showroom. Greater savings on bags of woodcraft knobs, spools, handles, etc., for do-it-yourselfers.

Payment: Cash, check, Master Charge, Visa.
Parking: Lot.

East Toledo

HIRZEL CANNING COMPANY
Wholesale Outlet
411 Lemoyne Road at Woodville
East Toledo, Ohio 43601   phone: 419-693-0531
(Wholesale outlet is across the drive from the main office.)

Hours: Monday, Wednesday, Friday, 8 am-3 pm

Peeled, whole canned tomatoes sold by the case only: 24-16-oz. cans; 24-28-oz. cans; 24-1-lb. cans.
Savings: Up to 40% on first quality product.

Payment: Cash, check for exact amount with identification.
Parking: Lot.

Elyria

PAPERBACK EXCHANGE
41100 Griswold Avenue
Elyria, Ohio 44035   phone: Ohio Residents: 1-800-362-7417
                                 Other: 216-323-1204

Hours: Monday-Saturday, 9 am-9 pm
       Sunday, 9 am-5 pm

Bookseller's Paperback Exchange has one of the largest book and paperback selections in Ohio. They have a new-book discount policy and deal extensively in used books.
Savings: Up to 80% on surplus stock paperback books with front covers ripped off.

Bookseller's Paperback Exchange stores are also located in Lorain and Parma, Ohio. This store has the most extensive inventory.

Payment: Cash, check with identification, Master Charge, Visa.
Parking: Lot.

Englewood

EVELYN SPRAGUE PORTION CONTROL MEATS
Division of Consolidated Foods Corporation
905 South Main Street
Englewood, Ohio 45322   phone: 513-836-2611
(Right off Interstate 70.)

Hours: Monday-Friday, 9 am-5 pm

Sell frozen meat products in bulk institutional sizes of 6, 10, and 12 lbs. each: beef patties; pork steak and patties; rib-eye, fillet, and T-bone steaks; etc. Cooked meat specialties include bar-b-que beef, chili with beans, beef tips, and sliced beef in gravy. Order at office window.
Savings: 33⅓% and up on quality frozen product sold in bulk.

Also: Kahn's hot dogs, Booth Chef Cut Cod, Rudy's Sausage, etc.

Payment: Cash, check for exact amount with identification.
Parking: In front of building.

Foster

CANNON TOWEL OUTLET
2091 West US 22 and Ohio 3
Montgomery Road
Symmes Township
Foster, Ohio 45039   phone: 513-683-7275

Hours: Monday-Saturday, 10 am-6 pm
        April 1-December 24—Sunday, 12 noon-5 pm

Outlet for Cannon first quality, seconds, and irregulars (minor flaws such as variations in the dye lot) in towels from the designer to the budget lines. Also Chatham blankets (baby, bunk, twin, full, queen, and king sizes) and blanket remnants. Seconds are excellent buys for camp, college, and vacation housing.
Savings: 30% to 70% on towel irregulars and seconds, blanket seconds, and remnants sold by the pound.

Payment: Cash, check for exact amount with identification, Master Charge, Visa.
Parking: Lot.

Fremont

GENERAL CUTLERY
1022 Oakwood Street
Fremont, Ohio 43420   phone: 419-332-2316

Hours: Monday-Friday, 8 am-4 pm
Manufacturer of quality knife blades and commercial butcher knives

under the General and private labels. Also makes steak knives, paring knives, and a variety of kitchen knives.

Savings: Up to 50% on seconds—knives with slight flaws in the handles—and overruns, when available.

Payment: Cash, check for exact amount with identification.
Parking: Lot.

INFANT ITEMS, INC.
1071 North Fifth Street
Fremont, Ohio 43420   phone: 419-332-7361
(Across from the Heinz Plant.)

Hours: Wednesdays, 10 am-12 noon
    Saturday morning sales scheduled periodically.

Write to be placed on mailing list for advance notice of sales.

Manufacturer of infants' clothing and accessories holds periodic clearance sales of infant gowns, bibs, towels, plush toys, samples, and sample fabrics.
Savings: 50%.

Payment: Cash, check with identification.
Parking: Lot.

Hamilton

COTTON MILL STORE
1230 Central Avenue
Hamilton, Ohio 45011   phone: 513-896-6575
(Corner of Central Avenue and Leshner Place.)

Hours: Monday-Saturday, 8 am-5 pm

See: Cincinnati, Ohio, Cotton Mill Store.

Savings: 35% to 80% on firsts, discontinueds, overruns, seconds, and irregulars in sheets, towels, blankets, bedspreads, tablecloths, and fabrics.

Payment: Cash, check for exact amount with identification, Visa.
Parking: Lot.

THE SHOE MARKET
2412 Dixie Highway
Hamilton Plaza Center
Hamilton, Ohio 45015
(Ohio 4.)

phone: 513-868-8493

Hours: Monday-Thursday, Saturday, 10 am-6 pm
Friday, 10 am-9 pm
See: Cincinnati, Ohio, The Shoe Market.

Savings: Up to 50% on first-quality name-brand men's, women's, and children's shoes.

Payment: Cash, check with identification, Master Charge, Visa.
Parking: Lot.

Hartville

ASPLIN BASKET COMPANY, INC.
224 East Maple Street
Hartville, Ohio 44632

phone: 216-877-9321

Hours: Monday-Friday, 7:30 am-4 pm
Saturday, 7:30 am-12 noon

Asplin makes wood-splint fruit and vegetable baskets, which are used to package farm produce. These baskets come with handles and covers in 8-quart, 16-quart, and 20-quart sizes and can be purchased in quantities of one dozen. (Single baskets are not available.)

Note: These baskets make excellent flower and picnic baskets and can be decorated or lined with fabric for use as sewing baskets, plant holders, and laundry or magazine baskets.

Savings: 50% and more when compared with other baskets available in retail stores.

Payment: Cash, check for exact amount with identification.
Parking: Lot.

Hudson

TOWEL BAR
72 North Main Street
Hudson Square Building
Hudson, Ohio 44236   phone: 216-653-2343

Hours: Monday-Saturday, 10 am–5 pm

The Towel Bar sells, at discount, bath furnishings and accessories made by Acme, Burlington, Cannon, Fieldcrest, Martex, Regal, and Vera. In addition, the store sells the irregular towels from Cannon and Martex by the pound.

Savings: About 60% on labeled towel irregulars sold by the pound. Average 20% on all other first quality merchandise.

Payment: Cash, check for exact amount with identification, Master Charge, Visa.
Parking: In rear.

Jackson Center

HOLLOWAY SPORTSWEAR, INC.
Jackson Center, Ohio 45334   phone: 513-596-6193

Factory is not open for retail sales to the public. Write for advance notice of annual sale, usually held the first week in October.

Manufacturers of athletic and sports apparel for men, women, girls, and boys: wool and nylon jackets, jerseys, warm-up clothes, and football, baseball, and softball uniforms.

Savings: 50% to 80% on overstocks, discontinueds, and some seconds at annual sale held in a location other than the factory.

Payment: Cash, check for exact amount with identification.
Parking: Lot.

Kent

EUCLID GARMENT MANUFACTURING COMPANY
333 Martinel Drive
Kent, Ohio 44240   phone: 216-673-7413

Hours: Monday–Friday, 8:30 am–4:30 pm

Men's work clothing in all-cotton or cotton-polyester blends: shopcoats, shirts, pants, coveralls, smocks, and sales coats.
Savings: 35% and up on first quality. Greater savings on seconds, when available.

Payment: Cash, check for exact amount with identification.
Parking: Lot.

Kenton

IMPERIAL CUP CORPORATION
808 Fountain Street
Kenton, Ohio 43326   phone: 419-673-0711

Hours: Monday–Friday, 8 am–5 pm

Manufacturer of hot and cold cups (7-oz. and 8¼-oz. sizes) and soup tubs and lids for vending machines, sold in case lots only (2,000 cups or soup tubs per case) through the front office.
Savings: About 40% to 50% on misprint hot and cold cups and tubs—sold in case lots only.

Payment: Cash only.
Parking: Lot.

Lancaster

ANCHOR HOCKING SHOP
621 North Memorial Drive
Lancaster, Ohio 43130   phone: 614-687-2090

Hours: Monday–Thursday, Saturday, 10 am–6 pm
       Friday, 10 am–8 pm
       Sunday, 12:30 pm–6 pm

Store sells many of the almost 2,500 items made by Anchor Hocking and subsidiaries at a price comparable to that charged by leading discount retailers.

Product lines include barware, stemware, tableware, bakeware, microwave ovenware, bud vases, what-nots, and open-stock Anchor Hocking patterns and designs.

Savings: 20% to 50% on discontinued and closeout styles, patterns, and items.

Payment: Cash, check with identification, Master Charge, Visa.
Parking: Lot.

Lodi

OHIO STEAK AND BARBECUE COMPANY
Bank Street
Lodi, Ohio 44254 phone: 216-948-2195
(On old US 224, now Ohio 421.)

Hours: Monday-Friday, 3:30 pm-6 pm
Call first to place order.
See: Columbus, Ohio, Ohio Steak and Barbecue Company.
Savings: 20% and up on ready-to-cook-and-serve products packaged in bulk for institutional use and home freezers.

Payment: Cash, check for exact amount with identification.
Parking: Lot.

Lorain

DALTON FACTORY STORE
2201 West Park Drive
Lorain, Ohio 44053 phone: 216-282-4510
(Off 21st Street.)

Hours: Monday, Wednesday, Saturday, 10 am-3 pm
See: Bedford, Ohio, Dalton Factory Outlet.
Savings: 50% to 75% on first quality; greater savings on seconds.

Also: Good savings on wool, jersey, and polyester fabrics.
No fitting rooms and no try-ons.

Payment: Cash, check for exact amount with identification.
Parking: Lot.

Maple Heights

HOUGH BAKERIES, INC., THRIFT STORE
15850 Broadway
Maple Heights, Ohio 44137   phone: 216-475-3728

Hours: Monday-Saturday, 9 am-6 pm
See: Cleveland, Ohio, Hough Bakeries, Inc., Thrift Store.
Savings: 40% to 60% on day-old bread and pastry seconds.

Payment: Cash, check for exact amount with identification, food stamps.
Parking: Lot.

MRS. SMITH'S PIES
14801 Broadway Avenue
Maple Heights, Ohio 44137   phone: 216-663-4800
(Between McCracken Road and Libby Road. In back of building.)

Hours: Monday-Saturday, 9 am-5 pm
Mrs. Smith makes 10" institutional sized pies for hotels and restaurants (8 servings or cuts per pie), fresh baked or frozen unbaked, including apple, banana, blueberry, cherry, peach, pineapple, rhubarb; coconut, chocolate, and lemon meringue; coconut and egg custard; and walnut and pecan nut.
Savings: 30% to 50% on broken, damaged, or imperfect pies.

Payment: Cash, check for exact amount with identification.
Parking: Lot.

Maumee

BALDUF'S THRIFT STORE
915 Kingsbury Street
Maumee, Ohio 43537   phone: 419-893-7637

Hours: Monday-Saturday, 10 am-6 pm
Day-old breads, baked goods, and dented canned goods.
Savings: Up to 50% on a variety of food items.

Payment: Cash and local checks only.
Parking: Lot.

Mayfield Heights

MATERNITY FACTORY OUTLET
Dan Howard Maternity Clothes
1517 Goldengate Shopping Center
Mayfield Heights, Ohio 44124　　　　　phone: 216-473-0433
(1 block west of Interstate 271 off Mayfield Road.)

Hours:　Monday, Friday, 10 am-9 pm
　　　　Tuesday, Wednesday, Thursday, Saturday, 10 am-6 pm
　　　　Sunday, 12 noon-5 pm

See: Chicago, Illinois, Maternity Factory Outlet.

Savings: 20% to 50% on first quality production overruns, overcuts, and samples. Larger savings on seconds.

Payment: Cash, check with identification, Master Charge, Visa.
Parking: Lot.

PEPPERIDGE FARM THRIFT STORE
1519 Golden Gate Plaza
Mayfield Heights, Ohio 44124　　　　　phone: 216-461-9381

Hours:　Monday, Tuesday, Wednesday, 9 am-6 pm
　　　　Thursday, Friday, 9 am-8 pm
　　　　Saturday, 9 am-5 pm

See: Downers Grove, Illinois, Pepperidge Farm Thrift Store.

Savings: 25% to 50%. For best bread selection, shop early in the morning.

Payment: Cash, check for exact amount with identification.
Parking: Lot.

Medina

SEARS CATALOG OUTLET STORE
913 North Court Street
Medina Shopping Center
Medina, Ohio 44256　　　　　phone: 216-725-7711

Hours: Monday-Thursday, 9 am-5:30 pm
Friday, 9 am-9 pm
Saturday, 9 am-5:30 pm

See: Chicago, Illinois, Sears Catalog Surplus Store.

This Sears store sells appliances including dishwashers, freezers, stoves, refrigerators, stereos, TVs, and vacuums.

Savings: 20% to 80% on surplus catalog items and returns.

Payment: Cash, check with identification, Sears charge card.
Parking: Lot.

SEARS CATALOG SURPLUS STORE
945 North Court Street
Medina Shopping Center
Medina, Ohio 44256   phone: 216-725-0541

Hours: Monday-Friday, 9:30 am-9 pm
Saturday, 9:30 am-5:30 pm

See: Chicago, Illinois, Sears Catalog Surplus Store.

Savings: 20% to 80% on surplus catalog items and returns.

Payment: Cash, check with identification, Sears charge card.
Parking: Lot.

Middletown

ENDICOTT-JOHNSON
340 City Centre Mart
Middletown, Ohio 45042   phone: 513-422-1402

Hours: Monday, Friday, 9:30 am-8:30 pm
Tuesday, Wednesday, Thursday, Saturday, 9:30 am-5:30 pm
Sunday, 12 noon-5 pm

Outlet for Endicott-Johnson Corporation, shoe manufacturers. Men's, women's, and children's dress shoes, tennis and work shoes, slippers, and rubber boots.

Savings: 50% and up on overbuys, discontinueds, rejects, and odd lots.

Payment: Cash, Master Charge, Visa.
Parking: Enclosed mall parking.

Millersburg

RASTETTER WOOLEN MILL
Star Route (State routes 39 and 62)
Millersburg, Ohio 44654   phone: 216-674-2103
(2 miles west of Berlin, 4½ miles east of Millersburg.)

Hours: Tuesday-Saturday, 8 am-5 pm

Small, family owned company manufactures wool comforters, down and feather pillows and comforters, and hand-woven throw rugs.

They also sell, at discount, firsts and seconds of sheepskins (2'-2½' wide to 3' long)—which can be used for car seats, wheel chair or bed pads, accent rugs, or wall hangings—and sheepskin jackets and vests. **Savings: About 25% or more on sheepskin seconds.**

Also: Excellent savings on wool blanket pieces sold by the pound (usually about 10" wide and running up to 6' long).

Payment: Cash, check for exact amount with identification.
Parking: Lot.

Monroe

CARTER'S FACTORY OUTLET
Monroe Shopping Center
Monroe, Ohio 45050   phone: 513-539-8351
(1 mile west of US 75 on Ohio 63.)

Hours: Monday-Saturday, 10 am-5 pm
       Sunday, 1 pm-5 pm

See: Franklin, Indiana, Carter's Factory Outlet.

Savings: 20% to 60% on all merchandise including Carter samples, closeouts, and irregulars.

Payment: Cash, check for exact amount with identification.
Parking: Large lot.

Nelsonville

BROOKS SHOES FACTORY OUTLET STORE
Meyers Street at rear of factory
Nelsonville, Ohio 45764
(Off US 33.)

phone: 614-753-1953

Hours: Monday-Saturday, 9 am-4:30 pm
Sunday, 12 noon-6 pm

Factory outlet store for William Brooks, manufacturer of men's shoes and boots and women's oxfords and dress shoes, retail priced from $36 to $60.
Savings: 40% and up on overruns, seconds, and factory-damaged shoes and boots.

Payment: Cash, check for exact amount, Master Charge, Visa.
Parking: Lot.

New Richmond

J & H CLASGENS COMPANY
Mill Store
500 Ohio Street
New Richmond, Ohio 45157

phone: 513-553-4177

Hours: Monday-Friday, 9 am-5 pm
Saturday, 9 am-12 noon

Old mill on the banks of the Ohio River. Outlet store sells knitting, weaving, rug, and crewel yarns in wool and orlon blends in a wide range of colors and weights and antique bobbins and spools.
Savings: 30% and up.

Payment: Cash, check with identification, Master Charge, Visa.
Parking: Side of mill.

North Olmsted

MATERNITY FACTORY OUTLET
Dan Howard Maternity Clothes
4591 Great Northern Boulevard
North Olmsted, Ohio 44138   phone: 216-734-0600
(Between Lorain and Brookpark Roads.)

Hours: Monday, Friday, 10 am-9 pm
       Tuesday, Wednesday, Thursday, Saturday, 10 am-6 pm
       Sunday, 12 noon-5 pm

See: Chicago, Illinois, Maternity Factory Outlet.

Savings: 20% to 50% on first quality production overruns, overcuts, and samples. Larger savings on seconds.

Payment: Cash, check with identification, Master Charge, Visa.
Parking: Lot.

Norwalk

FANNY FARMER QUALITY CANDIES
Old US 20 and Old State Road
East Main Street
Norwalk, Ohio 44851   phone: 419-668-2941

Hours: Monday-Friday, 8 am-5 pm
       Saturday, 9 am-5 pm

Fanny Farmer retail candy shop.
Savings: Up to 50% on 2½-lb. bags of mixed candy seconds, when available. Also some savings on store specials.

Payment: Cash, check for exact amount with identification.
Parking: Lot.

Parma

NEW YORK TEXTILES
5422 Pearl Road
Parma, Ohio 44129
(Near Ridge.)

phone: 216-842-4500

Hours: Monday, Thursday, 10 am-9 pm
Tuesday, Wednesday, Friday, 10 am-6 pm
Saturday, 10 am-5 pm

Manufacturer of Beauty Pleat Self-Pleat draperies. New York Textiles carries a wide range of decorator fabrics including slipcover and upholstery weights and drapery fabrics in a variety of textures, weights, weaves, and colors. They will custom make draperies to your measurements (and with your own fabric).
Savings: Up to 50% on first quality decorator fabrics.

Payment: Cash, check with identification, Master Charge, Visa.
Parking: In back of store.

Roseville

THE POT SHOP
Robinson-Ransbottom Pottery Company
County Road 32
Roseville, Ohio 43777

phone: 614-697-7355

Hours: Monday-Friday, 8 am-3 pm
Saturday, 8 am-10:30 am

Outlet for glazed and unglazed gardenware including flower pots, birdbaths, strawberry jars, pottery churns, water kegs, and stoneware planters. Also, brownware, decorated specialty pottery, pet feeders, and floral containers.
Savings: 35% and more on specials and seconds, when available.

Inquire about weekday tours through plant, said to be the oldest working pottery plant in the state.

Payment: Cash, check with identification.
Parking: In front of shop.

St. Marys

COTTON MILL STORE
134 East Spring Street
St. Marys, Ohio 45885   phone: 419-394-3064

Hours: Monday-Saturday, 9:30 am-5 pm
         Open Friday evenings until 9 pm
See: Cincinnati, Ohio, Cotton Mill Store.

Savings: 35% to 80% on firsts, discontinueds, overruns, seconds, and irregulars.

Payment: Cash, check, Master Charge, Visa.
Parking: Metered—nickels, dimes.

Scio

SCIORAMIC
Scio Pottery Company, Inc.
Eastport Road Extension
Scio, Ohio 43988   phone: 614-945-4101
(Across the street from the plant.)

Hours: Monday-Saturday, 12 noon-6 pm

Outlet for Scio Pottery mugs and dinnerware sets in service for 4, 6, and 8. Patterns include Avon, Blue Onion, Brownware, Currier and Ives, Dorset, Hazel, Meadow Blue, Platinum, Swirl, and Tempo.
Savings: 25% and up on first quality dinnerware sets; more on mugs.

Payment: Cash, check for exact amount with identification, Master Charge, Visa.
Parking: Lot.

Silverton

CANNON TOWEL OUTLET
6926½ Montgomery Road
Silverton, Ohio 45236   phone: 513-793-5996

Hours: Monday-Saturday, 10 am-6 pm
April 1-December 24—Sunday, 12 noon-5 pm
See: Foster, Ohio, Cannon Towel Outlet.

Savings: 30% to 70% on Cannon towel irregulars and seconds, Chatham blanket seconds, and remnants sold by the pound.

Payment: Cash, check for exact amount with identification, Master Charge, Visa.
Parking: Lot.

Solon

STOUFFER'S THRIFT STORE
5750 Harper Road
Solon, Ohio 44139   phone: 216-248-0700

Hours: Monday-Friday, 10 am-5 pm
Saturday, 9 am-3 pm

Outlet for Stouffer Foods frozen main dishes and side dishes including spinach, asparagus, and cheese souffles, potato and vegetable dishes, and meat entrees.
Savings: 25% to 50% on "tests," samples, closeouts, and seconds.

Payment: Cash, check for exact amount with identification.
Parking: Lot.

Strongsville

BROWNBERRY OVENS THRIFT STORE
8381 Pearl Road
Strongsville, Ohio 44146   phone: 216-243-5294

Hours: Monday-Friday, 9 am-7 pm
Saturday, 9 am-6 pm
Sunday, 10 am-5 pm

See: LaGrange Park, Illinois, Brownberry Ovens Thrift Store.

Savings: 33⅓% and up on day-old and seconds. Extra 10% savings on Tuesdays.

Payment: Cash, check for exact amount with identification.
Parking: In front.

Tiffin

TIFFIN GLASS COMPANY FACTORY OUTLET STORE
Towle Silver
Fourth Avenue and Vine Street
Tiffin, Ohio 44883   phone: 419-447-5313

Hours: Monday–Saturday, 9 am–5 pm
        June to October—Sunday, 12 noon–5 pm

Tiffin produces more than 50 crystal stemware patterns and 2 lines of casual crystal. The store carries seconds, when available, of many of these patterns, in addition to hand-blown crystal accessories such as paperweights, animals, and fruit; pitchers, vases, candy dishes, plates, mugs, and barware; and flowerpots and bowls from Libbey, L. E. Smith, and West Virginia Glass.
Savings: Average 50% on seconds or "less-than-perfect."

Tours of Tiffin can be arranged in advance. (Children under 6 are not permitted on tours.)

Payment: Cash, check, American Express, Diner's Club, Master Charge, Visa.
Parking: Lot.

Toledo

BASSETT NUT COMPANY
43 South Huron Street
Toledo, Ohio 43602   phone: 419-243-7544

Hours: Monday-Friday, 8:30 am–5 pm

Edible nuts sold in 1-lb. minimum packs: cashews, peanuts, macadamia nuts, almonds, pecans, and mixed nuts.
Savings: 35% and up on good quality nut meats.

Payment: Cash, check for exact amount with identification.
Parking: Street.

DISTINCTIVE COSTUMES, INC.
2223 Ashland Avenue
Toledo, Ohio 43620
(Right off Bancroft Avenue.)

phone: 419-246-7243

Hours: Monday-Saturday, 10 am-5:30 pm

Manufacturer of clown and Santa Claus costumes, specialty uniforms, and a basic leotard.

Savings: 20% and up on clearance costumes and sample costumes, with greatest savings in October, just before Halloween.

Also: Savings on fabrics, trims, and supplies for making costumes.

Payment: Cash, check for exact amount with identification.
Parking: Street.

LIBBEY GLASSWARE SALES ROOM
1205 Buckeye Street
Toledo, Ohio 43611
(Across from Libbey Plant.)

phone: 419-247-2374

Hours: Tuesday-Saturday, 9:30 am-5:30 pm

Retail showroom for Libbey's nationally advertised table glassware. A large selection of tumblers, stemware, glass and barware sets, pitchers, decanters, cannisters, crystal glass flowerpots, mushrooms, ginger jars, terrariums, ashtrays, etc.

Savings: Average 33⅓% on first quality glassware.

Payment: Cash, Master Charge, Visa.
Parking: Lot.

Twinsburg

BROWNBERRY OVENS THRIFT STORE
2000 Highland Boulevard
Twinsburg, Ohio 44087

phone: 216-425-7842

Hours: Monday-Saturday, 8 am-5:30 pm
See: LaGrange Park, Illinois, Brownberry Ovens Thrift Store.

Savings: 33⅓% and up on day-old and seconds. Extra 10% savings on Tuesdays.

Payment: Cash, check for exact amount with identification.
Parking: Lot.

Van Wert

FACTORY OUTLET
Van Wert Manufacturing Company
Main and Market Streets
Van Wert, Ohio 45891								phone: 419-238-3747

Hours: Monday, Tuesday, Thursday, Friday, 12:30 pm-4:30 pm

Store is located on first floor of Home Guards Temple Building. Polyfill insulated and quilted coats for women in sizes 8 to 28; jackets for men and boys in sizes small to XXXL. Also, nylon taffeta and corduroy warm-up and athletic jackets, lined and unlined, and unlined polyester double knit blazers for men and women.
Savings: 33⅓% to 80% on discontinueds, closeouts, and irregulars. Good savings on fabric piece goods, trimmings, zippers, and large fabric pieces for quilting.

Payment: Cash, check for exact amount with identification.
Parking: Metered—pennies, nickels, dimes.

KENNEDY MANUFACTURING COMPANY
QUALITY CONTROL REJECT OUTLET
201 North Cherry Street
Van Wert, Ohio 45891								phone: 419-238-2442

Hours: Monday-Friday, 9 am-4:30 pm
       Saturday, 8 am-12 noon

Manufacturer of high quality steel tool boxes, tool chests, tote trays, small parts organizers, and roller cabinets. Products that do not meet the high quality standards are sold in the Reject Outlet.
Savings: 50% on rejects.

Payment: Cash only.
Parking: Next to building.

Vermilion

THE POTTERY CUPBOARD #6
4340 Liberty Avenue
Vermilion, Ohio 44089   phone: 216-967-4070

Hours: Winter—Tuesday-Saturday, 10 am-5 pm
                  Sunday, 12 noon-5 pm
                  Closed Mondays
            Summer—Monday-Saturday, 10 am-5:30 pm
                  Sunday, 12 noon-5:30 pm
                  Open Friday evenings until 8 pm

The Pottery Cupboards are subsidiaries of the Anchor Hocking Corporation and carry first quality, closeouts, and seconds in glass bakeware and tableware; ceramic, glass, and plastic microwave ovenware; gourmet cooking items and giftware; and Taylor, Smith and Taylor dinnerware, Hall Pottery, and Indiana Glass.
Savings: Average 50% on seconds.

Mail order available through:
National Retailers Guild, Inc.
825 Phoenix Avenue
PO Box 268
Chester, West Virginia 26034
phone: 304-387-2626

Payment: Cash, check, Master Charge, Visa.
Parking: Lot.

Wapakoneta

B AND M PACKING COMPANY
Bohrer and Moore
711 North Dixie Highway
Wapakoneta, Ohio 45805   phone: 419-738-7719
(Old US 25. Building is located back from the highway down a long drive. Entrance is to left of the chimney on the loading dock and through the pull-up doors.)

Hours: Monday-Friday, 9 am-5 pm
            Saturday, 9 am-11 am

B and M processes meats under the B and M and Koneta Brand Lunchmeat labels. Pork and beef lunch meats including Dutch and

pepper loaves, 3 kinds of bologna, dried beef, old-fashioned wieners in 6- or 7-lb. bags, and coney sticks in 2-lb. bags.
Savings: 30% and up on loaves of lunch meat.

Also: Beef and pork special cuts at savings.

Payment: Cash, check for exact amount with identification.
Parking: Lot.

BUTCHER SHOP
Walter and Sons, Inc.
703 North Dixie Highway
Wapakoneta, Ohio 45895   phone: 419-738-2612
(Old US 25.)

Hours: Monday–Friday, 9 am–5 pm
Saturday, 9 am–2 pm

Retail outlet for portioned beef and pork products and sausage. Available in freezer packs are beef patties, oxtails, tongue, hearts, sweetbreads, neckbones, and T-bone, strip, and rib-eye steaks. Also chunk, slab, and sliced bacon, Canadian bacon, hamburger, wieners, turkey rolls, and beef sides or beef hindquarters.
Savings: 25% and up on freezer-pack restaurant quality meats.

Payment: Cash, check for exact amount with identification.
Parking: Lot.

Waverly

OHIO STEAK AND BARBECUE COMPANY
James Road
Waverly, Ohio 45690   phone: 614-947-7165
(Back of Big Bear Shopping Center.)

Hours: Monday–Friday, 3 pm–6 pm

See: Columbus, Ohio, Ohio Steak and Barbecue Company.

Savings: 20% and up on ready-to-cook-and-serve products packaged in bulk for institutional use and home freezers.

Call first to place order.

Payment: Cash, check for exact amount with identification.
Parking: Lot.

West Carrollton

SILCO DISPOSABLE PRODUCTS DIVISION
5335 Springboro Pike, Suite E and F
West Carrollton, Ohio 45439   phone: 513-293-9795

Hours: Monday-Friday, 8 am-5 pm

Industrial and commercial supplier now selling case lots of paper products directly to the consumer: toilet tissue, handiwipes, paper towels, and plastic leaf and garbage bags.
Savings: 20% to 50% on case lot orders.

Delivery of case orders in the greater Dayton area at no extra cost.

Payment: Cash, check.
Parking: Lot.

Westlake

PEPPERIDGE FARM THRIFT STORE
Cambridge Commons Shopping Center
26457 Center Ridge Road
Westlake, Ohio 44145   phone: 216-835-5743

Hours: Monday-Friday, 10 am-6 pm
       Saturday, 9 am-5 pm
See: Downers Grove, Illinois, Pepperidge Farm Thrift Store.
Savings: 25% to 50%.

For best selection, shop around 11 am.

Payment: Cash, check for exact amount with identification.
Parking: Lot.

Whitehall

PEPPERIDGE FARM THRIFT STORE
3741 East Broad Street
Whitehall, Ohio 43213   phone: 614-239-0221

Hours: Monday-Friday, 9 am-5:30 pm
        Saturday, 9 am-5 pm
See: Downers Grove, Illinois, Pepperidge Farm Thrift Store.
Savings: 25% to 50%.

For best selection, shop early when store opens.

Payment: Cash, check for exact amount with identification.
Parking: Lot.

Willoughby

DALTON OF AMERICA FACTORY STORE
4545 Dalton Boulevard
Willoughby, Ohio 44094   phone: 216-946-7799

Hours: Tuesday, Thursday, Saturday, 10 am-3 pm
See: Bedford, Ohio, Dalton Factory Outlet.
Savings: 50% on first quality; greater savings on seconds.

Also: 60" wide polyesters, wools, and knits sold by the yard.
Savings: 50%.

This is the largest of the Dalton Factory Stores. No fitting rooms. You may try on blouses or sweaters that button in front.

Payment: Cash, check for exact amount with identification.
Parking: Lot.

HOUGH BAKERIES, INC., SURPLUS STORE
4113 Erie Street
Willoughby, Ohio 44094   phone: 216-942-6617

Hours: Monday-Saturday, 8 am-6 pm
See: Cleveland, Ohio, Hough Bakeries, Inc., Thrift Store.
Savings: 40% to 60% on day-old bread and pastry seconds.

Payment: Cash, traveler's checks.
Parking: Street.

Wooster

REGAL WARE OUTLET STORE
770 Spruce Street
Wooster, Ohio 44691   phone: 216-262-3015
(Old Ohio 3.)

Hours: Monday-Friday, 8:30 am-4:30 pm

Outlet store for Regal Ware, manufacturers of sheet and cast aluminum cookware; teflon-coated stainless steel cookware; and porcelain, enamel, and color crafted cookware. Also coffee-makers (4-cup and 8-cup), percolators, frying pans, popcorn poppers, broilers, fondue pots, griddles, etc. Brand names include Regal, Duncan Hines, Accent, Imperial, etc.
Savings: 10% below retail on first quality products; up to 50% on seconds, discontinueds, and closeouts. Incredible buys in the "bargain box."

Payment: Cash, check for exact amount with identification.
Parking: Lot.

Zanesville

McCOY RETAIL STORE
Nelson McCoy Pottery Retail Store
US 22 and Ohio 93
Zanesville, Ohio 43701   phone: 614-454-2421
(3 miles south of Zanesville.)

Hours: Monday-Saturday, 9:30 am-6 pm
        Sunday, 12 noon-6 pm

Glazed pottery cookie jars, bowls, vases, planters, miniature straw-

berry pots, vases, and brownware dinnerware, serving pieces, and coffee mugs.
Savings: 50% on discontinueds and closeouts and up to 80% on seconds and irregulars.

Payment: Cash, check for under $10, Master Charge, Visa.
Parking: Lot.

OHIO POTTERY FACTORY OUTLET
US 40 West—National Road
Zanesville, Ohio 43701   phone: 614-452-1858
(Exit 151 off Interstate 70, Zanesville city limits.)

Hours: Open seven days, 9 am until dark

Outlet for Ohio Pottery, Imperial Glass, and Hall Pottery: garden statues, figures, birdbaths, plant pots, vases, bean pots, and sets of brownware, ironstone in various colors, and stoneware.
Savings: 50% on seconds with small flaws.

Payment: Cash, check, Master Charge, Visa.
Parking: Lot.

OLD TRAIL POTTERY
East Pike
Zanesville, Ohio 43701   phone: 614-453-7069
(½ block south of Zanesville/Interstate 70, Exit 157.)

Hours: Monday-Saturday, 10 am-5 pm

Outlet for Hall Pottery brownware settings. Dinner sets available in 4-place, 6-place, and 8-place settings. Also carry other local pottery lines and a large selection of flowerpots.
Savings: 50% on seconds with minor flaws in pattern or glaze.

Payment: Cash only.
Parking: Lot.

WISCONSIN

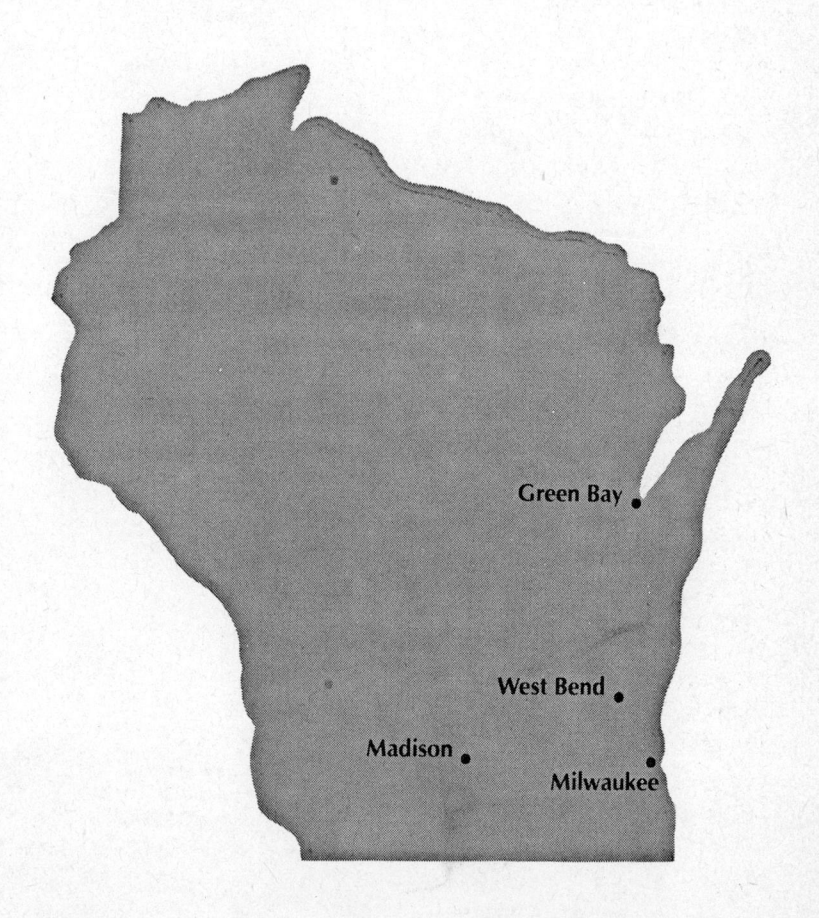

Antigo

WEINBRENNER FACTORY STORE
US 45 North—Next to Copp's Shopping Center
Antigo, Wisconsin 54409　　　　　　　　　phone: 715-623-4705
(Corner of US 45 and Wisconsin 52.)

Hours:　Monday-Saturday, 9 am-5 pm
　　　　Sunday, 12 noon-5 pm
　　　　Open Friday evenings until 9 pm

Weinbrenner manufactures golf shoes and outdoor, safety, and work shoes under the Thorogood, Wood 'N Stream, Mulligans, and Weinbrenner labels, which are sold through major sporting goods retailers and catalog sources.

The factory outlet sells men's boots and work boots and dress, sport, and work shoes in sizes 7 to 13, A, B, C, and D widths. Shoes are "factory damaged" with slight flaws, many of which have been corrected.
Savings: At least 50% on good quality footwear for men.

Payment: Cash, check with identification, Master Charge, Visa.
Parking: Lot.

Appleton

KNIT PIKKER FACTORY OUTLET
306 North Richmond Street
Appleton, Wisconsin 54911　　　　　　　phone: 414-739-1711
(Corner of Franklin and North Richmond Streets. Next to Zwicker Knitting Mills.)

Hours:　Monday, Friday, 10 am-8 pm
　　　　Tuesday, Wednesday, Thursday, Saturday, 10 am-5 pm

Outlet for Zwicker Knitting Mills knitwear, Quality Mills Apparel for all members of the family (from infants' wear to men's extra large), and Illinois Yarn Company hand knitting yarns.

A wide variety of knitwear for all the family: hats, scarves, mittens, gloves, sweaters, vests, and slipper sox.
Savings: 20% to 60% on factory overruns, company returns, sales representatives' samples, and discontinueds.

Payment: Cash, check for exact amount with identification.
Parking: Lot on corner.

PLANT STORE
Rich Products
Elm Tree Frozen Foods Corporation
3300 West College Avenue
Appleton, Wisconsin 54911   phone: 414-739-3111

Hours: Tuesday-Saturday, 10 am-6 pm

Unbaked frozen and fresh baked-off breads, rolls, 8" layer cakes (iced and uniced), sheet cakes (iced and uniced), pies, sweet rolls, and cookies.
Savings: 25% and up on frozen unbaked product. 50% and more on fresh, baked-off "baker's mistakes." (Elm Tree has a baker's school where bake-off techniques are taught.)

Payment: Cash, check for exact amount with identification.
Parking: Lot.

Arcadia

ARCADIA FURNITURE FACTORY MART
East Washington Street
Arcadia, Wisconsin 54612   phone: 608-323-7442
(Wisconsin 93.)

Hours: Monday, Tuesday, Wednesday, Friday, 9 am-5:30 pm
        Thursday, 9 am-9 pm
        Saturday, 9 am-5 pm
        Sunday, 1 pm-5 pm
        Thanksgiving to Christmas—Monday-Friday, 9 am-9 pm
                                  Saturday, 9 am-5 pm
                                  Sunday, 1 pm-5 pm

Outlet for Arcadia Furniture Corporation bookcases, end tables, and coffee tables in hickory, oak, pine, and pecan wood composition with vinyl surfaces. Six-foot bookcases are 24" wide and 12" deep and 30" wide and 15" deep.
Savings: Average 33⅓% less than retail on Arcadia Furniture Company bookcases.

Payment: Cash, check, Master Charge, Visa.
Parking: Lot.

Ashland

LARSON PICTURE FRAME, INC.
422 Third Street West
Ashland, Wisconsin 54806 phone: 715-682-5257
(Corner of Vaughan and Third.)

Hours: Monday, Tuesday, Wednesday, Friday, 8 am-5 pm
Thursday, 8 am-9 pm
Saturday, 9 am-5 pm

Manufacturer of all-wood picture frames from mini (5" × 7" and smaller) to 24" × 36". A variety of styles in walnut and light oak finishes.
Savings: 40% to 70% on seconds and overruns.

Payment: Cash, check for exact amount with identification, Master Charge, Visa.
Parking: Lot.

Baraboo

McARTHUR TOWELS, INC.
700 Moore Street
Baraboo, Wisconsin 53913 phone: 608-356-8922

Hours: Monday-Friday, 8 am-4:30 pm

Manufacturers of "thirsty," heavy-duty, long-lasting institutional towels, beach towels in colors (45"×72"), sport towels, and robes to order. Standard 20"×40" towels, comparable to quality towels sold in retail outlets, in white or white with stripes, in various weights. Sold by the dozen.
Savings: Up to 50%. Also, 65% or better on "grab bag," seconds, and irregulars sold by the pound—2 or 3 towels to the pound.

Also: Laundry bags and detergent in 125-lb. drums at good savings.

Payment: Cash, check for exact amount with identification.
Parking: Lot and street.

Beaver Dam

GARDNER BAKING COMPANY BAKERY THRIFT STORE
1010 De Clark Street
Beaver Dam, Wisconsin 53916 phone: 414-887-2233

Hours: Monday-Friday, 9 am-5 pm
       Saturday, 9 am-4 pm

Bakery outlet store for day-old product and some fresh including breads, hard and soft rolls, buns, English muffins, cakes, pies, doughnuts, sweet rolls, and snack pies, corn chips, taco and cheese snacks, and pretzels.
Savings: Up to 40% on day-old product.

Payment: Cash, check for exact amount with identification.
Parking: Lot.

Belgium

ALLEN EDMONDS SHOE BANK
775 Main Street
Belgium, Wisconsin 53004   phone: 414-285-7922
(1 mile west of Interstate 43, County Road D.)

Hours: Monday-Saturday, 9 am-5 pm

Outlet store for Allen Edmonds quality men's shoes, sizes 5 to 16 and AAAA to EEE widths.
Savings: 30% to 40% on factory-damaged and closeout shoes.

Payment: Cash, check for exact amount, Master Charge, Visa.
Parking: Street.

Beloit

CARPET SECONDS
1220 Cranston Road
Beloit, Wisconsin 53511   phone: 608-362-7113
(1 block west of Exit 190, Wisconsin 15.)

Hours: Monday-Friday, 8:30 am-8:30 pm
       Saturday, 9:30 am-4 pm

Synthetic fiber carpeting in seconds, closeouts, and discontinued patterns and colors from such carpet mills as Coronet and World. Available in 12' widths in assorted patterns and colors. Stair widths cut from the roll.
Savings: Up to 50%.

Payment: Cash, check with identification.
Parking: In front.

FREEMAN SHOE FACTORY OUTLET
Division of United States Shoe Corporation
Freeman Lane
Beloit, Wisconsin 53511   phone: 608-365-0964
(Wisconsin 15, one mile west of Interstate 90.)

Hours: Monday-Friday, 10 am-9 pm
       Saturday, 10 am-6 pm
       Sunday, 11 am-5 pm

The United States Shoe Corporation manufactures shoes for men, women, and children under a wide variety of labels including such well-knowns as Freeman, French Shriner, H.I.S., Free-Flex, William Joyce, Etienne Aigner, Amalfi, Pappagallo, Red Cross, and others.
Savings: Up to 50% on famous name brand shoes that are cancellations, overruns, or have slight factory imperfections.

Payment: Cash, check with identification, American Express, Master Charge, Visa.
Parking: Lot.

Berlin

MEDALIST SAND KNIT COMPANY
290 Junction Street
Berlin, Wisconsin 54923   phone: 414-361-0808

Twice-a-year factory warehouse weekend sale, usually held in April and October. Write or call for exact date of sale.

Note: Factory is not open for retail sales except for these two weekends each year.

Medalist Sand Knit manufactures athletic wear and casual recreation clothes for men, women, and children including football jerseys and pants, sweat suits, jogging shirts, slacks, and golf shirts.
Savings: Up to 50% on discontinueds, seconds, and a "little bit of everything" including cotton and polyester knit fabrics at the twice-a-year factory warehouse weekend sale.

Payment: Cash only.
Parking: Lot.

MID-WESTERN SPORT TOGS
150 Franklin Street
Berlin, Wisconsin 54923   phone: 414-361-2555

Hours: Monday-Friday, 8 am-5 pm
        September to May—Saturdays, 8 am-3 pm
        June to August—Saturdays, 8 am-12 noon

Manufacturer of top quality leather coats, jackets, handbags, vests, gloves, shoes, moccasins, slippers, boots, hats, and accessories (wallets, key cases, eyeglass cases, tobacco pouches, change purses, and cigarette cases).

Women's coats, jackets, and vests in small, medium, and large, size 32 and up; men's coats, jackets, and vests in sizes 38 to 50. Also: Children's jackets, vests, mittens.
Savings: Up to 50% on salesman's samples, factory seconds, and closeouts.

Payment: Cash, check, Master Charge, Visa.
Parking: Customer parking area in front.

UNIVERSAL FABRICS COMPANY, INC.
151 West Park Avenue
Berlin, Wisconsin 54923   phone: 414-361-1525

Factory overrun sale held several times a year. Call for exact date of next sale.

Universal manufactures jumpsuits and sweat suits for men and women in small, medium, and large sizes.
Savings: 30% off factory wholesale price for first quality overruns and discontinueds during the factory overrun sale.

Payment: Cash, check for exact amount with identification.
Parking: Lot.

Brookfield

BROWNBERRY OVENS THRIFT STORE
17365 West Bluemound Road
Brookfield, Wisconsin 53005 phone: 414-782-8950

Hours: Monday-Thursday, 9 am-6 pm
Friday, 9 am-7 pm
Saturday, 8 am-5 pm
Sunday, 10 am-4 pm

See: LaGrange Park, Illinois, Brownberry Ovens Thrift Store.

Savings: 33⅓% and up on day-old bread and seconds. Extra 10% savings on Tuesdays.

Payment: Cash only.
Parking: In front.

Chippewa Falls

MASON RETAIL SHOE STORE
307 North Bridge Street
Chippewa Falls, Wisconsin 54729 phone: 715-723-4323
(Next to J C Penney Store.)

Hours: Monday-Saturday, 9 am-5 pm
Open Thursday evenings until 9 pm

Outlet for Mason Shoe Company, manufacturers of dress and work shoes and sandals for men under the Chippewa, Velvet-Eez, Mason, Chief, Foot Preservers, and Mason Flex labels, in sizes 6 to 14, AA to EEEE widths.
Savings: From 40% up for closeouts and factory damaged.

Also: Store carries, when available, closeouts in women's shoes, sizes 5 to 10, at good savings.

Payment: Cash, check with identification.
Parking: Metered—pennies, nickels.

Cudahy

J C PENNEY CATALOG OUTLET STORE
5656 South Packard Street
Cudahy, Wisconsin 53110　　　　　　phone: 414-769-6210

Hours: Monday-Friday, 9:30 am-9 pm
　　　　Saturday, 9:30 am-5 pm
　　　　Sunday, 11 am-4 pm

See: Villa Park, Illinois, J C Penney Catalog Outlet Store.

Savings: 40% and up on catalog surplus and returned merchandise including clothing, furniture, and sports equipment.

Payment: Cash, check with identification, J C Penney charge card, Visa.
Parking: Lot.

Eau Claire

BUDGET DRAPERY
Wisconsin and Farrell Streets
Eau Claire, Wisconsin 54701　　　　phone: 715-835-7928

Hours: Monday-Friday, 8:30 am-4 pm
　　　　Saturday, 9 am-3 pm

Outlet for Robertson Factories, Inc., of Massachusetts, one of the country's largest manufacturers of custom-made and ready-made draperies and bedspreads for major catalog retailers.

Discontinued styles, returns, and slight irregulars in ready-made draperies and quilted and unquilted bedspreads in twin, full, queen, and king sizes. Also: Fabrics, fringes, and curtain rods.
Savings: 40% to 80% on discontinueds and slight irregulars.

For excellent savings on custom-made draperies for your home, measure your windows and bring measurements with you when you shop Budget Drapery. A wide range of fabrics are available including antique satins, sheers, casements, thermal back, open weave, printed cottons, and blends.

Payment: Cash, check with identification.
Parking: Lot.

Fond du Lac

DICK BROTHERS BAKERY THRIFT STORE
21 North Macy Street
Fond du Lac, Wisconsin 54935   phone: 414-922-0500

Hours: Monday–Friday, 9 am–5:30 pm
          Saturday, 9 am–3 pm

Bakery outlet store for day-old and some fresh products including breads, buns, English muffins, bread sticks, doughnuts, sweet rolls, and snack cakes. Brands include Butternut, Dick Brothers, Holsum, Olympic Meal, Hillbilly, Weight Watchers, and Country Hearth, which is made of all natural ingredients.

Savings: Up to 40% on day-old. Also, small savings on fresh products.

Payment: Cash only.
Parking: Lot.

FLORENCE EISEMAN, INC.
631 South Hickory Street
Fond du Lac, Wisconsin 54935   phone: 414-922-0030

Write to be placed on mailing list for notice of twice-a-year sale.

Manufacturing facility for Florence Eiseman, Inc., designers and manufacturers of excellent quality clothes for infants, toddlers, small girls and boys, and girls' preteens to size 14.

Twice-a-year sale, usually in April and October, runs for one or two weekends only. All samples, overruns, and discontinueds are sold.
Savings: 60% and more on top quality, beautifully-styled garments.

Payment: Cash, check for exact amount with identification.
Parking: Lot.

Fort Atkinson

JONES DAIRY FARM RETAIL STORE
Jones Street off Wisconsin 26
Fort Atkinson, Wisconsin 53538   phone: 414-563-2963
(Take 6th Street over tracks, then first right. Yellow brick building to the left of shipping dock.)

Hours: Monday-Friday, 8:30 am-12:25 pm
1 pm-4:15 pm
Saturday, 8 am-11:55 am

Top quality pork and pork products including sausages, roasts, chops, ribs, tenderloins, hams, bacon, and liver sausage.
Savings: Average 30% on seconds of manufactured items. Small savings on other products of quality surpassing most meat counters.
Payment: Cash only.
Parking: Large lot.

Green Bay

BACK DOOR STORE FACTORY OUTLET
1514 Morrow Street
Green Bay, Wisconsin 54302   phone: 414-437-4935

Hours: Monday-Saturday, 9 am-5 pm
Outlet for Fabry Glove and Mitten Company, Inc., manufacturer of fabric combined with leather, and all leather dress, sport, and work gloves under the Fabray and Saranac labels.
Savings: 50% and up on glove seconds and discontinueds.

Also: First quality sheepskin coats for men (sizes 36 to 46) and women (sizes 10 to 16) manufactured by Ardney in Milwaukee.
Savings: Up to 40%.

The Back Door also sells closeouts, discontinueds, irregulars, and seconds in moccasins and leather accessories and discounts some name label sportswear for women.

Payment: Cash, check with identification, Master Charge, Visa.
Parking: Lot.

THE CHEESE HUT
1123 Main Street
Green Bay, Wisconsin 54301   phone: 414-432-5062

Hours: Monday-Saturday, 9:30 am-5:30 pm
The Cheese Hut supplies cheese to other retail sources.

Available are more than 100 varieties of cheeses (bulk, packaged, or spreads) from local and Wisconsin cheesemakers. Custom packed gift

boxes can be sent UPS directly from store.
Savings: 30% and more on frequent specials.

Payment: Cash, check for exact amount with identification.
Parking: In rear of building in Sundial Laundromat area or parking lot next to laundromat.

VALLEY BUSINESS INTERIORS
1830 West Mason Street
Green Bay, Wisconsin 54303　　　　　　phone: 414-499-4822

Hours: Monday-Friday, 8:30 am-5 pm

Outlet for Krueger Metal Products, manufacturers of steel folding and stacking chairs and molded fiberglass chairs.
Savings: 50% on metal furniture seconds.

Payment: Cash, check with identification, Master Charge, Visa.
Parking: Lot.

Hartford

W. B. PLACE AND COMPANY
368 West Sumner Street
Hartford, Wisconsin 53027　　　　　　phone: 414-673-3130

Hours: Monday-Friday, 8 am-5 pm
　　　　Saturday, 8 am-12 noon

Manufacturer of leather and deerskin jackets, coats, gloves, mittens, and moccasins in pigskin suede, deerskin, and deer-tanned cowhide grain. Also small leather accessories like billfolds, key cases, and coin purses.
Savings: About 35% on small leather accessories. Greater savings if customer supplies skins.

Also: One-pound bags of assorted leather scraps are great buys for crafts people.

Payment: Cash, check with identification.
Parking: Lot.

Hudson

OUTLET 9—BUDGET DRAPERY
1300 Industrial Road South
Hudson, Wisconsin 54016   phone: 715-386-8318

Hours: Tuesday-Saturday, 9 am-4 pm
   Open Thursday evenings until 9 pm
   Closed Mondays
See: Eau Claire, Wisconsin, Budget Drapery.
Savings: 20% to 50%.

Payment: Cash, check with identification.
Parking: Lot.

Iron River

J-MART SPORTING GOODS
J-Mart of Johnson Tackle Corporation
Corner of Main Street in center of town.
Iron River, Wisconsin 54847   phone: 715-372-4272

Hours: Monday-Saturday, 8 am-5:30 pm
   Sunday, 9 am-1 pm
Outlet for Brule Corporation, manufacturer of fishing rods.
Savings: Up to 65% on fishing rod samples, overruns, closeouts, discontinueds, and seconds.

Payment: Cash, check with identification.
Parking: In front.

Janesville

JAEGER BAKING COMPANY THRIFT STORE
1533 Monterey Lane
Janesville, Wisconsin 53545   phone: 608-754-1912

Hours: Monday-Saturday, 8:30 am-6 pm
   Sunday, 10 am-3 pm
Day-old bakery outlet for breads, buns, rolls, pastries, snack items,

and cakes. Some fresh products.
Savings: 33⅓% to 50%.

Best time to shop: Tuesday and Thursday mornings.

Payment: Cash only.
Parking: Lot.

J H COLLECTIBLES OUTLET STORE
A Junior House, Inc., Company
31 South Main Street
Janesville, Wisconsin 53545   phone: 608-752-3120

Hours: Monday-Thursday, 10 am-5:30 pm
        Friday, 10 am-7 pm
        Saturday, 10 am-4:30 pm

See: Milwaukee, Wisconsin, J H Collectibles Outlet Store.

Savings: 50% and up on first quality overruns, samples, and discontinued items in women's better priced sportswear, sizes 4 to 15.

Five fitting rooms.

Payment: Cash, check for exact amount with identification.
Parking: Street.

MONTEREY MILLS OUTLET STORE
1725 Delavan Drive
Janesville, Wisconsin 53545   phone: 608-754-8309
(In the "old sugar beet factory.")

Hours: Monday-Friday, 9 am-4 pm
        Saturday, 8 am-12 noon

Outlet store for Monterey Mills, Inc., manufacturer of knitted high pile fabrics in 60" widths and in all colors. Remnants and yardage from bolts in short, medium, and long pile fabrics, crushed velvets, quilted piles, imitation fur, and rug fabrics in 60" widths with rubber latex, non-skid backing.

Savings: 50% and better on first quality, closeouts, overruns, and discontinueds. Greater savings on seconds.

Also: Bathroom tank sets, novelty rugs, area rugs, and bags of sheared fiber ends for use as washable stuffing at good savings.

Payment: Cash, check for exact amount with identification.
Parking: Lot.

NORWOOD MILLS, INC.
2101 Kennedy Road
Janesville, Wisconsin 53545   phone: 608-756-0321

Hours: Monday-Friday, 9 am-4 pm
     Saturday, 9 am-12 noon

Factory outlet store for knitted pile fabrics in discontinued firsts, overruns, and seconds.

Fur-like fabrics for bedspreads, rugs, upholstery, floorcoverings, clothing, and stuffed animals in simulated fox, mink, raccoon, bear, etc., and in a variety of shades and markings. "Furs" in 13 standard colors and variations including white, black, and pastels.

Non-skid backed rug fabrics in 5' and 6' widths in short to long plush piles. Also bathroom tank sets, rugs, and den rugs.
Savings: 50% and up.

Also: Bagged, sheared fiber for stuffing pillows, animals, etc., sold by bag.

Payment: Cash, check for exact amount with identification.
Parking: Street or lot.

GARDNER BAKING COMPANY BAKERY THRIFT STORE
1720 Old Humes Road
Janesville, Wisconsin 53545   phone: 608-754-5541
(US 14.)

Hours: Monday-Friday, 9 am-5:30 pm
     Saturday, 9 am-5 pm

See: Beaver Dam, Wisconsin, Gardner Baking Company Bakery Thrift Store.
Savings: Up to 40% on day-old. Small discount on fresh goods. Extra 10% savings for senior citizens.

Payment: Cash, check for exact amount with identification, food stamps.
Parking: Lot.

Jefferson

BORG TEXTILE OUTLET STORE
South Gardiner Street
Jefferson, Wisconsin 53549   phone: 414-674-2092
(Right behind City Hall.)

Hours: Monday–Friday, 11 am–4 pm
        Saturday, 9 am–12 noon

Outlet store for overruns and seconds of Borg's knitted deep pile fabrics, Borg, Borgana, and Borgazia.

The man made, fur-like fabrics are made in 54" to 60" widths in plaids, stripes, and solid colors. Some are in crushed velvet textures. Some fabrics have rubberized backings for use as floor coverings. (A one-yard, 60" width piece makes a perfect 3'×5' accent rug.)
Savings: 50% to 70%.

Also: Bagged knit waste for stuffing pillows, toys, etc., and from time to time, when available, "fur" pillows, cut rugs in varying sizes, "fur" throws, and 3- to 5-piece bath sets.

Payment: Cash only.
Parking: Street.

Kenosha

CARTER'S FACTORY OUTLET
K-Mart Shopping Center
52nd Street
Kenosha, Wisconsin 53140   phone: 414-652-9002

Hours: Monday–Saturday, 10 am–5 pm
        Sunday, 1 pm–5 pm

See: Franklin, Indiana, Carter's Factory Outlet.

Savings: 30% to 60% on Carter samples, closeouts, and irregulars.

Payment: Cash, check for exact amount with identification.
Parking: Lot.

CONTOUR HOSIERY, INC.
2410 52nd Street
Kenosha, Wisconsin 53140   phone: 414-657-7131

Hours: Friday, 9 am-2:30 pm
Saturday, 9 am-6 pm

Outlet for Cannon, Bijou, Contour, Rapture, Larkwood, and Springfoot women's pantyhose in support, sheer, and service weights, seamed and seamless, opaque and patterned. Also, maternity and outsize hose and a large selection of hosiery for nurses.
Savings: Up to 50%.

Also: Men's and boys' full-fashioned hose, sox, and wool stockings.
Savings: Up to 40%.

Surgical support hose for men and women are also sold.

Payment: Cash, check for exact amount with identification.
Parking: Side of building.

Kewaskum

REGAL WARE, INC.
143 Main Street
Kewaskum, Wisconsin 53040   phone: 414-626-2121, ext. 433

Hours: Monday-Friday, 9 am-5 pm
Saturday, 9:30 am-12 noon
June, July, August—Monday-Friday, 9 am-4:30 pm
Saturday, 9 am-12 noon

Outlet store for Regal cookware, accessories, and portable electric and home security products including stainless steel cookware, bakeware, and bowls; aluminum bakeware and accessories; drawn and cast aluminum cookware; porcelain-coated and decorated exterior cookware; SilverStone and Teflon II treated interior cookware.

Also: Drip coffee makers, percolators, griddles, slow cookers, indoor grills, corn poppers, fondues, commercial and party-size coffee makers, travel kits, portable burglar alarms, and security lights.

Brand names include Duncan Hines, Poly-Perk, Coffee-Miser, The Griller, Poly Pot, and Startler.
Savings: Up to 50% on seconds, discontinueds, and closeouts.

Payment: Cash, check with identification.
Parking: Street.

Kewaunee

KEWAUNEE EQUIPMENT COMPANY
401 Park Street
Kewaunee, Wisconsin 54216　　　　　　phone: 414-388-3232

Hours: Monday-Friday, 9 am-11 am
　　　　　　　　　　 1 pm-3 pm

Manufacturer of baby equipment: walkers, playpens, baby seats and swings, strollers, and potty-chairs.
Savings: 20% on firsts bought here at the factory.

Payment: Cash, check for exact amount with identification.
Parking: In front.

Lake Geneva

J H COLLECTIBLES OUTLET STORE
A Junior House, Inc., Company
830 Main Street
Fancy Fair Mall
Lake Geneva, Wisconsin 53147　　　　　phone: 414-248-1151

Hours: Monday-Sunday, 10 am-5 pm

See: Milwaukee, Wisconsin, J H Collectibles Outlet Store.

Savings: 50% and up on first quality overruns, samples, and discontinued items in women's better priced sportswear, sizes 4 to 15.

Five fitting rooms.

Payment: Cash, check for exact amount with identification.
Parking: Lot.

Laona

CONNOR TRUE VALUE SHOPPING CENTER
US 8
100 Mill Road
Laona, Wisconsin 54541　　　　　　　phone: 715-674-2811

Hours: Monday-Thursday and Saturday, 9 am-5 pm
　　　　　Friday, 9 am-8 pm

Outlet for Connor Forest Industries, manufacturers of prefinished

cabinets, nursery and juvenile furniture, educational toys, and the Williamsburg Chair.
Savings: About 20% on first quality, well constructed juvenile furniture, and up to 50% on seconds when available.

Payment: Cash, check for exact amount with identification.
Parking: Lot.

Little Chute

KAUKAUNA DAIRY PRODUCTS
Division of International Multifoods Corporation
Wisconsin 96
Little Chute, Wisconsin 54140   phone: 414-788-9887
(1 mile east of Little Chute.)

Hours: Monday-Friday, 8 am-4:30 pm

Selling directly from the plant: Kaukauna Club, Swiss, mozzarella, Muenster, colby, and a variety of processed domestic cheeses.
Savings: Up to 25%.

Payment: Cash, check with identification.
Parking: Lot in front of plant.

PAPER SECONDS
500 South Wilson Street
Little Chute, Wisconsin 54140   no telephone
(On the corner.)

Hours: Monday-Friday, 10 am-12 noon
                         1 pm-4:30 pm
               Saturday, 9:30 am to 12 noon

Paper outlet for napkins, plates, cups, party goods, gift wrap, and children's books.
Savings: 50% and up.

Payment: Cash, check for exact amount with Wisconsin identification.
Parking: Street.

Loyal

LOYAL CANNING CORPORATION
Loyal, Wisconsin 54446 phone: 715-255-8521

Hours: Monday-Friday, 8 am-12 noon
                      1 pm-5 pm

Packers of peas and whole kernel corn, sold by case only.
Savings: Up to 50% on "dents" (first quality product in dented cans), when available.

Payment: Cash, check with identification.
Parking: Lot.

Madison

BROWNBERRY OVENS THRIFT STORE
2733 Atwood Avenue
Madison, Wisconsin 53704 phone: 608-241-1275

Hours: Monday-Friday, 8:30 am-6 pm
       Saturday, 8:30 am-5 pm
       Sunday, 10 am-4 pm

See: LaGrange Park, Illinois, Brownberry Ovens Thrift Store.

Savings: 33⅓% and up on day-old and seconds. Extra 10% savings on Tuesdays and Sundays.

Payment: Cash only.
Parking: In front.

THE CANNERY
2701 Packers Avenue, Wisconsin 113
Madison, Wisconsin 53974 phone: 608-249-6969
(1 block north of airport entrance.)

Hours: Wednesday, Thursday, Friday, 9 am-4 pm
       Saturday, 9 am-3 pm
       Closed Sundays, Mondays, and Tuesdays

Outlet for Oconomowoc Canning Company. Top quality Land O' Lakes brand canned goods sold in half-case and case lots. Unlabeled vegetable "dents" sold in one-case lots.

Label products include vegetables, fruits, juices, soups, pickles, catsup, tomato sauce and paste, olives, mushrooms, peanut butter,

grape jelly, and strawberry preserves.
Savings: 40% to 60% on cases of dented cans of vegetable product. Average of 15% savings on top quality, labeled canned product.

Payment: Cash, check for exact amount with identification.
Parking: Lot.

KNIT PIKKER FACTORY OUTLET
6220 Monona Drive
Madison, Wisconsin 53713   phone: 608-222-7253

Hours: Monday, 9 am-8 pm
        Tuesday-Friday, 9 am-6 pm
        Saturday, 9 am-4 pm

See: Appleton, Wisconsin, Knit Pikker Factory Outlet.

Savings: 20% to 60% on knitwear for all members of the family: overruns, company returns, sales representatives' samples, and discontinueds.

Also: Knitting and needlepoint yarns.

Payment: Cash, check for exact amount with identification.
Parking: Lot.

Manitowoc

SCHUETTE BROTHERS MIRRO FACTORY OUTLET STORE
814 Jay Street
Manitowoc, Wisconsin 54220   phone: 414-684-5521

Hours: Monday, 12 noon-9 pm
        Tuesday, Wednesday, Thursday, 12 noon-5 pm
        Friday, 9 am-9 pm
        Saturday, 9 am-1 pm

Mirro Aluminum Company manufactures cookware, bakeware, Teflon, Silverstone, and porcelain-coated utensils, foil containers, and appliances that include coffee makers, popcorn poppers, electric fry pans, and pressure pans. Also, children's cooking, baking, camp, and tea sets. Brand names include Mirro, Mirromatic, Mirrocraft, Comet, and Kitchen Pride.

Also: Store carries an assortment of Mirro overstocks and irregulars

and a large variety of cookware and bakeware priced under $1.
Savings: From 40% to 65% on overstocks, irregulars, and discontinueds.

Payment: Cash, check for exact amount with identification.
Parking: Lot on west side of store.

Marinette

SARANAC FACTORY STORE
1316 Marinette Avenue
Marinette, Wisconsin 54143   phone: 715-732-2385

Hours: Winter—Monday-Saturday, 9 am-5 pm
         Sunday, 12 noon-4 pm
         Open Thursday evenings until 9 pm
      Summer—Monday-Friday, 9 am-9 pm
         Saturday, 9 am-6 pm
         Sunday, 11 am-6 pm

Exclusive outlet for several Wisconsin leather manufacturers. Men's, women's, and children's leather gloves for dress, sports, skiing, snowmobiling, gardening, and work.

Men's leather coats, sized 38 to 46; women's leather coats, 6 to 18. Also: Leather handbags, belts, wallets, and moccasins.
Savings: 30% to 50%.

Payment: Cash, check with identification, Master Charge, Visa.
Parking: Lot.

Marshfield

WEINBRENNER FACTORY STORE
Wisconsin 13 North
Marshfield, Wisconsin 54449   phone: 715-387-6125

Hours: Monday-Saturday, 9 am-5 pm
      Friday, 9 am-9 pm
      Sunday, 12 noon-5 pm

See: Antigo, Wisconsin, Weinbrenner Factory Store.

Savings: At least 50% on good quality, "factory damaged" footwear for men.

Payment: Cash, check with identification, Master Charge, Visa.
Parking: Lot.

Menomonee Falls

HOLIDAY CUPS, INC.
W. 158, N. 9278 Nor X Way
Menomonee Falls, Wisconsin 53051   phone: 414-251-8770

Hours: Monday-Friday, 8:30 am-4:30 pm

Manufacturer of hot and cold drinking cups.
Savings: Up to 70% on misprinted cups.

A sign in the lobby describes various types of cups and prices.

Payment: Cash, check for exact amount with identification.
Parking: Lot.

Merrill

WEINBRENNER FACTORY STORE
Pine Ridge Oasis
Merrill, Wisconsin 54452   phone: 715-536-5559
(¼ mile west of US 51, Freeway Exit 64.)

Hours: Monday-Saturday, 9 am-5 pm
        Sunday, 12 noon-5 pm
        Open Friday evenings until 9 pm

See: Antigo, Wisconsin, Weinbrenner Factory Store.

Savings: At least 50% on good quality, "factory damaged" footwear for men.

Payment: Cash, check with identification, Master Charge, Visa.
Parking: Lot.

Milwaukee

AMBROSIA CHOCOLATE COMPANY
528 West Highland Avenue
Milwaukee, Wisconsin 53202   phone: 414-271-2081

Hours: Monday-Friday, 9:30 am-5:30 pm
        Saturday, 9:30 am-4 pm

Ambrosia makes 100 different kinds of candies including 50 hard candy varieties, a dietetic candy line, and chocolate specialties for cooking and eating. Blueberry, cherry, lemon, orange, peanut, and

chocolate chips for baking, jelly beans, and fresh nuts are among the items carried in the store.
Savings: Average 33⅓% with up to 50% on broken candy bars sold in 1½-lb. bags.

Mail orders accepted.

Payment: Cash, check for exact amount with Wisconsin identification.
Parking: Employees' lot; enter through 6th Street.

BRILL BROTHERS, INC.
2102 West Pierce Street
Milwaukee, Wisconsin 53201 phone: 414-672-6300

Write to have name put on mailing list for notice of once-a-year sale.

Manufacturer of men's and boys' outerwear, sportswear, and jackets in nylon, leather, wool, cotton, and blends. Also, school and team jackets, parkas, and some women's coats. Labels are Timberline, Golden Thread, Walkie Talkies.

Men's sizes 34 to 54; women's sizes 6 to 18; boys' and girls' sizes 3 to 20.

Once-a-year sale, usually in early December, of samples, overruns, irregulars, and discontinueds.
Savings: 50% and up.

Payment: Cash, check for exact amount with identification.
Parking: Lot.

THE CHOCOLATE HOUSE FACTORY OUTLET STORE
4121 South 35th Street
Milwaukee, Wisconsin 53221 phone: 414-281-7803

Hours: Monday-Friday, 9 am-5 pm
Saturday, 8:30 am-1 pm
Closed Saturdays in June, July, and August

Chocolate House makes fancy, quality dipped chocolates including nougats, creams, fruits, caramels, and nuts.
Savings: Up to 50% on seconds and overruns in bulk and packaged chocolates. Special holiday candy features.

Payment: Cash only.
Parking: Lot.

THE CLOTHES RACK
201 North Water Street
Milwaukee, Wisconsin 53208   phone: 414-271-4650
(Stuart Manufacturing Company—fifth floor.)

Hours: Monday-Friday, 8 am-4 pm
       Saturday, 8 am-12 noon

Outlet for Stuart Manufacturing Company, manufacturers of better priced ladies' and junior sportswear under nationally known and advertised labels. Jackets, skirts, blouses, shirts, sweaters, pants, and mix and match ensembles in sizes 3 to 16. Five dressing rooms.
Savings: 50% and up on samples, overruns, and closeouts.

Payment: Cash, check for exact amount with identification.
Parking: Street.

EVERITT KNITTING COMPANY
234 West Florida Street
Milwaukee, Wisconsin 53204   phone: 414-276-4647
(Store located in main building: walk through office.)

Hours: November to March—Monday-Friday, 10 am-3:30 pm

Write to be put on mailing list for November opening date.

Knitwear for girls, boys, and women. Sweaters, skirts, shirts, vests, pants, hats, scarves, and mittens.
Savings: Up to 50% on overruns, discontinueds, and irregulars.

Also: Excellent savings on 58" to 66" wide knitted fabrics and knit ribbing sold by the yard. Scraps sold by the pound. Acrilan and cotton yarns in all colors.

Payment: Cash, check with identification.
Parking: Street.

FLORENCE EISEMAN, INC.
301 North Water Street
Milwaukee, Wisconsin 53202   phone: 414-272-3222

Write to be placed on regular mailing list for notice of quarterly fabric sales.

Manufacturer of excellent quality clothing for children. Quarterly factory fabric sales of first quality, imported (often manufactured to

Florence Eiseman special order) bolt-ends, remnants, and cuttings from mills in England, France, Italy, and Switzerland.

Also: Trims, edgings, embroidered frontings, etc.
Savings: 50% and up.

Note: Sales begin on Friday and run through the following week.

Payment: Cash, check with identification, Master Charge, Visa.
Parking: Lot.

FRED USINGER, INC.
1030 North 3rd Street
Milwaukee, Wisconsin 53203   phone: 414-276-9100

Hours: Monday-Saturday, 8:30 am-5 pm

Milwaukee's famous sausage maker posts a store list of imperfects, when available, of knackwurst; frankfurters; bratwurst; mettwurst; tea wurst; blood, liver, and summer sausages; pastrami; roast pork; ham; and many more.

Take a number and wait your turn.
Savings: 25% and up on good-tasting "imperfects."

Payment: Cash.
Parking: Metered—nickels, dimes.

J C PENNEY CATALOG OUTLET STORE
103rd Street and Silver Spring Road
Milwaukee, Wisconsin 53201   phone: 414-464-1111

Hours: Monday-Friday, 9:30 am-9 pm
       Saturday, 9:30 am-5 pm
       Sunday, 12 noon-5 pm

See: Villa Park, Illinois, J C Penney Catalog Outlet Store.

Savings: 50% and up on catalog surplus and returned merchandise including furniture.

All mechanical items are serviced free before they're offered for sale.

Payment: Cash, check with identification, J C Penney charge card, Visa.
Parking: Lot.

J H COLLECTIBLES OUTLET STORE
A Junior House Inc. Company
710 South Third Street
Third and National Avenues
Milwaukee, Wisconsin 53240

phone: 414-744-5080
(Ask for outlet store.)

Hours: Monday-Saturday, 10 am-4 pm

Write to be placed on mailing list for advance notice of quarterly fabric sales.

Junior House manufactures a better quality women's sportswear line in sizes 4 to 15 including skirts, shirts, blouses, pants, jackets, and sweaters. Five fitting rooms.

Savings: 50% and up on first quality overruns, samples, and discontinued items.

Payment: Cash, check for exact amount with identification.
Parking: Lot.

KNIT PIKKER FACTORY OUTLET
500 South Third Street
Milwaukee, Wisconsin 53213

phone: 414-271-4703

Hours: Monday-Friday, 9 am-4 pm
Saturday, 9 am-2 pm

See: Appleton, Wisconsin, Knit Pikker Factory Outlet.

Savings: 20% to 60% on knitwear for all members of the family: overruns, company returns, sales representatives' samples, and discontinueds.

Also: Knitting and needlepoint yarns.

Payment: Cash, check for exact amount with identification.
Parking: Street.

MELCO CLOTHING COMPANY, INC.
200 South Water Street
Milwaukee, Wisconsin 53204
(Near North Water Street Bridge.)

phone: 414-273-6682

Hours: Saturday only, 8:30 am-12 noon

Large weekend sales scheduled three times a year. Send stamped, self-addressed, business sized envelope for advance notice of sales, usually held in February, June, and October.

Warehouse outlet for men's clothing (national brands and Melco label) including suits in sizes 37 to 52 (regular, long, and short lengths), sports coats, leather coats, slacks, rainwear, and outerwear.
Savings: 50% and more on all clothing during the three-times-a-year weekend sales, which begin at noon on Friday and continue until 4 pm on Sunday.

Payment: Cash sales only on Saturday morning. Master Charge and Visa accepted during the three-day weekend sales.
Parking: Lot.

MILWAUKEE SOAP COMPANY
1526 North 31st Street
Milwaukee, Wisconsin 53208   phone: 414-344-5300

Hours: Monday-Friday, 8 am-4:30 pm
Savings: 30% to 35% on controlled suds detergents; 30% on unwrapped, unlabeled paper products (towels and tissues), sold by case only.

Also: Dish detergents, window cleaners, bar soaps, and cleaning supplies at good savings.

Will deliver in Milwaukee if order is $60 or more.

Payment: Cash, check for exact amount.
Parking: Lot.

MILWAUKEE SOAP COMPANY
5661 South 27th Street
Milwaukee, Wisconsin 53221   phone: 414-282-7880

Hours: Monday, Friday, 10 am-9 pm
        Tuesday, Wednesday, Thursday, 10 am-6 pm
        Saturday, 9 am-5 pm
Savings: 30% to 35%.

Payment: Cash, check for exact amount.
Parking: Lot.

MILWAUKEE SOAP COMPANY
142nd and Greenfield Avenue
Milwaukee, Wisconsin 53220   phone: 414-784-5821
(In Greenfield Plaza Shopping Center, Sunny Slope and Greenfield, Ranch Road side—far southwest corner.)

Hours: Monday, Friday, 9 am-9 pm
Tuesday, Wednesday, Thursday, 10 am-6 pm
Saturday, 9 am-5 pm
Savings: 30% to 35%.

Payment: Cash, check for exact amount with identification.
Parking: Lot.

MRS. KARL'S BAKERY THRIFT STORE
1923 West Pierce Street
Milwaukee, Wisconsin 53204   phone: 414-383-7920

Hours: Monday-Friday, 8:30 am-7 pm
Saturday, 8:30 am-5 pm
Sunday, 9 am-3 pm

Day-old bakery outlet for breads, rolls, layer and dessert cakes, doughnuts, and pastries.
Savings: Up to 50% on day-old.

Payment: Cash, check for exact amount with identification.
Parking: Side lot.

THE ODD LOT SHOE STORE
1007 North 3rd Street at State
Milwaukee, Wisconsin 53203   phone: 414-271-1964

Hours: Monday-Saturday, 9:30 am-5:30 pm

Factory outlet for men's dress and sports shoes with Weyenburg, Nunn Bush, and Stacy-Adams labels. Store also sells closeouts from other well-known shoe manufacturers.
Savings: 33⅓% to 50% on seconds, discontinueds, and closeouts—odds and ends of first quality merchandise.

Payment: Cash, check from Wisconsin residents with identification, Master Charge, Visa.
Parking: Metered—nickels, dimes.

THE ODD LOT SHOE STORE
Point Loomis Shopping Center
3555 South 27th Street at Morgan Avenue
Milwaukee, Wisconsin 53221   phone: 414-672-2771

Hours: Monday-Friday, 10 am-9 pm
        Saturday, 9:30 am-6 pm
        Sunday, 12 noon-5 pm

Savings: 20% to 50%.

Payment: Cash, check from Wisconsin residents with identification, Master Charge, Visa.
Parking: Lot.

THE ODD LOT SHOE STORE
Mill Road Shopping Center
6540 North 76th Street at Mill Road
Milwaukee, Wisconsin 53207   phone: 414-353-0540

Hours: Monday-Friday, 10 am-9 pm
        Saturday, 10 am-5:30 pm
        Sunday, 12 noon-5 pm

Savings: 33⅓% to 50%.

Payment: Cash, check from Wisconsin residents with identification, Master Charge, Visa.
Parking: Lot.

THE ODD LOT SHOE STORE
2944 South 108th Street
Southtown Shopping Center
Milwaukee, Wisconsin 53200   phone: 414-327-7770

Hours: Monday-Friday, 10 am-9 pm
        Saturday, 10 am-6 pm
        Sunday, 12 noon-5 pm

Savings: 33⅓% to 50%.

Payment: Cash, check from Wisconsin residents with identification, Master Charge, Visa.
Parking: Lot.

ODDS 'N ENDS SHOP
231 East Chicago Street
Milwaukee, Wisconsin 53203   phone: 414-272-5084
(In basement.)

Hours: Monday-Friday, 9 am-4 pm
Saturday, 8 am-12 noon
Open from mid-August to February 1

Outlet for Reliable Knitting Works, manufacturers of knit headwear, scarves, dickeys, knee sox, and washable slippers for men, women, and children under the labels Mukluks, Polar Boots, Scuffies, and Footlights.
Savings: 50% and up on first quality overruns and irregulars.

Also: Yarns at excellent savings. Write to be put on mailing list for August reopening date and for special sales notices.

Payment: Cash, check for exact amount with identification.
Parking: Street.

OSTER CORPORATION SERVICE DEPARTMENT
Division of Sunbeam Oster Corporation
5055 North Lydell Avenue
Milwaukee, Wisconsin 53217   phone: 414-332-8300

Hours: Monday-Friday, 7 am-4 pm
See: Chicago, Illinois, Sunbeam Appliance Service Company.
Savings: Up to 40% on reconditioned and overstock appliances with full one-year warranties.

Payment: Cash, check for exact amount with identification.
Parking: Street.

PEPPERIDGE FARM THRIFT STORE
3902 North 76th Street
Milwaukee, Wisconsin 53213   phone: 414-461-0050

Hours: Monday-Friday, 9 am-6 pm
        Saturday, 9 am-5 pm

See: Downers Grove, Illinois, Pepperidge Farm Thrift Store.

Savings: 25% to 50%.

For best selection, shop around 1 pm-2 pm.

Payment: Cash, check for exact amount with identification.
Parking: Lot.

THRIFTY LIQUOR AND PIPE MART
7218 West Greenfield Avenue
Milwaukee, Wisconsin 53200   phone: 414-453-2050

Hours: Monday-Friday, 9 am-9 pm
        Saturday, 9 am-7 pm
        Open Sundays from Thanksgiving to January 1, 10 am-4 pm

Thrifty sells cigar seconds (cigars that don't meet the high "all colors must match in a box" standards) from American companies and, when available, some seconds in import brands.

Savings: Average 50% on cigar seconds.

Also: Pipe seconds and pipe tobacco seconds that aren't up to the top level standards for particular blends.

Savings: Up to 75% on pipe seconds. Incredibly high on tobacco seconds.

Payment: Cash.
Parking: Street.

Mishicot

ANDERCRAFT WOODS
Church Street
Mishicot, Wisconsin 54228   phone: 414-755-4014
(Straight east of Fox Hills.)

Hours: Saturday, 9 am–4 pm
Sunday, 1 pm–4 pm
Monday, 8 am–5 pm

Andercraft makes a complete line of white cedar wood rustic planters for indoor and outdoor use (priced from around $3 to $22), bird feeders, wooden nativity sets, wall sconces, and craft items.
Savings: 25% to 55% on seconds and overruns.

Payment: Cash, check for exact amount with identification.
Parking: Lot.

Neenah

JERSILD STORE
318 First Street
Neenah, Wisconsin 54956   phone: 414-725-6912

Hours: Monday–Saturday, 10 am–4:30 pm

Direct outlet for Jersild Knitting Company, makers of knitted outerwear since 1895. Overruns, closeouts, and seconds in gloves, mittens, caps, blankets, and women's pants and in women's sweaters (sizes 34 to 42).

Also available are men's sweaters in small to extra large.
Savings: 50% and up on factory closeouts and seconds.

Also: Knit fabrics and yarns at good savings.

Payment: Cash, check for exact amount with identification, Master Charge, Visa.
Parking: Lot.

New Glarus

SWISS MISS
Wisconsin 69
New Glarus, Wisconsin 53574   phone: 608-527-2514

Hours: Monday–Saturday, 9 am–5 pm
Sunday, 12 noon–5 pm

Prime outlet for the two Upright Swiss Embroideries, Inc. plants,

manufacturers of Schiffli embroidered cottons, linens, woolens, knits, and satins in widths—depending on fabric—of up to 108".
Four floors of fashion fabrics, border prints, lace all-overs, lace trims, etc.
Savings: Up to 50% for first quality.

Also: Handkerchiefs, aprons, scarves, blankets.

Payment: Cash, check for exact amount with identification.
Parking: Large lot.

Oconomowoc

BROWNBERRY OVENS THRIFT STORE
1 Meadow Road
Oconomowoc, Wisconsin 53066   phone: 414-567-0667

Hours: Monday-Friday, 8:30 am-5:30 pm
       Saturday, 8:30 am-5 pm
       Sunday, 10 am-4 pm
See: LaGrange Park, Illinois, Brownberry Ovens Thrift Store.
Savings: 33⅓% and up on day-old and seconds. Extra 10% savings on Tuesdays and Sundays.

Payment: Cash only.
Parking: Lot.

THE CANNERY
616 East Wisconsin Avenue
Oconomowoc, Wisconsin 53066   phone: 414-567-6053

Hours: Wednesday, Thursday, Friday, 9 am-4 pm
       Saturday, 10 am-3 pm
       Closed on Sundays, Mondays, and Tuesdays
See: Madison, Wisconsin, The Cannery.
Savings: 40% to 60% on vegetable product "dents." Average of 15% savings on top quality, labeled cases of canned goods.

Payment: Cash, check for exact amount with identification.
Parking: Lot.

Oshkosh

THE LENOX SHOP
Lenox Candles
627 Bay Shore Drive
Oshkosh, Wisconsin 54901   phone: 414-231-9655
(On the shores of Lake Winnebago.)

Hours: Monday-Saturday, 9:30 am-5 pm

Manufacturer of candles, candle holders, floral rings, soaps, and bath products. Lenox and Carolina products.

Shop carries a complete line of gift items, Lenox china, and crystal and Imperial glass. Seconds room in the back.
Savings: 50% and more on seconds.

Payment: Cash, check with identification, Master Charge, Visa.
Parking: Lot.

Platteville

GARDNER BAKING COMPANY BAKERY THRIFT STORE
State Highway 151
Platteville, Wisconsin 53818   phone: 608-348-2211
(2 blocks east of main intersection of town.)

Hours: Monday-Friday, 12:30 pm-5 pm
　　　　Saturday, 11:30 am-4 pm
　　　　Closed Wednesdays

See: Beaver Dam, Wisconsin, Gardner Baking Company Bakery Thrift Store.

Savings: Up to 40% on day-old product.

Shop Monday and Thursday for best selection.

Payment: Cash, check for exact amount with identification.
Parking: Lot.

Plover

BAKE RITE THRIFT STORE
Mrs. Carter's Quality Bread
1001 Hoover Avenue
Plover, Wisconsin 54467　　　　　　　　phone: 715-344-3900

Hours: Monday–Saturday, 9 am–5 pm

Bakery outlet next to plant for day-old Mrs. Carter's breads, rolls, butter buns, bread cubes, cakes, sweet rolls, etc.
Savings: 33⅓% to 50%.

Shop Tuesdays for best selection. Tuesday is also "Senior Citizens' Day," and senior citizens get 10% off on all purchases.

Payment: Cash only.
Parking: Lot.

Rice Lake

KNIT PIKKER FACTORY OUTLET
113 North Main Street
Rice Lake, Wisconsin 54868　　　　　　　phone: 715-234-9480

Hours:　Monday–Friday, 9 am–5 pm
　　　　Saturday, 9 am–1 pm
　　　　Open Thursday evenings until 7 pm

See: Appleton, Wisconsin, Knit Pikker Factory Outlet

Savings: 20% to 60% on knitwear for all members of the family: overruns, company returns, sales representatives' samples, and discontinueds.

Also: Knitting and needlepoint yarns.

Payment: Cash, check for exact amount with identification.
Parking: Street—2 hour limit.

Ripon

FOX RIVER GLOVE FACTORY OUTLET
113 West Fond du Lac Street
Ripon, Wisconsin 54971　　　　　　　　phone: 414-748-5845

Hours: Monday-Thursday, 9 am-5 pm
Friday, 9 am-9 pm
Saturday, 9 am-5 pm

Outlet for Fox River Glove Company. Also sells irregulars, samples, and closeout items from many Wisconsin manufacturers.

Men's, women's, and children's gloves and mittens in canvas, deerskin, knit, and cotton for hunting, snowmobiling, skiing, gardening, and heavy work.

Men's, women's, and children's moccasins and casual leather footwear. Athletic, thermal, skating, slipper and sweat socks, stockings, and pantyhose. Also, ladies' leather handbags made by Fox River Glove Company.

Savings: Up to 50% on first quality, seconds, closeouts, and irregulars.

Also: Genuine leather (smooth and suede) jackets for men (sizes 34 to 52) and men's and women's knit goods, ski jackets, and clothing.

Payment: Cash, check for exact amount with identification.
Parking: Street.

Schofield

GARDNER BAKING COMPANY BAKERY THRIFT STORE
Wisconsin 29, just east of US 51
Schofield, Wisconsin 54476   phone: 715-359-2949

Hours: Monday-Saturday, 9 am-5:30 pm

See: Beaver Dam, Wisconsin, Gardner Baking Company Bakery Thrift Store.

Savings: Up to 40% on day-old product.

Shop Tuesday or Wednesday for best selection.

Payment: Cash, check for exact amount with identification, food stamps.
Parking: Lot.

MARATHON LUGGAGE COMPANY
215 Ross Street
Schofield, Wisconsin 54476   phone: 715-359-3202

Hours: Monday-Friday, 9 am-5 pm
Saturday, 9 am-12 noon

Manufacturer of foot lockers, trunks, and roller skate cases. Metal

covered wood frames from 30" × 16" × 12" to 36" × 20" × 22".
Savings: 30% to 50% on factory seconds and closeouts in luggage, trunks, and attaché cases.

Payment: Cash, check for exact amount with Wisconsin identification.
Parking: Lot.

Sheboygan

LEV-CO FACTORY SHOE OUTLET
1211 Indiana Avenue
Sheboygan, Wisconsin 53081   phone: 414-452-8506

Hours: Monday–Friday, 9 am–8 pm
       Saturday, 9 am–5 pm

Outlet for Leverenz men's and boys' dress shoes and Jung Company work shoes. Dress and work boots and shoes in sizes 6 to 14 up to EEE widths.
Savings: Up to 50% on samples, closeouts, discontinueds, and some factory damaged.

Payment: Cash, check for exact amount with identification.
Parking: Lot.

Stevens Point

HERRSCHNER'S, INC.
Hoover Road
Stevens Point, Wisconsin 54481   phone: 715-341-0560
(1 block west of US 51, 1 mile south of US 10.)

Hours: Monday–Saturday, 9 am–5 pm

Large catalog retailer for quality needlecraft, hobby kits, and accessories.
Savings: 33⅓% to 50% on mail order needlepoint kit returns, discontinued kits and accessories, and seconds in such items as stamped canvas (usually found in back of the store).

Payment: Cash, check for exact amount with identification, Master Charge, Visa.
Parking: Lot.

Stoughton

ORTEGA
Division of Heublein
Cooper Avenue—Industrial Park
Stoughton, Wisconsin 53589   phone: 608-873-8197
(Order at desk.)

Hours: Monday-Friday, 8 am-4:30 pm

Manufacturer of Mexican-American foods: taco shells, seasonings, and sauce. They sell taco kits by the case only—12 kits to a case, 10 tacos in each kit.
Savings: About 30% on taco kits purchased by the case.

Payment: Cash, check for exact amount with identification.
Parking: Street.

Tomah

GARDNER BAKING COMPANY BAKERY THRIFT STORE
1210 North Superior Avenue
Tomah, Wisconsin 54660   phone: 608-373-2411

Hours: Monday-Friday, 8:30 am-5:30 pm
       Saturday, 8:30 am-5 pm

See: Beaver Dam, Wisconsin, Gardner Baking Company Bakery Thrift Store.
Savings: Up to 40% on day-old product.

Payment: Cash, check for exact amount with identification.
Parking: Lot.

Watertown

ROCK RIVER FOODS, INC.
925 South Twelfth Street
Watertown, Wisconsin 53094   phone: 414-261-2314
(Enter store at front entrance.)

Hours: Monday-Friday, 8 am-12 noon
                     1 pm-4:45 pm

Fin and Tail and Rock River products: batter fried and breaded fish,

onion rings, shrimp, and cocktail and tartar sauces. Fish used includes catfish, perch, haddock, cod, and shrimp.
Savings: Up to 50% on irregular sized or broken pieces of fish.

Payment: Cash, check for exact amount with identification.
Parking: Lot.

Waukesha

OLD TAVERN FOOD PRODUCTS, INC.
230 Prairie Avenue
Waukesha, Wisconsin 53186   phone: 414-542-5301

Hours: Monday-Friday, 8 am-4:30 pm
       Saturday, 8 am-1 pm

Large mail order cheese packers of Old Tavern Club Cheese and assorted cheese spreads in cups and stoneware jars, cutting cheeses, assortments of sausages, and honey.
Savings: Average 20% on cheese purchased here without individual packaging.

Payment: Cash, check for exact amount with identification.
Parking: Private lot.

PALMER COMPANY, INC.
1200 Sentry Drive
Waukesha, Wisconsin 53186   phone: 414-547-2246

Hours: Monday-Friday, 8 am-4:45 pm

Building maintenance and janitorial supplies sold by the quart or gallon include floor, wall, and window cleaners; wax strippers; and wood floor and vinyl floor waxes.
Savings: 20% to 50% on wood, vinyl, and synthetic waxes sold by the gallon. Up to 50% on "Speede Clean," a wax stripper or wall cleaner (as compared with prices on comparable products sold in retail outlets).

Payment: Cash, check for exact amount with identification.
Parking: Street.

Waupaca

KNIT PIKKER FACTORY OUTLET
810 Churchill Street
Waupaca, Wisconsin 54981   phone: 715-258-5616
(Located in plant on right-hand side.)

Hours: Monday-Friday, 9 am-4 pm
Saturday, 10 am-2 pm

See: Appleton, Wisconsin, Knit Pikker Factory Outlet.

Savings: 20% to 60% on knitwear for all members of the family: overruns, company returns, sales representatives' samples, and discontinueds.

Also: Knitting and needlepoint yarns.

Payment: Cash, check for exact amount with identification.
Parking: Street.

Waupun

E & E SALES
Discount Food Warehouse
201 Young Street
Waupun, Wisconsin 53963   phone: 414-324-2916

Hours: Wednesday-Saturday, 9 am-5 pm

First quality and "dents" in canned fruits, vegetables, juices, sauces, pickles, and jellies sold in full-case or half-case quantities. Some items available in individual units.

Savings: 25% to 50% on "dents" (first quality product in dented can), closeouts, and specials.

Smaller savings on other products including baked goods, cereals, household items, and paper products.

Payment: Cash, check with identification.
Parking: Small lot or on street.

THE HANDCRAFTERS, INC.
Division of Nasco Industries
1 West Brown Street
Waupun, Wisconsin 53963   phone: 414-324-2031

Hours: Monday, Tuesday, Thursday, Friday, 10 am-4 pm

Manufacturer of recreational and educational supplies and arts and craft supplies and materials.

Savings: Better than 50% on overruns and seconds.

Payment: Cash, check with identification.
Parking: Lot.

Wausau

THE CANNERY
111 West Bridge Street
Wausau, Wisconsin 54401   phone: 715-845-2529

Hours: Wednesday, Thursday, Friday, 9 am-5 pm
      Saturday, 9 am-3 pm
      Closed on Sundays, Mondays, and Tuesdays

See: Madison, Wisconsin, The Cannery.

Savings: 40% to 60% on vegetable product "dents." Average of 15% savings on top quality, labeled cases of canned goods.

Payment: Cash, check for exact amount with identification.
Parking: Lot.

West Allis

KNIT PIKKER FACTORY OUTLET
2942 South 108th Street
West Allis, Wisconsin 53227   phone: 414-327-7010

Hours: Monday-Wednesday, 9 am-5 pm
      Thursday and Friday, 9 am-9 pm
      Saturday, 10 am-5 pm

See: Appleton, Wisconsin, Knit Pikker Factory Outlet.

Savings: 20% to 60% on knitwear for all members of the family: over-

runs, company returns, sales representatives' samples, and discontinueds.

Also: Knitting and needlepoint yarns.

Payment: Cash, check for exact amount with identification.
Parking: Lot.

SEARS CATALOG SURPLUS STORE
10635 West Greenfield Avenue
West Allis, Wisconsin 53214   phone: 414-259-0033

Hours: Monday-Friday, 9:30 am-9 pm
        Saturday, 9 am-4 pm
        Sunday, 12 noon-4 pm

See: Chicago, Illinois, Sears Catalog Surplus Store.

Savings: 20% to 80%.

Payment: Cash, check with identification, Sears charge card.
Parking: Lot.

West Baraboo

GARDNER BAKING COMPANY BAKERY THRIFT STORE
401 Linn Street
West Baraboo, Wisconsin 53913   phone: 608-356-4743

Hours: Monday-Friday, 9 am-5 pm
        Saturday, 9 am-4 pm

See: Beaver Dam, Wisconsin, Gardner Baking Company Bakery Thrift Store.

Savings: Up to 40% on day-old product.

Shop Monday and Thursday afternoons for best selection.

Payment: Cash only.
Parking: Lot.

West Bend

AMITY LEATHER PRODUCTS COMPANY
Amity Distribution Center
Rolf's Road off Wisconsin 33
West Bend, Wisconsin 53095   phone: 414-338-6506

Hours: Monday-Friday, 8 am-4:30 pm
        Saturday, 8 am-1 pm
        Open until 4:30 pm on Saturdays from Thanksgiving to Christmas

Outlet for Amity and Rolf overruns, closeouts, and seconds in leather accessories: billfolds, eyeglass cases, key cases, cigarette cases, French purses, card cases, travel and shoe kits, brush sets, wallets for men and women, credit card cases, briefcases, etc.
Savings: 40% and more.

Also: Plastic, leather, and fabric remnants and sample cuts at good savings.

Payment: Cash, check for exact amount with identification.
Parking: Large lot.

E. K. FACTORY OUTLET STORE
151 Wisconsin Street
West Bend, Wisconsin 53095   phone: 414-334-3455

Hours: Monday-Friday, 8 am-4:30 pm
        Saturday, 8 am-1 pm
        Open until 3 pm on Saturdays during November and December

Factory outlet store for Enger Kress, fine leather crafters since 1885. Men's and women's billfolds, key cases, pocket secretaries, clutch purses, grab bags, cigarette cases, eyeglass cases, travel accessories, personal leathergoods accessories, manicure kits, and matching sets.
Savings: 25% on new items; up to 70% on seconds and irregulars.

Call ahead to reserve a place in a morning or afternoon plant tour.

Payment: Cash, check, Visa, Wisconsin Master Charge.
Parking: Lot.

THE EXPLORER SHOP
253 South Main Street
West Bend, Wisconsin 53095   phone: 414-338-1500

Hours: Monday-Thursday, 10 am-4:30 pm
        Friday, 10 am-8:30 pm
        Saturday, 9:30 am-4:30 pm

Outlet for men's and women's leather accessories including key and card cases, handbags, French and clutch purses, wallets, secretaries, and belts. Also, Kenro plastic dinnerware, platters, and trays in first quality, closeouts, and irregulars.

Savings: Between 30% and 60% on leather goods and Kenro closeouts, irregulars, and seconds.

Also: Closeouts on stainless steel flatware and gift items handmade in the area. Priced reasonably.

Payment: Cash, check for exact amount with identification.
Parking: Metered—nickels.

WEST BEND COMPANY
Division of Dart Industries
445 Western Avenue
West Bend, Wisconsin 53095   phone: 414-334-2311
(Off Chestnut.)

Hours: Monday-Thursday, 9:30 am-5 pm
        Friday, 9:30 am-6 pm
        Saturday, 9 am-1 pm
        Open Saturdays until 3 pm from Thanksgiving to Christmas

Outlet store for West Bend, manufacturers of electric housewares including automatic coffee makers serving 6 to 100 cups, bun warmers, griddle servers, broilers, chafing dishes, automatic skillets, crock pots, corn poppers, woks, and humidifiers.

Decorator cookware in stainless steel, porcelain on aluminum, and porcelain on steel in multiple sizes, patterns, and colors.

Baking and cooking pans, stainless steel mixing bowls, decorated kitchen cannister sets, humidors, salad servers, thermal hot or cold drink servers, and tea kettles in all colors and finishes.

Savings: 35% to 70% on a large variety of overruns, discontinueds, and seconds.

Payment: Cash, check for exact amount with identification.
Parking: Lot.

WEST BEND WOOLEN MILLS OUTLET STORE
1125 East Washington Street
West Bend, Wisconsin 53095   phone: 414-334-7052

Hours: Monday and Friday, 9 am-9 pm
        Tuesday, Wednesday, Thursday, Saturday, 9 am-5:30 pm
        Sunday, 1 pm-5 pm
        Open Monday-Friday, 9 am-9 pm from Thanksgiving to Christmas

Outlet for Badger Manufacturing and Midwest Outerwear, clothing for the entire family from underwear and hosiery to outerwear. Firsts, seconds, and overruns from 31 manufacturers.

Complete range of sizes for children, women from 8 to 48 (with a good selection in the larger sizes), and men's to size 60. Fitting rooms. **Savings: 40% to 60% on discontinueds, closeouts, and seconds.**

Payment: Cash, check with identification.
Parking: Lot.

CATEGORY INDEX

APPLIANCES
Illinois
Factory Outlet Store, General Time Service	Wheeling	83
Jewel Catalog Outlet Merchandise Clearance Center	Crystal Lake	52
	Wauconda	83
Montgomery Ward Franklin Park Warehouse Liquidation Center	Franklin Park	62
Sears Catalog Surplus Store	Carol Stream	23
Sears Retail Store Outlet	Melrose Park	68
Sunbeam Appliance Service Company	Chicago	47
	Downers Grove	57
	Evergreen Park	61
	Niles	74

Indiana
Sears Catalog Surplus Store	Highland	99

Michigan
Sears Catalog Surplus Store	Flint	128

Minnesota
Northland Aluminum Products, Inc.	Minneapolis	170
Sears Catalog Surplus Store	Bloomington	152
	Fridley	158
	St. Paul	183
Sears Retail Store Outlet	Minneapolis	170
Ward's Warehouse, Montgomery Ward Bargain Outlet Store	St. Paul	183

Ohio
Regal Ware Outlet Store	Wooster	255
Sears Catalog Outlet Store	Medina	240
Sears Catalog Surplus Store	Cincinnati	202
	Medina	241

Wisconsin
J C Penney Catalog Outlet Store	Milwaukee	282
Oster Corporation Service Department	Milwaukee	287
Regal Ware, Inc.	Kewaskum	273
Schuette Brothers Mirro Factory Outlet Store	Manitowoc	277
Sears Catalog Surplus Store	West Allis	299
West Bend Company	West Bend	301

BABY EQUIPMENT. See also Clothing—Infants

Illinois
American Family Scale Company, Inc.	Chicago	26

Indiana
Cosco Company Store	Columbus	91

Ohio
Stork Baby Furniture and Toy Company	Cleveland	218

Wisconsin
Connor True Value Shopping Center	Laona	274
Kewaunee Equipment Company	Kewaunee	274

BEDSPREADS

Illinois
Stead Textile Company, Inc.	Chicago Heights	50
Story, Inc.	Algonquin	18

Indiana
Aero Blinds and Draperies	Indianapolis	100
The Drapery Mart	Carmel	90
Nettle Creek Industries	Richmond	111

Ohio
Cotton Mill Store	Cincinnati	196–97
	Dayton	227–28
	Hamilton	234
	St. Marys	246
Whiting Manufacturing Company, Inc.	Cincinnati	207

Wisconsin
Budget Drapery	Eau Claire	265
Outlet 9—Budget Drapery	Hudson	269

BEVERAGES

Illinois
Lasser Beverage Company	Chicago	39

BOOKS

Illinois
Book Value International, Inc.	Northbrook	75
Kroch's and Brentano's Bargain Book Center	Chicago	39
Monastery Hill Bindery	Chicago	42

Minnesota
Lerner Publications, Inc., "Hurt Books" Room	Minneapolis	166

Ohio
Paperback Exchange	Elyria	232

Wisconsin
Paper Seconds	Little Chute	275

CARPETING. See Floor Coverings

CHINA/GLASSWARE. See also Pottery

Illinois
Berggren Trayner Corporation	Libertyville	66
Crate & Barrel	Chicago	32
	Oak Brook	75
	Vernon Hills	82
	Wilmette	84
Pickard China	Antioch	18

Indiana
Indiana Glass Company	Dunkirk	92

Ohio
Anchor Hocking Shop	Lancaster	237
The Factory Outlet Store	Deerfield	230
Imperial Glass Hay Shed	Bellaire	191
Libbey Glassware Sales Room	Toledo	249
The Pottery Cupboard #6	Vermilion	251
Tiffin Glass Company Factory Outlet Store	Tiffin	248

CIGARS

Ohio
Ibold Cigar Company, Inc.	Cincinnati	198

Wisconsin
Thrifty Liquor and Pipe Mart	Milwaukee	288

CLOCKS

Illinois
Factory Outlet Store, General Time Service	Wheeling	83
Guaranty Clock Company	Chicago	38
Lava Simplex Internationale, Inc.	Chicago	40
Volna Limited	Chicago	49
The Westclox Company	Peru	77

Michigan
Sligh Furniture Company and Trend Clocks, Inc.	Holland	133

CLOTHING—Accessories

Illinois
Besley Tie Shops, Inc.	Chicago	28
Brody, Inc.	Elgin	59
Factory Fashion Center	Chicago	35
Factory Outlet Store, General Time Service	Wheeling	83
Royal Knitting Mills	Chicago	44
The Westclox Company	Peru	77

Indiana
Blue Bell Factory Outlet	Warsaw	116
The Corral	Columbia City	90
Excello Factory Store	Seymour	112
Frederic H. Burnham Company	Michigan City	106
Jasper Glove Company, Inc.	Jasper	103

Michigan
Red Flannel Factory	Cedar Springs	122
Red Flannel Factory Outlet Store	Rockford	143

Minnesota
Marceau Sports, Inc.	Minnetonka	171
Uber Glove Company	Owatonna	172

Ohio
Fecheimer Brothers Company	Cincinnati	198
Montgomery Ward Distribution Center Budget Store	Cincinnati	201

Wisconsin
Amity Leather Products Company	West Bend	300
Back Door Store Factory Outlet	Green Bay	267
E. K. Factory Outlet Store	West Bend	300
Everitt Knitting Company	Milwaukee	281
The Explorer Shop	West Bend	301

Fox River Glove Factory Outlet	Ripon	292
J C Penney Catalog Outlet Store	Milwaukee	282
Jersild Store	Neenah	289
Knit Pikker Factory Outlet	Appleton	258
	Madison	277
	Milwaukee	283
	Rice Lake	292
	Waupaca	297
	West Allis	298
Mid-Western Sport Togs	Berlin	263
Odds 'N Ends Shop	Milwaukee	287
Saranac Factory Store	Marinette	278
W. B. Place and Company	Hartford	268

CLOTHING—Boys

Illinois

Chicago Knitting Mills	Chicago	31
Factory Fashion Center	Chicago	35
J C Penney Catalog Outlet Store	Villa Park	83
Jewel Catalog Outlet Merchandise Clearance Center	Crystal Lake	52
	Wauconda	83
Leo's Advance Theatrical Company	Chicago	40
Montgomery Ward Catalog Liquidation Center	Chicago	42
Montgomery Ward Catalog Outlet	Rolling Meadows	80
Royal Knitting Mills	Chicago	44
Sears Catalog Surplus Store	Carol Stream	23
	Chicago	45
	Wheeling	84

Indiana

Blue Bell Factory Outlet	Warsaw	116
Carhartt Midwest Factory Outlet	Evansville	94
Carter's Factory Outlet Store	Franklin	98
The Corral	Columbia City	90
Factory Outlet Store, Elder Manufacturing Company	Fort Branch	97
Sears Catalog Surplus Store	Highland	99

Michigan

Anke Manufacturing Company	Hillsdale	132
Cameo Factory Outlet	Grand Rapids	131
Denton Mills, Inc.	Centreville	123
Great Lakes Sportswear Industries, Inc.	Detroit	124
Harvard of Hillsdale Factory Outlet	Brighton	122
Harvard of Hillsdale Factory Outlet Store	Clinton	123

308 Index • Clothing—Boys

Harvard of Hillsdale, Inc.	Litchfield	136
Harvard Trouser Company, Inc.	Pittsford	141
Royal Down Products, Inc.	Belding	120
Sears Catalog Surplus Store	Detroit	126
	Flint	128
Wolverine Sportswear Company	Ludington	138

Minnesota

Bemidji Woolen Mills	Bemidji	150
The Factory Store, Sharpee Manufacturing Company	Minneapolis	164
H. W. Carter and Sons, Inc.	Park Rapids	173
	Staples	184
J C Penney Outlet Store	St. Paul	178
Montgomery Ward Catalog Surplus Store	St. Paul	181
Munsingwear Remnant Room	St. Paul	181
Sears Catalog Surplus Store	Bloomington	152
	Fridley	158
	St. Paul	183

Ohio

Carolina Factory Outlet	Cincinnati	196
Carter's Factory Outlet	Brunswick	191
	Monroe	242
Down-Lite Products	Cincinnati	197
Factory Outlet	Van Wert	250
Holloway Sportswear, Inc.	Jackson Center	236
J C Penney Catalog Outlet Store	Cincinnati	198
	Columbus	222
Mid-American Textiles, Inc.	Columbus	222
Mill Outlet, Palm Beach/Austin Hill	Newport, KY	208
Mill Sample Store	Cincinnati	200
Montgomery Ward Distribution Center Budget Store	Cincinnati	201
Sears Catalog Surplus Store	Cincinnati	202
	Columbus	224
	Medina	241
Sears Catalog Surplus Store Distribution Center	Columbus	225
Velva Sheen Misprint Store	Cincinnati	206-07

Wisconsin

Brill Brothers, Inc.	Milwaukee	280
Carter's Factory Outlet	Kenosha	272
Contour Hosiery, Inc.	Kenosha	272
Everitt Knitting Company	Milwaukee	281
Florence Eiseman, Inc.	Fond du Lac	266

Fox River Glove Factory Outlet	Ripon	292
J C Penney Catalog Outlet Store	Cudahy	265
Knit Pikker Factory Outlet	Appleton	258
	Madison	277
	Rice Lake	292
	Waupaca	297
	West Allis	298
Medalist Sand Knit Company	Berlin	262
Mid-Western Sport Togs	Berlin	263
Sears Catalog Surplus Store	West Allis	299
West Bend Woolen Mills Outlet Store	West Bend	302

CLOTHING—Girls

Illinois

BeeLine Fashions	Bensenville	21
Chicago Knitting Mills	Chicago	31
Factory Fashion Center	Chicago	35
J C Penney Catalog Outlet Store	Villa Park	83
Jewel Catalog Outlet Merchandise Clearance Center	Crystal Lake	52
	Wauconda	83
Leo's Advance Theatrical Company	Chicago	40
Montgomery Ward Catalog Liquidation Center	Chicago	42
Montgomery Ward Catalog Outlet	Rolling Meadows	80
Royal Knitting Mills	Chicago	44
Sears Catalog Surplus Store	Carol Stream	23
	Chicago	45
	Wheeling	84

Indiana

Blue Bell Factory Outlet	Warsaw	116
Carter's Factory Outlet Store	Franklin	98
The Corral	Columbia City	90
Factory Outlet Store, Elder Manufacturing Company	Fort Branch	97
Sears Catalog Surplus Store	Highland	99

Michigan

Anke Manufacturing Company	Hillsdale	132
Baby Bliss, Inc., Outlet Store	Middleville	139
Bargain Corner Outlet Store	Grand Rapids	131
Cameo Factory Outlet	Grand Rapids	131
Denton Mills, Inc.	Centreville	123
Great Lakes Sportswear Industries, Inc.	Detroit	124
Harvard of Hillsdale Factory Outlet	Brighton	122
Harvard of Hillsdale Factory Outlet Store	Clinton	123

Harvard of Hillsdale, Inc.	Litchfield	136
Harvard Trouser Company, Inc.	Pittsford	141
Red Flannel Factory	Cedar Springs	122
Red Flannel Factory Outlet Store	Rockford	143
Royal Down Products, Inc.	Belding	120
Sears Catalog Surplus Store	Detroit	126
	Flint	128

Minnesota

Bemidji Woolen Mills	Bemidji	150
Cluett Factory Outlet	Eveleth	155
The Factory Store, Sharpee Manufacturing Company	Minneapolis	164
Grandmother's Attic	Cannon Falls	153
J C Penney Outlet Store	St. Paul	178
Montgomery Ward Catalog Surplus Store	St. Paul	181
Munsingwear Remnant Room	St. Paul	181
Sears Catalog Surplus Store	Bloomington	152
	Fridley	158
	St. Paul	183

Ohio

Carolina Factory Outlet	Cincinnati	196
Carter's Factory Outlet	Brunswick	191
	Monroe	242
Down-Lite Products	Cincinnati	197
Holloway Sportswear, Inc.	Jackson Center	236
J C Penney Catalog Outlet Store	Cincinnati	198
	Columbus	222
Mid-American Textiles, Inc.	Columbus	222
Mill Sample Store	Cincinnati	200
Montgomery Ward Distribution Center Budget Store	Cincinnati	201
Polly Flinders Girls Dresses	Cincinnati	202
Sears Catalog Surplus Store	Cincinnati	202
	Columbus	224
	Medina	241
Sears Catalog Surplus Store Distribution Center	Columbus	225
Velva Sheen Misprint Store	Cincinnati	206-07

Wisconsin

Carter's Factory Outlet	Kenosha	272
Everitt Knitting Company	Milwaukee	281
Florence Eiseman, Inc.	Fond du Lac	266
Fox River Glove Factory Outlet	Ripon	292
J C Penney Catalog Outlet Store	Cudahy	265

Knit Pikker Factory Outlet	Appleton	258
	Madison	277
	Rice Lake	292
	Waupaca	297
	West Allis	298
Medalist Sand Knit Company	Berlin	262
Mid-Western Sport Togs	Berlin	263
Sears Catalog Surplus Store	West Allis	299
West Bend Woolen Mills Outlet Store	West Bend	302

CLOTHING—Infants

Illinois
Rubens Baby Factory	Chicago	45
Winona Knitting Mills, Inc., Outlet Store	Downers Grove	57

Indiana
Carter's Factory Outlet Store	Franklin	98

Michigan
Baby Bliss, Inc., Outlet Store	Middleville	139
Bargain Corner Outlet Store	Grand Rapids	131
Gerber Products Company Outlet Store	Fremont	130
Kessler, Inc., Factory Outlet	Wayland	147

Minnesota
Grandmother's Attic	Cannon Falls	153
Winona Knitting Mills, Inc., Sales Room	Winona	186
Winona Knitting Mills Outlet Store	Red Wing	174

Ohio
Carter's Factory Outlet	Brunswick	191
	Monroe	242
Stork Baby Furniture and Toy Company	Cleveland	218

Wisconsin
Carter's Factory Outlet	Kenosha	272
Knit Pikker Factory Outlet	Appleton	258
	Madison	277
	Rice Lake	292
	Waupaca	297
	West Allis	298

CLOTHING—Men. See also Uniforms

Illinois
BeeLine Fashions	Bensenville	21
Brody, Inc.	Elgin	59
Chicago Knitting Mills	Chicago	31

312 Index • Clothing—Men

The Factory Letout	Belleville	21
Gingiss Formalwear Warehouse	Chicago	37
H. W. Gossard Company Factory Outlet Store	Batavia	20
	Effingham	58
J C Penney Catalog Outlet Store	Villa Park	83
Jewel Catalog Outlet Merchandise Clearance Center	Crystal Lake	52
	Wauconda	83
Lingerie and Fabric Shop	Cicero	50
Montgomery Ward Catalog Liquidation Center	Chicago	42
Montgomery Ward Catalog Outlet	Rolling Meadows	80
Royal Knitting Mills	Chicago	44
Sears Catalog Surplus Store	Carol Stream	23
	Chicago	45
	Wheeling	84
Winona Knitting Mills, Inc., Outlet Store	Downers Grove	57

Indiana

Berco, Inc.	Berne	88
Blue Bell Factory Outlet	Warsaw	116
Carhartt Midwest Factory Outlet	Evansville	94
The Corral	Columbia City	90
Edmonton Manufacturing Company	Rochester	112
Excello Factory Store	Seymour	112
Factory Outlet Store, Elder Manufacturing Company	Fort Branch	97
Factory Outlet Store, Jaymar-Ruby, Inc.	Michigan City	105
Gohn Brothers Manufacturing Company	Middlebury	107
H. W. Gossard Company Factory Outlet Store	Huntingburg	100
	Logansport	104
	Sullivan	113
Quality Discount Apparel	Gary	98
	Merrillville	104
Sears Catalog Surplus Store	Highland	99

Michigan

Anke Manufacturing Company	Hillsdale	132
Cameo Factory Outlet	Grand Rapids	131
Denton Mills, Inc.	Centreville	123
Great Lakes Sportswear Industries, Inc.	Detroit	124
Harvard of Hillsdale Factory Outlet	Brighton	122
Harvard of Hillsdale Factory Outlet Store	Clinton	123

Harvard of Hillsdale, Inc.   Litchfield   136
Harvard Trouser Company, Inc.   Pittsford   141
H. W. Gossard Company Factory
   Outlet Store   Escanaba   127
    Ishpeming   134
    Sault Ste. Marie   144
Red Flannel Factory   Cedar Springs   122
Red Flannel Factory Outlet Store   Rockford   143
Royal Down Products, Inc.   Belding   120
Sears Catalog Surplus Store   Detroit   126
    Flint   128
Wolverine Sportswear Company   Ludington   138

Minnesota
Bemidji Woolen Mills   Bemidji   150
Cluett Factory Outlet   Eveleth   155
D. B. Rosenblatt, Inc.   Fergus Falls   157
    Minneapolis   163
J C Penney Outlet Store   St. Paul   178
Kurysch Manufacturing Company
   Outlet Store   St. Paul   179
Milbern Men's Clothing   St. Paul   180
Milton Clothing   St. Paul   180
Montgomery Ward Catalog Surplus
   Store   St. Paul   181
Munsingwear Remnant Shop   St. Paul   181
Sears Catalog Surplus Store   Bloomington   152
    Fridley   158
    St. Paul   183
Wiman Corporation   Princeton   173
Winona Knitting Mills, Inc., Sales Room   Winona   186
Winona Knitting Mills Outlet Store   Red Wing   174

Ohio
Brooks Shoes Factory Outlet Store   Columbus   219-20
Carolina Factory Outlet   Cincinnati   196
Dalton of America Factory Store   Willoughby   254
Dalton Factory Store   Lorain   238
Down-Lite Products   Cincinnati   197
Euclid Garment Manufacturing
   Company   Kent   236
Factory Outlet   Van Wert   250
Fecheimer Brothers Company   Cincinnati   198
Hercules Outlet Store   Columbus   221
Holloway Sportswear, Inc.   Jackson Center   236
Imperial Sportswear "Name Brand"
   Store   Cleveland   211
Infant Items, Inc.   Fremont   234

J C Penney Catalog Outlet Store	Cincinnati	198
	Columbus	222
Lion Knitting Mills Company	Cleveland	213
Mid-American Textiles, Inc.	Columbus	222
Mill Outlet, Palm Beach/Austin Hill	Newport, KY	208
Mill Sample Store	Cincinnati	200
Montgomery Ward Distribution Center Budget Store	Cincinnati	201
Ohio Mill Factory Fashions	Cleveland	215
Rastetter Woolen Mill	Millersburg	242
Sears Catalog Surplus Store	Cincinnati	202
	Columbus	224
	Medina	241
Sears Catalog Surplus Store Distribution Center	Columbus	225
Velva Sheen Misprint Store	Cincinnati	206–07
Work Smart Store—Factory Outlet	Cleveland	218

Wisconsin

Back Door Store Factory Outlet	Green Bay	267
Brill Brothers, Inc.	Milwaukee	280
Contour Hosiery, Inc.	Kenosha	272
Fox River Glove Factory Outlet	Ripon	292
J C Penney Catalog Outlet Store	Cudahy	265
Jersild Store	Neenah	289
Knit Pikker Factory Outlet	Appleton	258
	Madison	277
	Rice Lake	292
	Waupaca	297
	West Allis	298
Medalist Sand Knit Company	Berlin	262
Melco Clothing Company, Inc.	Milwaukee	283
Mid-Western Sport Togs	Berlin	263
Saranac Factory Store	Marinette	278
Sears Catalog Surplus Store	West Allis	299
Universal Fabrics Company, Inc.	Berlin	263
West Bend Woolen Mills Outlet Store	West Bend	302

CLOTHING—Women. See also Uniforms

Illinois

Arbetman Brothers and Blair	Aurora	19
BeeLine Fashions	Bensenville	21
Brody, Inc.	Elgin	59
Carmen Foundations Factory Store	Chicago	29
Chicago Knitting Mills	Chicago	31
Decatur Garment Company Outlet Store	Decatur	53

Clothing—Women • Index

Factory Fashion Center	Belvidere	21
	Chicago	35
	Lindenhurst	66
Factory Outlet Store, Martha Manning Company	Mount Vernon	71
Herrin Apparel Retail Store	Herrin	63
H. W. Gossard Company Factory Outlet Store	Batavia	20
	Effingham	58
J C Penney Catalog Outlet Store	Villa Park	83
Jewel Catalog Outlet Merchandise Clearance Center	Crystal Lake	52
	Wauconda	83
Leo's Advance Theatrical Company	Chicago	40
Lingerie and Fabric Shop	Cicero	50
Martha Manning Company	Collinsville	51
	Mascoutah	67
Maternity Factory Outlet	Chicago	41
	Downers Grove	56
	Homewood	64
	Niles	73
	Riverside	79
	Schaumburg	81
Miss America Store	Berwyn	22
Montgomery Ward Catalog Liquidation Center	Chicago	42
Montgomery Ward Catalog Outlet	Rolling Meadows	80
Phil Maid, Inc.	Chicago	42
Pinckneyville Garment Company	Pinckneyville	77
Prevue Fashions	Aurora	19-20
	Elgin	59
Royal Knitting Mills	Chicago	44
Sears Catalog Surplus Store	Carol Stream	23
	Chicago	45
	Wheeling	84
Sewing Factory Outlet Store	Zion	85
Smoler Brothers, Inc.	Chicago	46
Winona Knitting Mills, Inc., Outlet Store	Downers Grove	57

Indiana

Blue Bell Factory Outlet	Warsaw	116
Carhartt Midwest Factory Outlet	Evansville	94
Carter's Factory Outlet Store	Franklin	98
The Company Store	New Castle	108
The Corral	Columbia City	90

316 Index • Clothing—Women

Eastmoor Company Factory Outlet Store	Michigan City	105
Edmonton Manufacturing Company	Rochester	112
Edwards Manufacturing Company	Evansville	95
Excello Factory Store	Seymour	112
Factory Fashion Center	Elkhart	93
	LaPorte	104
H. W. Gossard Company Factory Outlet Store	Huntingburg	100
	Logansport	104
	Sullivan	113
Lane Bryant Outlet Store	Indianapolis	101
Sears Catalog Surplus Store	Highland	99
Society Lingerie, Inc.	Michigan City	106

Michigan

Anke Manufacturing Company	Hillsdale	132
Cameo Factory Outlet	Grand Rapids	131
Denton Mills, Inc.	Centreville	123
Great Lakes Sportswear Industries, Inc.	Detroit	124
Harvard of Hillsdale Factory Outlet	Brighton	122
Harvard of Hillsdale Factory Outlet Store	Clinton	123
Harvard of Hillsdale, Inc.	Litchfield	136
Harvard Trouser Company, Inc.	Pittsford	141
H. W. Gossard Company Factory Outlet Store	Escanaba	127
	Ishpeming	134
	Sault Ste. Marie	144
Patchwork Stores	Grand Haven	130
	Grand Rapids	132
	Manistee	138
	Traverse City	146
Red Flannel Factory	Cedar Springs	122
Red Flannel Factory Outlet Store	Rockford	143
Royal Down Products, Inc.	Belding	120
Sears Catalog Surplus Store	Detroit	126
	Flint	128
Wolverine Sportswear Company	Ludington	138

Minnesota

Bemidji Woolen Mills	Bemidji	150
Cluett Factory Outlet	Eveleth	155
The Coat Store	St. Paul	176
D. B. Rosenblatt, Inc.	Fergus Falls	157
	Minneapolis	163
Doug's Factory Outlet Store	Minneapolis	163

Clothing—Women • Index

The Factory Store, Sharpee Manufacturing Company	Minneapolis	164
J C Penney Outlet Store	St. Paul	178
Kurysch Manufacturing Company Outlet Store	St. Paul	179
Maternity Factory Outlet	Minneapolis	167-68
Milaca Mills, Inc., Store	Milaca	160
Montgomery Ward Catalog Surplus Store	St. Paul	181
Munsingwear Remnant Shop	St. Paul	181
Sears Catalog Surplus Store	Bloomington	152
	Fridley	158
	St. Paul	183
Wiman Corporation	Princeton	173
Winona Knitting Mills, Inc., Sales Room	Winona	186
Winona Knitting Mills Outlet Store	Red Wing	174

Ohio

Brooks Shoes Factory Outlet Store	Columbus	219-20
Carolina Factory Outlet	Cincinnati	196
Carter's Factory Outlet	Brunswick	191
	Monroe	242
Dalton of America Factory Store	Willoughby	254
Dalton Factory Outlet	Bedford	189
Dalton Factory Store	Canton	193
	Cleveland	210
	Lorain	238
Down-Lite Products	Cincinnati	197
Factory Outlet	Van Wert	250
Fecheimer Brothers Company	Cincinnati	198
Holloway Sportswear, Inc.	Jackson Center	236
Imperial Sportswear "Name Brand" Store	Cleveland	211
J C Penney Catalog Outlet Store	Cincinnati	198
	Columbus	222
Jerrie Lurie Factory Fabric Outlet Store	Cleveland	212
Lion Knitting Mills Company	Cleveland	213
Love-Fore Outlet	Cincinnati	200
Maternity Factory Outlet	Mayfield Heights	240
	North Olmsted	244
Mid-American Textiles, Inc.	Columbus	222
Mill Outlet, Palm Beach/Austin Hill	Newport, KY	208
Mill Sample Store	Cincinnati	200
Montgomery Ward Distribution Center Budget Store	Cincinnati	201
Ohio Mill Factory Fashions	Cleveland	215

Rastetter Woolen Mill	Millersburg	242
Sears Catalog Surplus Store	Cincinnati	202
	Columbus	224
	Medina	241
Sears Catalog Surplus Store Distribution Center	Columbus	225
Section Factory Outlet	Cincinnati	203
Velva Sheen Misprint Store	Cincinnati	206–07

Wisconsin

Back Door Store Factory Outlet	Green Bay	267
Brill Brothers, Inc.	Milwaukee	280
Carter's Factory Outlet	Kenosha	272
The Clothes Rack	Milwaukee	281
Everitt Knitting Company	Milwaukee	281
Florence Eiseman, Inc.	Fond du Lac	266
Fox River Glove Factory Outlet	Ripon	292
J C Penney Catalog Outlet Store	Cudahy	265
Jersild Store	Neenah	289
J H Collectibles Outlet Store	Janesville	270
	Lake Geneva	274
	Milwaukee	283
Knit Pikker Factory Outlet	Appleton	258
	Madison	277
	Rice Lake	292
	Waupaca	297
	West Allis	298
Medalist Sand Knit Company	Berlin	262
Mid-Western Sport Togs	Berlin	263
Saranac Factory Store	Marinette	278
Sears Catalog Surplus Store	West Allis	299
Universal Fabrics Company, Inc.	Berlin	263
West Bend Woolen Mills Outlet Store	West Bend	302

COOKWARE

Illinois

Berggren Trayner Corporation	Libertyville	66
Crate & Barrel	Chicago	32
	Oak Brook	75
	Vernon Hills	82
	Wilmette	84
Paul Revere Shoppe	Clinton	51
Sunbeam Appliance Service Company	Chicago	47
	Downers Grove	57
	Evergreen Park	61
	Niles	74

Indiana
    Factory Store, General Housewares
        Corporation — Terre Haute — 114

Minnesota
    Northland Aluminum Products, Inc. — Minneapolis — 170

Ohio
    General Cutlery — Fremont — 233
    Regal Ware Outlet Store — Wooster — 255
    Wearever Aluminum Factory Outlet — Chillicothe — 194

Wisconsin
    Oster Corporation Service Department — Milwaukee — 287
    Regal Ware, Inc. — Kewaskum — 273
    Schuette Brothers Mirro Factory Outlet
        Store — Manitowoc — 277
    West Bend Company — West Bend — 301

DETERGENTS/CLEANERS

Illinois
    Armour Dial Men's Club Store — Chicago — 26
    Arrow Soap — Chicago — 27

Indiana
    Cosco Company Store — Columbus — 91

Minnesota
    National Purity Soap and Chemical
        Company — Minneapolis — 169

Wisconsin
    Milwaukee Soap Company — Milwaukee — 284–85
    Palmer Company, Inc. — Waukesha — 296

DRAPERIES

Illinois
    Stead Textile Company, Inc. — Chicago Heights — 50
    Whiteside Drapery Fabricators, Inc. — Zion — 86

Indiana
    Aero Blinds and Draperies — Indianapolis — 100
    The Drapery Mart — Carmel — 90
    Nettle Creek Industries — Richmond — 111

Ohio
    King Bag and Manufacturing Company — Cincinnati — 200
    New York Textiles — Parma — 245
    Whiting Manufacturing Company, Inc. — Cincinnati — 207

Wisconsin
Budget Drapery	Eau Claire	265
Outlet 9—Budget Drapery	Hudson	269

FABRICS
Illinois
Arbetman Brothers and Blair	Aurora	19
Decatur Garment Company Outlet Store	Decatur	53
Elenhank Designers	Riverside	78
The Factory Letout	Belleville	21
Factory Outlet Store, Martha Manning Company	Mount Vernon	71
Grist "Mill Ends" and Things	Carpentersville	23
Herrin Apparel Retail Store	Herrin	63
H. W. Gossard Company Factory Outlet Store	Batavia	20
	Effingham	58
Lingerie and Fabric Shop	Cicero	50
Loomcraft Textiles	Chicago	41
Martha Manning Company	Collinsville	51
	Mascoutah	67
Phil Maid, Inc.	Chicago	42
Pinckneyville Garment Company	Pinckneyville	77
Prevue Fashions	Aurora	19–20
	Elgin	59
Sand-Man Couch Company	Thomasboro	82
Sewing Factory Outlet Store	Zion	85
Smoler Brothers, Inc.	Chicago	46
Stead Textile Company, Inc.	Chicago Heights	50
Story, Inc.	Algonquin	18
Whiteside Drapery Fabricators, Inc.	Zion	86

Indiana
The Company Store	New Castle	108
The Drapery Mart	Carmel	90
Eastmoor Company Factory Outlet Store	Michigan City	105
Fabric Gallery	Berne	88
Factory Fashion Center	Elkhart	93
Gohn Brothers Manufacturing Company	Middlebury	107
H. W. Gossard Company Factory Outlet Store	Huntingburg	100
	Logansport	104
	Sullivan	113
Mastercraft, Inc.	Shipshewana	113

Fabrics • Index

Nettle Creek Industries	Richmond	111
Shane Uniform Factory Outlet	Evansville	96
Society Lingerie, Inc.	Michigan City	106
Yager Furniture Company	Berne	89

Michigan

Baker Furniture Company	Holland	133
Cameo Factory Outlet	Grand Rapids	131
Frankenmuth Woolen Mill Company	Frankenmuth	128
Harvard of Hillsdale, Inc.	Litchfield	136
H. W. Gossard Company Factory Outlet Store	Ishpeming	134
Kessler, Inc., Factory Outlet	Wayland	147
Marüshka Fabric Outlet Store	Spring Lake	145
Patchwork Stores	Grand Haven	130
	Grand Rapids	132
	Manistee	138
	Traverse City	146
Wolverine Sportswear Company	Ludington	138

Minnesota

Bro-Tex Company	St. Paul	175
The Coat Store	St. Paul	176
D. B. Rosenblatt, Inc.	Fergus Falls	157
	Minneapolis	163
Doug's Fabric Outlet Store	Minneapolis	163
Eastern Woolen Company Fabrics Plus	St. Paul	178
The Factory Store, Sharpee Manufacturing Company	Minneapolis	164
Faribo Woolens, Inc.	Faribault	156
Home Beautiful Enterprises, Inc.	Minneapolis	165
Milaca Mills, Inc., Store	Milaca	160
Mill End Fabrics	Minneapolis	168
Munsingwear Remnant Room	Minneapolis	169
	St. Paul	181

Ohio

Benjamin Hey Company	Cincinnati	194
Carolina Mill Wholesale Fabrics	Cleveland	209
Cotton Mill Store	Cincinnati	196–97
	Dayton	227–28
	Hamilton	234
	St. Marys	246
Dalton of America Factory Store	Willoughby	254
Dalton Factory Store	Canton	193
	Cleveland	210
	Lorain	238
Distinctive Costumes, Inc.	Toledo	249

Factory Outlet	Van Wert	250
Infant Items, Inc.	Fremont	234
Jerrie Lurie Factory Fabric Outlet Store	Cleveland	212
King Bag and Manufacturing Company	Cincinnati	200
Mill Outlet, Palm Beach/Austin Hill	Newport, KY	208
New York Textiles	Parma	245
Polly Flinders Girls Dresses	Cincinnati	202
Section Factory Outlet	Cincinnati	203
Tannery Hill Furniture Manufacturing Company, Inc.	Ashtabula	188
Whiting Manufacturing Company, Inc.	Cincinnati	207

Wisconsin

Amity Leather Products Company	West Bend	300
Borg Textile Outlet Store	Jefferson	272
Florence Eiseman, Inc.	Milwaukee	281
Jersild Store	Neenah	289
J H Collectibles Outlet Store	Milwaukee	283
Knit Pikker Factory Outlet	Appleton	258
	Madison	277
	West Allis	298
Medalist Sand Knit Company	Berlin	262
Monterey Mills Outlet Store	Janesville	270
Norwood Mills, Inc.	Janesville	271
Swiss Miss	New Glarus	289

FLOOR COVERINGS

Illinois

Jewel Catalog Outlet Merchandise Clearance Center	Crystal Lake	52
	Wauconda	83
Montgomery Ward Franklin Park Warehouse Liquidation Center	Franklin Park	62
Sears Retail Store Outlet	Melrose Park	68

Indiana

Kirby's	North Vernon	109

Michigan

Frankenmuth Woolen Mill Company	Frankenmuth	128

Wisconsin

Borg Textile Outlet Store	Jefferson	272
Carpet Seconds	Beloit	261
Monterey Mills Outlet Store	Janesville	270
Norwood Mills, Inc.	Janesville	271

FOOD—Baked Goods

Illinois

Baltic Bakery	Chicago	28
Brownberry Ovens Thrift Store	LaGrange Park	64
	Prospect Heights	78
Davidson's Bakeries Surplus Store	Chicago	33
Dressel's Bakery	Chicago	34
	Oak Lawn	76
	Willowbrook	85
Entenmann's, Inc., Thrift Store	Hanover Park	62
	Morton Grove	70
	Naperville	72
	Oak Lawn	76
	Schaumburg	80
Fasano Pie Thrift Store	Chicago	36
Flavor Kist	Chicago	36
	Countryside	52
	Downers Grove	55
Kitchens of Sara Lee Thrift Store	Chicago	38
	Deerfield	54
	Downers Grove	56
	Mount Prospect	71
Mama Cookie Bakeries, Inc.	Chicago	41
Pepperidge Farm Thrift Store	Downers Grove	56
	Niles	73
	Oak Lawn	76
	Schaumburg	81
Resale Cookie Company	Norridge	74
Tom Tom Tamale and Bakery Company	Chicago	48
Zion Industries	Zion	86

Indiana

Bunny Bread Company Thrift Store	Evansville	94
Colonial Thrift Store	Evansville	95
Heyerly Bakery Company, Inc.	Ossian	109
Honey Fluff Donut Shop	Evansville	96
Kitchens of Sara Lee Thrift Store	Whiting	116
Roselyn Bakery Surplus Store	Indianapolis	102
Sap's Bakeries, Inc.	Columbus	91

Michigan

American Biscuit Company Thrift Store	Battle Creek	119
Brownberry Natural Breads	Livonia	137
Kwast Bakery	Lansing	135
Pepperidge Farm Thrift Store	Birmingham	121
	Livonia	137
Russell-Phinney Pies, Inc., Thrift Bakery	Detroit	126

324 Index • Food—Baked Goods

Schafer Bakeries, Inc., Thrift Store	Battle Creek	119
United Biscuit Company Surplus Store	Grand Rapids	132

Minnesota

Best Maid Cookie Company	Minneapolis	162
Brownberry Ovens Thrift Store	Bloomington	151
	Crystal	154
Daisy Thrift Store	Minneapolis	162
	St. Paul	176-77
Egekvist Thrift Store	Minneapolis	164
Middle East Bread	St. Paul	180
Willmar Cookie Company, Inc., Outlet Store	Willmar	185

Ohio

Balduf's Thrift Store	Maumee	239
Brownberry Ovens Thrift Store	Akron	188
	Cincinnati	194
	Columbus	220
	Dayton	227
	Strongsville	247
	Twinsburg	249
H. C. Cecutti Bakery Company	Columbus	221
Hough Bakeries, Inc., Surplus Store	Willoughby	255
Hough Bakeries, Inc., Thrift Store	Cleveland	210
	Maple Heights	239
Mehaffie Pie Company	Dayton	228
Mrs. Smith's Pies	Maple Heights	239
Pepperidge Farm Thrift Store	Columbus	224
	Dayton	229
	Mayfield Heights	240
	Westlake	253
	Whitehall	254
Quality Bakery Company	Columbus	224
Schwebel's Thrift Bakery	Cleveland	216-17
Spring Water Cookie Company	Cincinnati	205
Tedeschi's Bakery, Inc.	Columbus	227

Wisconsin

Bake Rite Thrift Store	Plover	292
Brownberry Ovens Thrift Store	Brookfield	264
	Madison	276
	Oconomowoc	290
Dick Brothers Bakeries Thrift Store	Fond du Lac	266

Food—Canned Goods • Index

Gardner Baking Company Bakery Thrift Store	Beaver Dam	260
	Janesville	271
	Platteville	291
	Schofield	293
	Tomah	295
	West Baraboo	299
Jaeger Baking Company Thrift Store	Janesville	269
Mrs. Karl's Bakery Thrift Store	Milwaukee	285
Pepperidge Farm Thrift Store	Milwaukee	288
Plant Store, Elm Tree Frozen Foods	Appleton	259

FOOD—Canned Goods

Illinois
Armour Dial Men's Club Store	Chicago	26

Indiana
Leichty's Foods, Inc.	Berne	89
Ossian Canning Company, Inc.	Ossian	110
Ray Brothers and Noble Canning Company	Hobbs	99
Swayzee Packing Company, Inc.	Swayzee	114

Michigan
Burnette Farms Packing Company	Keeler	134
Gerber Products Company Outlet Store	Fremont	130
Honee Bear	Lawton	136
Huron Farms Decatur Storage, Inc.	Decatur	124

Minnesota
Big Stone, Inc.	Arlington	150
The Faribault Canning Company	Faribault	155
Olivia Canning Company Warehouse	Olivia	172

Ohio
Balduf's Thrift Store	Maumee	239
H. C. Cecutti Bakery Company	Columbus	221
Hirzel Canning Company	East Toledo	232

Wisconsin
The Cannery	Madison	276
	Oconomowoc	290
	Wausau	298
E & E Sales	Waupun	297
Loyal Canning Corporation	Loyal	276

FOOD—Cheese

Illinois
Randolph Packing Company	Chicago	43

Indiana
Graham Farms Cheese Corporation	Elnora	94

Minnesota
Associated Milk Producers, Inc.	Clarkfield	154
Treasure Cave, Inc., Retail Store	Faribault	156

Ohio
Matthews Meats, Inc.	Cleveland	214
Schrier Lunch and Dairy Bar	Bucyrus	192

Wisconsin
The Cheese Hut	Green Bay	267
Kaukauna Dairy Products	Little Chute	275
Old Tavern Food Products, Inc.	Waukesha	296

FOOD—Ethnic

Illinois
Kosher Zion Sausage Company	Chicago	39
Tom Tom Tamale and Bakery Company	Chicago	48
Vienna Sausage Manufacturing Company	Chicago	48

Minnesota
The Kramarczak Sausage Company Deli and Bakery	Minneapolis	166
Middle East Bread	St. Paul	180

Ohio
H. C. Cecutti Bakery Company	Columbus	221
Tedeschi's Bakery, Inc.	Columbus	227

Wisconsin
Ortega	Stoughton	295

FOOD—Frozen

Illinois
Danielson Food Products	Chicago	33
Kitchens of Sara Lee Thrift Store	Chicago	38
	Deerfield	54
	Downers Grove	56
	Mount Prospect	71
Pepperidge Farm Thrift Store	Downers Grove	56
	Niles	73
	Oak Lawn	76
	Schaumburg	81

Pick Fisheries, Inc.	Chicago	43
Indiana		
Kitchens of Sara Lee Thrift Store	Whiting	116
Uncle Charlie's Meats	Evansville	97
Michigan		
Pepperidge Farm Thrift Store	Birmingham	121
	Livonia	137
Silver Mill Frozen Foods, Inc.	Eau Claire	127
Smeltzer Orchard Company	Frankfort	129
Minnesota		
Captain Ken's Firehouse Beans, Inc.	St. Paul	176
Ohio		
B and M Packing Company	Wapakoneta	251
Butcher Shop	Wapakoneta	252
Evelyn Sprague Portion Control Meats	Englewood	232
Henry H. Beaver Packing Company, Inc.	Delaware	231
Matthews Meats, Inc.	Cleveland	214
Mehaffie Pie Company	Dayton	228
Mister Sirloin	Cleveland	215
Ohio Steak and Barbecue Company	Columbus	223
	Dayton	229
	Lodi	238
	Waverly	252
Pepperidge Farm Thrift Store	Columbus	224
	Dayton	229
	Mayfield Heights	240
	Westlake	253
	Whitehall	254
Quality Bakery Company	Columbus	224
State Fish, Inc.	Cleveland	217
Stouffer's Thrift Store	Solon	247
Wisconsin		
Pepperidge Farm Thrift Store	Milwaukee	288
Plant Store, Elm Tree Frozen Foods	Appleton	259

FOOD—Meat/Fish

Illinois

Charles Hollenbach, Inc.	Chicago	30
Crawford Sausage Company	Chicago	33
Danielson Food Products	Chicago	33
Kosher Zion Sausage Company	Chicago	39
Pick Fisheries, Inc.	Chicago	43
Randolph Packing Company	Chicago	43

Slotkowski Sausage Company	Chicago	46
Sparrer Sausage Company	Chicago	47
Tom Tom Tamale and Bakery Company	Chicago	48
Vienna Sausage Manufacturing Company	Chicago	48

Indiana

Liechty's Foods, Inc.	Berne	89
Staub and Smith Meat Market and Packing Company	Indianapolis	102
Uncle Charlie's Meats	Evansville	97

Michigan

Regal Packing Company	Detroit	125

Minnesota

Chip Steak and Provision Company	Mankato	160
Eisen Sausage, Inc.	Waldorf	185
The Kramarczak Sausage Company Deli and Bakery	Minneapolis	166
La Salle Food Processing Association	La Salle	160
Pioneer Sausage Company	St. Paul	182

Ohio

B and M Packing Company	Wapakoneta	251
Butcher Shop	Wapakoneta	252
Evelyn Sprague Portion Control Meats	Englewood	232
Henry H. Beaver Packing Company, Inc.	Delaware	231
Marks and Sons Company	Cleveland	214
Matthews Meats, Inc.	Cleveland	214
Mister Sirloin	Cleveland	215
Ohio Steak and Barbecue Company	Columbus	223
	Dayton	229
	Lodi	238
	Waverly	252
State Fish, Inc.	Cleveland	217
Stouffer's Thrift Store	Solon	247

Wisconsin

Fred Usinger, Inc.	Milwaukee	282
Jones Dairy Farm Retail Store	Fort Atkinson	266
Rock River Foods, Inc.	Watertown	295

FOOD—Mushrooms

Illinois

G. & G. D. Hasselman Supreme Meadow Mushrooms	Elk Grove Village	60

Food—Snacks • Index

Indiana
- Brighton Mushroom Farm — Howe — 100

Michigan
- Michigan Mushroom Growers, Ltd. — Niles — 140

Minnesota
- Lehmann's Mushrooms — St. Paul — 179

FOOD—Nuts

Illinois
- Ace Pecan Company — Elk Grove Village — 60
- Georgia Nut Company — Chicago — 37
- J. B. Sanfilippo and Son, Inc. — Des Plaines — 54
- Ricci Nuts — Chicago — 44

Minnesota
- Midwest Northern Nut Company, Inc. — Minneapolis — 168

Ohio
- Bassett Nut Company — Toledo — 248
- Capco Nuts — Cleveland — 209
- Dayton Nut Specialties, Inc. — Dayton — 228
- Hillson Nut Company, Inc. — Cleveland — 210
- Krema Products — Columbus — 222

Wisconsin
- Ambrosia Chocolate Company — Milwaukee — 279

FOOD—Pet

Ohio
- S. E. Mighton Company — Bedford — 190

FOOD—Snacks

Illinois
- Brownberry Ovens Thrift Store — LaGrange Park — 64
- Brownberry Ovens Thrift Store — Prospect Heights — 78
- Cracker Jack — Chicago — 31
- Pepperidge Farm Thrift Store — Downers Grove — 56
- Pepperidge Farm Thrift Store — Niles — 73
- Pepperidge Farm Thrift Store — Oak Lawn — 76
- Pepperidge Farm Thrift Store — Schaumburg — 81

Indiana
- Bunny Bread Company Thrift Store — Evansville — 94
- Colonial Thrift Store — Evansville — 95

Michigan
- Brownberry Natural Breads — Livonia — 137

330 Index • Food—Snacks

Pepperidge Farm Thrift Store	Birmingham	121
	Livonia	137

Minnesota
Brownberry Ovens Thrift Store	Bloomington	151
	Crystal	154
Daisy Thrift Store	Minneapolis	162
	St. Paul	176-77
Happy's Potato Chip Company	St. Anthony	174

Ohio
Brownberry Ovens Thrift Store	Akron	188
	Cincinnati	194
	Columbus	220
	Dayton	227
	Strongsville	247
	Twinsburg	249
Capco Nuts	Cleveland	209
Pepperidge Farm Thrift Store	Columbus	224
	Dayton	229
	Mayfield Heights	240
	Westlake	253
	Whitehall	254
Schwebel's Thrift Bakery	Cleveland	216-17

Wisconsin
Brownberry Ovens Thrift Store	Brookfield	264
	Madison	276
	Oconomowoc	290
Dick Brothers Bakery Thrift Store	Fond du Lac	266
Gardner Baking Company Bakery Thrift Store	Beaver Dam	260
	Janesville	271
	Platteville	291
	Schofield	293
	Tomah	295
	West Baraboo	299
Jaeger Baking Company Thrift Store	Janesville	269
Pepperidge Farm Thrift Store	Milwaukee	288

FOOD—Sweets

Illinois
Affy Tapple, Inc.	Chicago	25
Andrews Caramel Apples	Chicago	26
Beich's Candy	Bloomington	22
E. J. Brach and Son	Chicago	34
Fannie May Candies	Chicago	35
J. B. Sanfilippo and Son, Inc.	Des Plaines	54

Minnesota
Abdallah Candy Store	Burnsville	152
	Minneapolis	161
Goggin Party Shop	Stillwater	184
J. A. Goggin Candy Company	Stillwater	184
Villager Foods, Inc., Factory Discount Store	Jackson	158

Ohio
Capco Nuts	Cleveland	209
Fanny Farmer Quality Candies	Norwalk	244
Mullane Taffy Company	Cincinnati	201

Wisconsin
Ambrosia Chocolate Company	Milwaukee	279
The Chocolate House Factory Outlet Store	Milwaukee	280

FOOTWEAR

Illinois
Bass Shoe Factory Outlet	Champaign	24
Chernin's Shoes	Chicago	30
	Downers Grove	55
	Matteson	68
	Morton Grove	70
Chicago Shoe Outlet	Chicago	32
Sears Catalog Surplus Store	Carol Stream	23
	Chicago	45
	Wheeling	84

Indiana
M. G. Grundman and Sons, Inc.	Vincennes	115

Michigan
Little Red Shoe House	Big Rapids	120
	Manistee	138
	Muskegon	139
	North Muskegon	140
	Portland	142
	Rockford	142
	South Haven	145
Shaw Shoe Store	Coldwater	123

Minnesota
Walt's Shoe Service	Red Wing	173

Ohio
Bressan Shoes Factory Outlet	Alliance	188
Brooks Shoes Factory Outlet Store	Columbus	219-20
	Nelsonville	243
Endicott-Johnson	Middletown	241

Safety Footwear, Inc.	Cleveland	216
Shoe Factory Store	Columbus	225-26
The Shoe Market	Cincinnati	203-04
	Dayton	230
	Hamilton	235

Wisconsin

Allen Edmonds Shoe Bank	Belgium	261
Fox River Glove Factory Outlet	Ripon	292
Freeman Shoe Factory Outlet	Beloit	262
Lev-Co Factory Shoe Outlet	Sheboygan	294
Mason Retail Shoe Store	Chippewa Falls	264
Odd Lot Shoe Store	Milwaukee	285-86
Odds 'N Ends Shop	Milwaukee	287
Saranac Factory Store	Marinette	278
Weinbrenner Factory Store	Antigo	258
	Marshfield	278
	Merrill	279

FURNITURE

Illinois

The Bartley Collection, Ltd.	Lake Forest	65
Butcher Block & More Factory Store	Chicago	29
Montgomery Ward Catalog Liquidation Center	Chicago	42
Montgomery Ward Catalog Outlet	Rolling Meadows	80
Montgomery Ward Franklin Park Warehouse Liquidation Center	Franklin Park	62
Sand-Man Couch Company	Thomasboro	82
Sears Catalog Surplus Store	Carol Stream	23
Sears Retail Store Outlet	Melrose Park	68
Volna Limited	Chicago	49

Indiana

Brittany Furniture Industries	Paoli	110
Cosco Company Store	Columbus	91
Hoffman Office Supply, Inc.	Jasper	103
Mastercraft, Inc.	Shipshewana	113
Peters-Revington Manufacturing Company	Delphi	92
Sears Catalog Surplus Store	Highland	99
Yager Furniture Company	Berne	89

Michigan

Baker Furniture Company	Holland	133
Burwood Products Company Factory Outlet	Traverse City	146
College Wood Products	Berrien Springs	120

Garden Supplies • Index

Gallerie La Barge	Saugatuck	144
Lu Van, Inc.	Belding	119
The Pine Shop Store	Big Rapids	121
Sears Catalog Surplus Store	Detroit	126
	Flint	128
Sligh Furniture Company and Trend Clocks, Inc.	Holland	133

Minnesota

Gottlieb Furniture and Carpet Company	Bloomington	151
	Minneapolis	164
Sears Catalog Surplus Store	Bloomington	152
	Fridley	158
	St. Paul	183
Sears Retail Store Outlet	Minneapolis	170
The Unpainted Place	Minneapolis	171

Ohio

J C Penney Catalog Outlet Store	Columbus	222
Sears Catalog Surplus Store	Cincinnati	202
	Medina	241
Stork Baby Furniture and Toy Company	Cleveland	218
Tannery Hill Furniture Manufacturing Company, Inc.	Ashtabula	188

Wisconsin

Arcadia Furniture Factory Mart	Arcadia	259
Connor True Value Shopping Center	Laona	274
J C Penney Catalog Outlet Store	Milwaukee	282
Sears Catalog Surplus Store	West Allis	299
Valley Business Interiors	Green Bay	268

GAMES. See Sporting Goods/Recreational Supplies
GARDEN SUPPLIES

Illinois

Haeger Potteries	East Dundee	58
Hahn Industries	Cullom	53

Indiana

Jasper Glove Company, Inc.	Jasper	103
Wilson Brothers	Roachdale	111

Minnesota

Hans Rosacher Rose Acres	Minneapolis	165

Ohio

Libbey Glassware Sales Room	Toledo	249
McCoy Retail Store	Zanesville	255

Index • Garden Supplies

Ohio Pottery Factory Outlet	Zanesville	256
The Pot Shop	Roseville	245
Silco Disposable Products Division	West Carrollton	253

Wisconsin

Andercraft Woods	Mishicot	288

GIFTWARE

Illinois

American Family Scale Company, Inc.	Chicago	26
Berggren Trayner Corporation	Libertyville	66
Bowl of Beauty Thrift Store	Melrose Park	68
Crate & Barrel	Chicago	32
	Oak Brook	75
	Vernon Hills	82
	Wilmette	84
Guaranty Clock Company	Chicago	38
Haeger Potteries	East Dundee	58
Lava Simplex Internationale, Inc.	Chicago	40
Macomb Pottery Company	Macomb	67
Monastery Hill Bindery	Chicago	42
Paul Revere Shoppe	Clinton	51
Pickard China	Antioch	18
The Pottery Barn	Monmouth	70
Sunbeam Appliance Service Company	Chicago	47
	Downers Grove	57
	Evergreen Park	61
	Niles	74
The Westclox Company	Peru	77

Indiana

Indiana Glass Company	Dunkirk	92
The Pottery Cupboard #13	Nashville	108

Ohio

Anchor Hocking Shop	Lancaster	237
Candle Tree Factory Outlet	Cincinnati	195
The Glass Corner	Barnesville	189
Guernsey Glass Company, Inc.	Cambridge	193
Imperial Glass Hay Shed	Bellaire	191
Infant Items, Inc.	Fremont	234
Libbey Glassware Sales Room	Toledo	249
McCoy Retail Store	Zanesville	255
National Potters Outlet Store	Cleveland	215
The Pottery Cupboard #6	Vermilion	251
Regal Ware Outlet Store	Wooster	255
Tiffin Glass Company Factory Outlet Store	Tiffin	248

Wearever Aluminum Factory Outlet	Chillicothe	194
Worldwide Games, Inc.	Delaware	231

Wisconsin

Amity Leather Products Company	West Bend	300
E. K. Factory Outlet Store	West Bend	300
The Explorer Shop	West Bend	301
The Lenox Shop	Oshkosh	291
Mid-Western Sport Togs	Berlin	263
Oster Corporation Service Department	Milwaukee	287
Regal Ware, Inc.	Kewaskum	273
Saranac Factory Store	Marinette	278
Schuette Brothers Mirro Factory Outlet Store	Manitowoc	277
West Bend Company	West Bend	302

GLASSWARE. See China/Glassware
HANDCRAFTS. See also Fabrics, Picture Frames

Illinois

Bowl of Beauty Thrift Store	Melrose Park	68
Caron Yarn Company	Mendota	69
Caron Yarn Outlet Store	Moline	69
	Oregon	77
Lingerie and Fabric Shop	Cicero	50
Story, Inc.	Algonquin	18
V.I.P. Yarn Outlet	Rochelle	79

Indiana

A. F. Billings Company	Wabash	115
The Drapery Mart	Carmel	90
Fabric Gallery	Berne	88
Factory Fashion Center	Elkhart	93
Kirby's	North Vernon	109
Kirby's Outlet	Nashville	107
Mastercraft, Inc.	Shipshewana	113
Society Lingerie, Inc.	Michigan City	106

Michigan

Baker Furniture Company	Holland	133
Davidson's Old Mill Yarn of Eaton Rapids	Eaton Rapids	126
Frankenmuth Woolen Mill Company	Frankenmuth	128

Minnesota

Bemidji Woolen Mills	Bemidji	150
Boland Manufacturing Company	Winona	186
Eastern Woolen Company Fabrics Plus	St. Paul	178

Glass House Studio, Inc.	St. Paul	178
Point of Sales, Inc.	Cannon Falls	153

Ohio

Asplin Basket Company, Inc.	Hartville	235
Benjamin Hey Company	Cincinnati	194
Cambridge Tile Center	Cincinnati	195
Cannon Towel Outlet	Foster	233
	Silverton	246
Cotton Mill Store	Cincinnati	196–97
	Dayton	227–28
	Hamilton	234
	St. Marys	246
Factory Outlet	Van Wert	250
Franklin Art Glass Studios, Inc.	Columbus	220
Jerrie Lurie Factory Fabric Outlet Store	Cleveland	212
J & H Clasgens Company	Cincinnati	199
	New Richmond	243
Kennedy Manufacturing Company Quality Control Reject Outlet	Van Wert	250
Lamrite	Bedford	190
Mid-American Textiles, Inc.	Columbus	222
Polly Flinders Girls Dresses	Cincinnati	202
Rastetter Woolen Mill	Millersburg	242
Trait Tex Industries	Cleveland	218
Worldwide Games, Inc.	Delaware	231

Wisconsin

Borg Textile Outlet Store	Jefferson	272
Budget Drapery	Eau Claire	265
Everitt Knitting Company	Milwaukee	281
The Handcrafters, Inc.	Waupun	297
Herrschner's, Inc.	Stevens Point	294
Jersild Store	Neenah	289
Knit Pikker Factory Outlet	Appleton	258
	Madison	277
	Milwaukee	283
	Rice Lake	292
	Waupaca	297
	West Allis	298
Monterey Mills Outlet Store	Janesville	270
Norwood Mills, Inc.	Janesville	271
Odds 'N Ends Shop	Milwaukee	287
Outlet 9—Budget Drapery	Hudson	269
W. B. Place and Company	Hartford	268

HOME ACCESSORIES. *See also* **Clocks, Draperies, Floor Coverings, Furniture, Lamps**

Illinois

Alpha-Batics	Northbrook	74
American Family Scale Company, Inc.	Chicago	26
The Bartley Collection, Ltd.	Lake Forest	65
Bowl of Beauty Thrift Store	Melrose Park	68
Butcher Block & More Factory Store	Chicago	29
Condecor, Inc.	Mundelein	72
Crate & Barrel	Chicago	32
	Oak Brook	75
	Vernon Hills	82
	Wilmette	84
Factory Outlet Store, General Time Service	Wheeling	83
Grist "Mill Ends" and Things	Carpentersville	23
Haeger Potteries	East Dundee	58
Harvey Manufacturing Company	Cary	24
J C Penney Catalog Outlet Store	Villa Park	83
Jewel Catalog Outlet Merchandise Clearance Center	Crystal Lake	52
	Wauconda	83
Macomb Pottery Company	Macomb	67
Monastery Hill Bindery	Chicago	42
Sears Catalog Surplus Store	Carol Stream	23
	Chicago	45
	Wheeling	84
Sears Retail Store Outlet	Melrose Park	68
Silvestri Corporation	Chicago	45
Specialty Trunk and Suitcase Company	Chicago	47
Volna Limited	Chicago	49
The Westclox Company	Peru	77

Indiana

Aero Blinds and Draperies	Indianapolis	100
A. F. Billings Company	Wabash	115
Cosco Company Store	Columbus	91
The Drapery Mart	Carmel	90
Fabric Gallery	Berne	88
Factory Store, General Housewares Corporation	Terre Haute	114
Hoffman Office Supply, Inc.	Jasper	103
Indiana Glass Company	Dunkirk	92
Kirby's	North Vernon	109
Nettle Creek Industries	Richmond	111
The Pottery Cupboard #13	Nashville	108

Sears Catalog Surplus Store	Highland	99
Wilson Brothers	Roachdale	111

Michigan

Burwood Products Company Factory Outlet	Traverse City	146
Cameo Factory Outlet	Grand Rapids	131
Frankenmuth Woolen Mill Company	Frankenmuth	128
Gallerie La Barge	Saugatuck	144
Marüshka Fabric Outlet Store	Spring Lake	145
Merillat Warehouse Outlet	Adrian	118
Olsen Knife Company, Inc.	Howard City	134
Sears Catalog Surplus Store	Detroit	126
	Flint	128
Sligh Furniture Company and Trend Clocks, Inc.	Holland	133

Minnesota

Bemidji Woolen Mills	Bemidji	150
Boland Manufacturing Company	Winona	186
The Box Shop	Minneapolis	162
Faribo Manufacturing Company	Faribault	156
Faribo Woolens, Inc.	Faribault	156
The Gallery	Kenyon	159
Gottlieb Furniture and Carpet Company	Bloomington	151
	Minneapolis	164
The Holes Webway Company	St. Cloud	175
J C Penney Outlet Store	St. Paul	178
Montgomery Ward Catalog Surplus Store	St. Paul	181
Point of Sales, Inc.	Cannon Falls	153
Sears Catalog Surplus Store	Bloomington	152
	Fridley	158
	St. Paul	183

Ohio

Anchor Hocking Shop	Lancaster	237
Asplin Basket Company, Inc.	Hartville	235
Candle Tree Factory Outlet	Cincinnati	195
Cannon Towel Outlet	Foster	233
	Silverton	246
Down-Lite Products	Cincinnati	197
The Glass Corner	Barnesville	189
Guernsey Glass Company, Inc.	Cambridge	193
J C Penney Catalog Outlet Store	Cincinnati	198
	Columbus	222
King Bag and Manufacturing Company	Cincinnati	200

Lamp Factory Outlet Store	Cleveland	212-13
McCoy Retail Store	Zanesville	255
Montgomery Ward Distribution Center Budget Store	Cincinnati	201
National Potters Outlet Store	Cleveland	215
Ohio Pottery Factory Outlet	Zanesville	256
The Pottery Cupboard #6	Vermilion	251
Rastetter Woolen Mill	Millersburg	242
Sears Catalog Surplus Store	Cincinnati	202
	Columbus	224
	Medina	241
Sears Catalog Surplus Store Distribution Center	Columbus	225
Tiffin Glass Company Factory Outlet Store	Tiffin	248
Towel Bar	Hudson	236
Whiting Manufacturing Company, Inc.	Cincinnati	207

Wisconsin

Andercraft Woods	Mishicot	288
Borg Textile Outlet Store	Jefferson	272
Budget Drapery	Eau Claire	265
Connor True Value Shopping Center	Laona	274
J C Penney Catalog Outlet Store	Cudahy	265
The Lenox Shop	Oshkosh	291
Outlet 9—Budget Drapery	Hudson	269
Paper Seconds	Little Chute	275
Sears Catalog Surplus Store	West Allis	299

HOME IMPROVEMENT PRODUCTS

Illinois

General Bathroom Products Corporation	Elk Grove Village	60
Montgomery Ward Home Improvement Sales Center	Franklin Park	61
Sears Retail Store Outlet	Melrose Park	68

Michigan

Baker Furniture Company	Holland	133
Grand Rapids Brick Company	Grand Rapids	131
Kurtis Kitchen and Bath Center	Ann Arbor	118
	Detroit	125
	Farmington Hills	128
	Lincoln Park	136
	Warren	146
United Glazed Products, Inc.	Lansing	135

Minnesota
- Medallion Outlet Store — Fergus Falls — 157
- Merillat Industries, Inc. — Lakeville — 159

Ohio
- Black and Decker Manufacturing Company — Cleveland — 208
- Cambridge Tile Center — Cincinnati — 195
- Skil Product Service Center — Cleveland — 217
- Valley Kitchens Tri-County Factory Outlet — Cincinnati — 205

Wisconsin
- J C Penney Catalog Outlet Store — Milwaukee — 282

HOME WORKSHOP SUPPLIES

Illinois
- Jewel Catalog Outlet Merchandise Clearance Center — Crystal Lake — 52
  - Wauconda — 83
- Montgomery Ward Home Improvement Sales Center — Franklin Park — 61

Ohio
- Black and Decker Manufacturing Company — Cleveland — 208
- Euclid Garment Manufacturing Company — Kent — 236
- House of Plastics — Cleveland — 211
- Kennedy Manufacturing Company Quality Control Reject Outlet — Van Wert — 250
- Skil Product Service Center — Cleveland — 217

HOSIERY

Illinois
- H. W. Gossard Company Factory Outlet Store — Batavia — 20
  - Effingham — 58

Indiana
- Blue Bell Factory Outlet — Warsaw — 116
- The Corral — Columbia City — 90
- Excello Factory Store — Seymour — 112
- Frederic H. Burnham Company — Michigan City — 106
- H. W. Gossard Company Factory Outlet Store — Huntingburg — 100
  - Logansport — 104
  - Sullivan — 113

Michigan
    H. W. Gossard Company Factory
        Outlet Store   Escanaba   127
                               Sault Ste. Marie   144

Ohio
    Mill Sample Store   Cincinnati   200

Wisconsin
    Contour Hosiery, Inc.   Kenosha   272
    Fox River Glove Factory Outlet   Ripon   292
    West Bend Woolen Mills Outlet Store   West Bend   302

LAMPS

Illinois
    Haegar Potteries   East Dundee   58
    Lava Simplex Internationale, Inc.   Chicago   40

Ohio
    Lamp Factory Outlet Store   Cleveland   212-13

LINENS. *See also* Bedspreads

Illinois
    R. A. Briggs and Company   Lake Zurich   65

Ohio
    Cannon Towel Outlet   Foster   233
                               Silverton   246
    Cotton Mill Store   Cincinnati   196-97
                               Dayton   227-28
                               Hamilton   234
                               St. Marys   246
    Whiting Manufacturing Company, Inc.   Cincinnati   207

Wisconsin
    McArthur Towels, Inc.   Baraboo   260

LUGGAGE

Illinois
    Specialty Trunk and Suitcase Company   Chicago   47

Minnesota
    Pedro's of St. Paul   St. Paul   182

Wisconsin
    Marathon Luggage Company   Schofield   293

MATTRESSES

Illinois
Champaign Mattress Factory	Champaign	24
Schaumburg Mattress Factory	Schaumburg	81

Indiana
Mastercraft, Inc.	Shipshewana	113

Michigan
College Wood Products	Berrien Springs	120

PAPER/PAPER PRODUCTS

Illinois
Arvey Paper and Supplies Center	Chicago	27
	Hillside	63
Graphic Two	Chicago	37
Graphic 14	Libertyville	66
Skokie Paper Point	Niles	73

Indiana
Arvey Paper and Supplies Center	Indianapolis	101

Michigan
Paper and Graphic Supplies Center	Oak Park	141
	Warren	147

Minnesota
Arvey Paper and Supplies Center	Minneapolis	161
Litin Paper Company	Minneapolis	167

Ohio
Hollo's Papercraft	Brunswick	192
Imperial Cup Corporation	Kenton	237
Silco Disposable Products Division	West Carrollton	253

Wisconsin
Holiday Cups, Inc.	Menomonee Falls	278
Milwaukee Soap Company	Milwaukee	284–85
Paper Seconds	Little Chute	275

PICTURE FRAMES

Illinois
Condecor, Inc.	Mundelein	72

Minnesota
Picture Frame Supply Company	Minneapolis	170

Wisconsin
Larson Picture Frame, Inc.	Ashland	260

PIPES

Michigan
Malaga Briar Pipe Company — Royal Oak — 143

Wisconsin
Thrifty Liquor and Pipe Mart — Milwaukee — 288

PLASTICS

Ohio
House of Plastics — Cleveland — 211

Wisconsin
The Explorer Shop — West Bend — 301

POTTERY

Illinois
Haeger Potteries — East Dundee — 58
Macomb Pottery Company — Macomb — 67
The Pottery Barn — Monmouth — 70

Indiana
Kirby's Outlet — Nashville — 107
The Pottery Cupboard #13 — Nashville — 108

Ohio
McCoy Retail Store — Zanesville — 255
National Potters Outlet Store — Cleveland — 215
Ohio Pottery Factory Outlet — Zanesville — 256
Old Trail Pottery — Zanesville — 256
The Pot Shop — Roseville — 245
The Pottery Cupboard #6 — Vermilion — 251
Scioramic — Scio — 246

SHOES. See Footwear

SPORTING GOODS/RECREATIONAL SUPPLIES

Illinois
B & W Golf Ball Company — Chicago — 29
Jewel Catalog Outlet Merchandise Clearance Center — Crystal Lake — 52
— Wauconda — 83

Indiana
Blessings School — Elkhart — 93
Farm and Home Saddlery — Indianapolis — 101

Michigan
Anke Manufacturing Company — Hillsdale — 132
Harvard of Hillsdale Factory Outlet — Brighton — 122

Index • Sporting Goods/Recreational Supplies

Harvard of Hillsdale Factory Outlet Store	Clinton	123
Harvard of Hillsdale, Inc.	Litchfield	136
Harvard Trouser Company, Inc.	Pittsford	141
Helin Tackle Company	Detroit	125
Royal Down Products, Inc.	Belding	120

Minnesota

Animal Fair Seconds Store	Chanhassen	154
Bemidji Boat Company, Inc.	Bemidji	150
J C Penney Outlet Store	St. Paul	178
Kurysch Manufacturing Company Outlet Store	St. Paul	179
Lakeside Games	Minneapolis	166

Ohio

Distinctive Costumes, Inc.	Toledo	249
Factory Outlet	Van Wert	250
Holloway Sportswear, Inc.	Jackson Center	236
Love-Fore Outlet	Cincinnati	200
Mid-American Textiles, Inc.	Columbus	222
Mill Sample Store	Cincinnati	200
Worldwide Games, Inc.	Delaware	231

Wisconsin

J C Penney Catalog Outlet Store	Cudahy	265
	Milwaukee	282
J-Mart Sporting Goods	Iron River	269
Medalist Sand Knit Company	Berlin	262

UNIFORMS

Illinois

Advance Uniform Company	Chicago	25

Indiana

Lane Bryant Outlet Store	Indianapolis	101
Shane Uniform Factory Outlet	Evansville	96

Ohio

Fecheimer Brothers Company	Cincinnati	198

Notes

Notes

Notes

Notes